CONSPIRACY

The Fear of Subversion in American History

CONSPIRACY
The Fear of Subversion in American History

Edited by

Richard O. Curry
University of Connecticut

Thomas M. Brown
Upsala College

HOLT, RINEHART AND WINSTON, INC.
New York Chicago San Francisco Atlanta
Dallas Montreal Toronto London Sydney

Cover illustration: "Exactly! There's A Plot
To Make Us Look Foolish"—from *Herblock's Here and Now*
(Simon and Schuster, 1955).

Library of Congress Catalog Card Number: 77–176370
ISBN: 0–03–084152–6
Printed in the United States of America
2 3 4 5 065 9 8 7 6 5 4 3 2 1

Contents

Introduction

This book focuses attention on a disturbing theme in American history: the tendency of political leaders and their followers to view the world in conspiratorial terms.[1] From the colonial period to the present, some Americans have attributed the disruptions produced by war, protest, and economic depression to subversive influences at work in American society. According to these alarmed citizens, politics is not an open process but a secret plot. As Richard Hofstadter points out, "there is a great difference between locating conspiracies *in* history and saying that history *is,* in effect, a conspiracy, between singling out those conspiratorial acts that do on occasion occur and weaving a vast fabric of social explanation out of nothing but skeins of evil plots."

Four major questions arise from a consideration of fears of conspiracy in American history. First, we must ask *when* these fears have been pervasive enough to affect national politics. Second, we must make clear *against whom* the numerous anticonspiracy crusades in our history have been directed. Third, we must ask *why* such fears exist. Finally, we need to know *what effects* the fear of subversion has had in shaping both political attitudes and specific government policies.

---

1 Although this book concerns the United States, it must be stressed that fears of conspiracy are by no means peculiar to American history. The theoretical piece in this collection by Franz Neumann is based upon models drawn from modern European history.

Although fears of conspiracy have existed throughout American history, this is not nearly as important as their virulence at a given time. As the articles in this collection make clear, fear of conspiracy is most intense during periods of national crisis. During World War I, for example, American citizens of German ancestry were treated as a potential fifth column. After the Japanese attack on Pearl Harbor, the West Coast was gripped by panic, and repressive measures, including deportation, were instituted against Japanese Americans. Senator Joseph R. McCarthy's erroneous but widely believed charge that government agencies, especially the State Department, were infested by Communist agents was a response to the tensions and frustrations of the Cold War in the early 1950s.

Domestic crises, especially severe social and economic dislocations, have also evoked conspiratorial interpretations. The Populists, impoverished by the agricultural depression of the 1890s, believed that international bankers were engaged in a secret plot to reduce American farmers to peonage. Labor leaders, in the wake of the violence that attended the rise of unions, were denounced as anarchists or agents of the Comintern. The Great Crash of 1929 was blamed by some observers on the intrigues of international Jewish bankers.

A prime example of fears of conspiracy resulting from a combination of pressures in both foreign and domestic affairs occurred during the 1790s. The Hamiltonians and Jeffersonians took turns accusing each other of treason and subversion. Jefferson's followers were denounced by Federalists as Jacobins who would introduce the French Reign of Terror to America. Conversely, Jeffersonians declared that Federalists were monarchists bent on destroying the Bill of Rights.

The only major examples of fears of conspiracy directed against purely domestic rather than foreign enemies were the attacks on "the great slave power conspiracy" of the 1840s and 1850s, southern fear of an abolitionist-inspired slave rebellion, and the alarm of the Lincoln administration over the "Copperhead" conspiracy during the Civil War. Even here, however, it must be noted that the mounting sectional crisis during the 1850s caused many northerners and southerners to regard their respective sections almost as foreign nations. During the war itself, conservative Union Democrats in the North were anathematized by Republicans with the label "Copperheads"—that is, traitors or Confederate sympathizers who favored southern independence.

Scholars have also noted that fear of conspiracy characterizes periods when traditional social and moral values are undergoing change. As David Brion Davis observes, much of the rhetoric of the anti-Masonic crusade, as well as the persecution of the Mormons and the anti-Catholic hysteria during the antebellum years, can be explained in these terms. Moreover, the article in this collection by Hiram Wesley Evans, an Imperial Wizard of the Ku Klux Klan, vividly reflects the alarm over social changes that the Klan opposed but could not prevent. In short, changes in traditional modes of behavior are often laid at the door of conspirators who would weaken the national moral fiber for the benefit of corrupt and dangerous foreign powers. It would be wrong, however, to conclude that fears of conspiracy are confined only to groups that oppose social change. The strife before and during the American Revolution and the Civil War demonstrates the tendency of reformers and revolutionaries to perceive political events within a conspiratorial framework.

In attempting to gauge the significance of fears of conspiracy in American politics, some scholars believe that the denunciation of subversion in high places is little more than a sham, a crude tactic designed to discredit political opponents whose domestic policies are the real target. Thus, Federalists who opposed Jefferson's social and economic ideas sought to link him with atheism and the French Reign of Terror, and Republican opponents of the New Deal hoped to drive Democrats from power by accusing them of advocating socialism and appointing Soviet agents to high government offices. While this approach to the omnipresence of conspiratorial rhetoric in American political life may be correct, it by no means solves the problem posed by fears of conspiracy. Most writers agree that such tactics cannot be successful unless large numbers of people fervently believe that conspiracies constitute a danger to American security and ideals. In an effort to explain why these fears are widespread, some scholars have used modern sociological and psychological theories of behavior.

In this book the articles by Franz Neumann and Gordon Allport emphasize the importance of societal disruption, alienation, and personality disorders in accounting for the success of demagogues. While a particular demagogue may or may not believe in the existence of the subversives he excoriates, the important point is his role as a catalyst: he appeals to people who must rationalize failure by externalizing it, by attributing personal or societal defects to foreign plotters who serve as scapegoats.

The concept of status politics is another theory used by scholars to explain the appeal of anticonspiracy crusades. Seymour Martin Lipset, a leading advocate of the status interpretation, argues that status-oriented rhetoric "appeals . . . not only [to] groups which have risen in the economic structure, who may be frustrated in their desire to be accepted socially by those who hold status, but [to] groups possessing status as well, who feel that various social changes threaten their own claims to high social position, or enable previously lower-status groups to claim equal status with them." As a result, such groups relieve their anxieties and frustrations by concluding that conspiratorial groups occupy or are attempting to seize the bastions of power in government, the churches, the press, and the universities. It must be kept in mind, however, that these sociological and psychological explanations of fears of conspiracy are theoretical propositions at best, requiring massive evidence to establish their validity as generalizations.

Sociological and psychological interpretations are open to the objection that they make fears of conspiracy solely the work of an extremist, usually right-wing, fringe of society. It is extremely important to note that fears of conspiracy are not confined to charlatans, crackpots, and the disaffected. Anticonspiratorial rhetoric has been a factor in major-party politics throughout most of our history. The passage of the Alien and Sedition Acts during the 1790s, the enactment of the Espionage Act during World War I, the Palmer raids during the Red Scare of 1919–1920, and the evacuation of Japanese Americans from the West Coast during World War II clearly show that fears of conspiracy have had their greatest impact in American society at the level of national politics. From George Washington to Richard Nixon, American presidents have uttered grim warnings against conspiracies. Fears of subversion are very much a part of the mainstream of politics.

In addition to the questions we have raised, numerous other problems exist in connection with the fear of conspiracy in American history. To what extent are these fears shaped by ideological convictions, and what effects do they have on ideology? What is the connection between the fear of subversion and traditional American opposition to centralized power? In what circumstances and in what specific ways has religion shaped the content of anticonspiratorial rhetoric? In the twentieth century has the demand for bipartisanship in foreign policy reflected a widely shared belief that dissent is the work of conspirators and not simply the result of honest differences about international objectives? Is conspiracy fear an extreme version of a continuous demand for national unity? Has a fiercely competitive economic system bred a tendency to be on guard against the wiles of others? Is there a general insecurity in American life that demands simple, *ad hominem* explanations of political and historical change?

Scholars, as the article by Higham suggests, are in disagreement about the effects of such fears on American society. Have fears of conspiracy directed at minority groups, such as Jews and Catholics, hindered their assimilation into American society? Are elections affected by the use of anticonspiratorial propaganda? For example, the impact of two separate anti-Catholic movements, the Know-Nothing crusade of the 1850s and the American Protective Association of the 1890s, were quite different. The APA had little discernible effect on national politics, whereas the Know-Nothing party was a significant force.

Whatever conclusion we may reach about these questions, one point seems plain enough: in times of crisis those most responsible for promoting national unity and protecting democratic values have sometimes done violence to both. There is tragedy here, and irony enough to provide even the most optimistic student of American history with cause for reflection.

1

The Image of the Beast: Anti-Papal Rhetoric in Colonial America

Thomas More Brown

The first essay in this book deals with the origins of American fears of conspiracy, the long process by which the American mind was shaped to regard conspiracy as a normal part of politics. Thomas More Brown locates the origins of anticonspiratorial rhetoric in the often expressed hatred of Roman Catholicism and fear of the activities of Pope during the colonial period. He traces such fears into the sixteenth-century English Reformation—indeed, into traditional Christian attitudes toward good and evil, God and the Devil. Although many historians regard fears of conspiracy as weapons used by antidemocratic forces to thwart social and political change, Brown suggests that in the colonial period antipapal rhetoric gave support to Enlightenment ideas and the American Revolution.

In the colonial period of American history no intellectual tradition was more prominent, or more omnipresent, than anti-Catholicism. It was found in sermons and almanacs, political treatises and poems; it was as vigorous in 1760 as it was in 1607. The attacks on "popery"

 A fully annotated version of this paper is available at Upsala College, East Orange, N.J., through interlibrary loan.

were not merely expressions of disagreements over theology or disputes about liturgy and church structure. What made them relevant to colonial Americans, and makes them interesting to us, was their high political content. They were permeated with a fear that the Pope was constantly engineering conspiracies to undermine Protestant nations. The endless repetition of this message slowly shaped an American mentality that regarded foreign-based conspiracies as a normal part of political reality.

The survival and the vitality of this rhetoric in a land far removed from European religious wars and inhabited by few Catholics forces us to question its significance in American politics and culture. During 150 years of the colonial period the message underwent a slow transformation, from a conception of the Pope as Antichrist, an emissary of Satan, to a metaphorical version of the Pope as a typical tyrant against whom men suspected of tyranny and conspiracy were measured. This rhetoric was a device for justifying the political practices and structures adopted by colonial Americans; it was also a conduit through which new political theories could be conveyed. If its importance is the light it sheds on colonial political thought, it must be recognized that antipapal rhetoric, especially the tendency to depict the Pope as an arch conspirator, has its roots in religion. What foreign power, after all, could be more malign than the Devil himself? Whose agents could be more deadly? The consciousness of evil as a power, as a palpable presence forever seeking the subversion of souls, is one of the greatest legacies of popular Christianity.

Theologians, to be sure, had asserted that evil is not a positive force. Saint Augustine, objecting to the Manichean theory of good and evil as powers warring for control of the universe, defined evil as the absence of good. Saint Thomas Aquinas insisted that evil does not exist, since all existence derives from God, who could not create his antithesis. The Devil, however, did exist; he was the angelic leader driven by unnatural pride to rebel against God, a revolt made possible by his free will. He sought to lead men along the same path of defiance of the Deity. Good Christians saw life as a war of self-defense, aided by Christ, the Virgin, and the saints, against the evil one.

The Protestant Reformation tapped this great source of popular belief, wedding it to a literature that specifically identified the Pope with the Devil. Attacks on the temporal power and spiritual authority of the papacy were not new. The eleventh-century Investiture Dispute had produced a flood of antipapal polemic, and the fourteenth century *Defensor Pacis* by Marsiglio of Padua was considered so powerful an indictment of the political pretensions of the Pope that Thomas Cromwell, Henry VIII's advisor, had portions of it translated into English in 1535 on behalf of the king's quarrel with Rome. The fourteenth-century Conciliar Movement saw a considerable literature challenging the right of Popes to overrule General Councils of the Church. But this outpouring of pamphlets and letters rarely identified the Pope as the agent of Satan, and little of it declared the Pope to be Antichrist.

There was another tradition of religious writing and thought, however, that did assert that the Pope was Antichrist. Numerous sects and movements in late medieval Europe prophesied the imminence of the second coming of Christ and called men to abandon worldly things in preparation for his return. The Protestant Reformers, always chary about the accusation that they represented something new, an abandonment of the ancient Christian Church, argued that the real church had lived underground through the long centuries of papal domination. Its existence could be inferred from sudden eruptions into the light of history—Albigensians, the followers of Joachim of Fiore (who in the late twelfth century predicted the imminent collapse of the papacy), Wycliff, and Hus. These protoreformers, as they came to be regarded, had lashed out at the worldliness, the profligacy, and the arrogance of the papacy. The Reformers were aware of this literature and saw in it a weapon in their war with Rome. Thus, in 1545, Martin Luther saluted the Council of Trent with a tract, "Against the Roman Papacy An Institution of the Devil."

The Protestant Reformers saw themselves participating in a movement more profound than a mere challenge to papal power. They understood themselves to be warriors of God in his awesome destruction of Antichrist; they were chosen to usher in the thousand-year reign of the saints promised in the Book of Revelations. The energy, intensity, and certitude of the Reformers were based on the conviction that they were witnessing and aiding in a great turning point in sacred history. Their war with the papacy and its triumphant outcome were forecast in Scripture.

The Reformers produced elaborate interpretations of the Book of the Revelation of St. John that explained the hidden meaning of the Evangelist's apocalyptic vision. The problem in Revelations was the identity of a red dragon that sprouted seven heads. This monster gave power to several earthly beasts, the most important of which is ridden by a whore dressed in scarlet. Reformers identified the dragon as the Devil and the beast with the scarlet whore as his earthly manifestation, the Antichrist, appearing as the Pope. According to John Bale, whose

Image of Both Churches (1548) is one of the first formal expositions of the Book of Revelations in English, the seven heads of the dragon symbolize seven historical appearances of the Devil. The seventh head is filled with "all carnal wisdom . . . all devilish policies and crafts: this is the papacy here in Europe, which is the general Antichrist of the whole world."

Bale found in the Book of Revelation a scenario for the history and future of the world, a history marked by the domination of the arrogant and avaricious Antichrist, the Roman Pontiff. This domination was no historical accident, but the result of a deliberate plot. William Tyndale's *Practice of Prelates* (1531) bared the origins of the plot: The Pope was subjected to the same temptation that the Devil spread before Christ, but the Pope succumbed.

> And the pope, after he had received the kingdom of the world of the devil, and was become the devil's vicar, took up in a like manner all Christendom on high, and brought them from the meekness of Christ unto the high hill and pride of Lucifer, and shewed them all the kingdoms of the earth, saying: Fall down and worship me, and I will give you these.

Among the Christians thus debauched the most important was the Emperor Constantine, who, according to Church tradition, had received the Empire from the Pope in return for fealty.

As a result of this Satanic grant of power, Tyndale suggests, "The bishops with the Pope have a certain conspiration and secret treason against the whole world." Through the confessional box they "know all secrets," by tithes they had drained the wealth of Christendom into the coffers of the Church, and by excommunication and interdict they had terrorized princes into docility and obedience to Rome.

Reform theologians differed among themselves over the precise chronology of Antichrist's reign, which the Book of Revelations was interpreted to measure 1260 years. Generally, however, they saw the beginning of papal power in the reign of Constantine. By the sixteenth century, therefore, the end of Antichrist's dominion was in sight, the great "Beast" was slowly dying as the papacy lost its grip. The Reformation, as Bale bluntly put it, presented all men with a stark choice, "either we are citizens in the New Jerusalem with Jesus Christ, or else, in the superstitious Babylon with Antichrist the vicar of Satan."

This interpretation had tremendous appeal—it made vivid and real the work of the Devil. Satan was no longer a force or a fallen angel, a mysterious and scarcely imaginable power of the air. He was an immensely rich and corrupt earthly power, with armies, diplomats, and secret agents. The Pope, indeed, was not simply an agent of Satan, he was an alter ego; the fate of the Pope was intimately bound up with the fate of Satan. As the Book of Revelations was interpreted God was about to devastate Satan, and God's people would destroy the papacy in preparation for the return to earth of Christ.

The world, then, became a battleground where upright Christians must combat the wiles, the subtle plots, and the military offensives of the papacy, which had "conspired against all commonwealths, and . . . made [for itself] several kingdoms, wherein it is lawful, unpunished, to work all abomination." The only recourse of God's people was to set up kingdoms dedicated to his work. Armed with this cosmic interpretation of history, Englishmen could make sense out of the turbulent upheavals of their own country in the sixteenth century. John Foxe in his immensely influential *Book of Martyrs* (1563 and numerous enlarged editions) explained to the Antichrist that the veil was torn from a hitherto inscrutable history:

> You see now, your doings, so wicked, cannot be hid; your cruelty is come to light; your murders be evident; your pretty practices, your subtle sleights, your secret conspiracies, your filthy lives are seen, and stink before God and man.

There crept into this rhetoric xenophobia and an identification of the papacy with the governments of France and Spain. Patriotism and religion combined to sanctify both the divine right claims of the Stuart monarchs and the Bible commonwealth of the Puritans in America.

All historical events and all apparently secular enterprises could be placed within the framework of the war against Antichrist. Foreign attacks on England or rebellion against the monarchy were seen as conspiracies launched by a desperate Satan. In 1640, for example, John Pym relayed to the House of Commons rumors of conspiracy involving English Catholics, Irish rebels, and Spain. "If this treason had taken effect," he declared, "our souls had been enthralled to the spiritual tyranny of Satan, our consciences to the ecclesiastical tyranny of the Pope, our lives, our persons and estates, to the civil tyranny of an arbitrary, unlimited, confused government." The greatest demonstration of the implacable enmity of Antichrist to the English Reformation was the Spanish Armada, and its destruction was a sign that the papacy was failing.

In the destruction of the Armada, Englishmen could take little comfort, however. The papacy was failing slowly; Antichrist, as events and pamphlets constantly reminded Englishmen, was like "the dragon . . . driven into his den, yet his sting and poison still in force." The sting of the papacy was felt again and again. James I, intended victim of the Gunpowder Plot of 1605, ascribed the whole "monstrous, rare . . . treacherous attempt" to papal agents and increased the persecution of Roman priests in England. It was in this atmosphere of an embattled England, beset by enemies, threatened by subversive plots, and informed by an endless stream of sermons and books, that the Pope and his French and Spanish allies were the visible presence of Antichrist, that Englishmen sailed forth to settle America.

To the theologically aware Englishman of the late sixteenth century America, however fabulous its reputed wealth, had to be discussed in terms other than a mere recitation of economic advantages. The Spanish had carved out an empire, not simply for themselves, but for the Pope; gold from America financed the Great Armada. America, like distant Sweden, could be viewed as a strategic base in the great international war against the antichristian Pope of Rome. It presented English leaders with both an opportunity and a danger.

Colonization of America was perceived as a religious necessity, for Spain had stolen a march on the Reformation, "When the Babylonish Inchantress . . . compassed sea and land, to make six, eight, or ten million Romish proselites" of American Indians. As Hakluyt pointed out to Queen Elizabeth in his famous "Discourse of Westerne Planting," settlement of America by English Protestants would give "such a mayme to the Pope and to that side, as never hapned [sic] to the sea of Rome by the practise of the late kinge of famous memory [Henry VIII] . . . or by all the former practices of all the protestant princes of Germanie."

There were dangers in the great venture. Even as honest Englishmen prepared to journey to Virginia, those "blinde guides the *Jesuites* . . . maligne and deprave this voyage, and we are well assured they have filled all corners of this kingdome, with all base reports and slanders of this action." Pamphlets urging the colonization of America often specified that Roman Catholics were to be banned from the new plantations, "for they will ever be plotting and conspiring, to root you out if they can; howsoever they sweare, flatter and equivocate beleeve them not. . . ." North America would be reserved for the King of England and the church of which he was head.

While Englishmen loyal to king and church planned to settle Virginia, the Puritans kept England in turmoil. The Church of England, they complained, too much resembled the Church of Rome: it retained many of the ceremonies and vestments of the Roman Church; it included, by law, all baptised Englishmen as had the Church of Rome; and it was governed by bishops, whom Puritans regarded as the Pope's general staff.

The Puritan insistence that the Church of England was almost a mirror image of the Roman Church outraged English bishops and seemed to the king dangerously close to treason. Worse, the Puritans claimed that they were not just a part of the Anglican Church, but the only part of it approved by God. James I and Charles I, with the aid of Archbishop Laud, launched a campaign to root Puritans out of the English Church.

The Puritans who came to New England did not see the move as a retreat from the great struggle to overthrow Antichrist. Rather, they would establish a sanctuary wherein they could construct a church purged of Romish corruptions, which would serve as a model for the world to emulate. The Reformation would receive its direction and ultimate goal from the Puritan City on a Hill. Even in this remote corner, however, the enemies of God and his people were a constant threat.

Increase Mather, as late as 1682, argued that the Church of Rome, though declining, was still dangerous, for, "a dying Beast will bite cruelly . . . since he is going out of the world, we may expect he will give a cruel bite at the Church of God." The Puritan fear of heresy was conditioned by the necessity for vigilance in the face of a vengeful Antichrist. John Cotton was especially alarmed that New England, removed from the European theatre of religious wars, might experience an outbreak of "the carnall and sinfull pity that is found in any state that shall be sparing of spilling the . . . bloud of the Priests and Jesuites . . . the Lord loathes this kinde of lenity and gentlenesse, and indulgence and toleration of such kinde of persons." New England ministers insisted that only a vigilant and unrelenting state could suppress Romanist heresies and ward off papal intrigues.

Subversives, asserted John Cotton, were ubiquitous.

> . . . No port can be so secretly wacht but they will enter in, no Gates of Princes Pallaces so secret but they will enter them . . . It is indefferent to them whether yee imploy them in Church worke, they can domineer there; or whether you imploy them in state matters, they are as free, and as busy there, in Courts of Princes, and the states of Commonwealths, as impetuous there, and as cunning, and as domineering, and Lordly there as they are in the Church.

Antichrist would strike not simply with armadas and armies, but with "lying wonders, with efficacie of delusions," the subtle corruptions spread by the most dangerous papal agents, the Jesuits.

The Society of Jesus was believed to be tirelessly engaged in "conspiracie and treason against the state: and that, unavoidably, by suffering such locusts to run up and downe the Countrey, to poison the hearts of men by their corrupt wayes and meanes: for their Ministers . . . draw men from their Allegiance due their Native Prince, to a forraine State. . . ." Inspired by such rhetoric and noting that the Thirty Years' War posed a threat to Protestant communities, the General Court of Massachusetts feared the "secret underminings and solicitations of those of the Jesuitical Order" and banned Jesuits from the colony. Nearly every colony passed similar laws.

The Devil, however, could not be stopped by a few laws barring the entry of subversive Jesuits. New England Puritans feared Roman inroads from less obvious sources. Dissension in the churches, challenges like those of Roger Williams and Ann Hutchinson, had their origin in pride, and a refusal to accept discipline. Such pride, Puritans argued, permitted the Bishop of Rome to dominate and destroy the primitive church. John Cotton warned his people that

> The more learned and witty you bee, the more fit to act for Satan will you bee if the Lord leave you . . . pride not yourselves . . . in these . . . or else they will be improved to the service of the Devill, and his instrument, the great and Monstrous Beast, the Roman Catholique visible Church, and the head thereof, the holy Father the Pope, as they call him.

Attacks on the polity of New England Congregationalism and challenges to the authority of the magistrates must inevitably lead the dissenter to Rome. Cotton conceived of the papacy not simply as Antichrist, but as anticommonwealth. New England's insistence on obedience amounted to a demand for loyalty in time of war.

Internal dissent was not the only door by which Satan and his papal emmissaries might wreak havoc in Massachusetts. Equally dangerous was the Church of England. Cotton argued that the Reformation was threatened not solely by direct papal assault, but by sympathizers. He distinguished between those "that had the Mark of the Beast"—the clergy ordained in the Roman Church—and those who, although not part of the Roman Church, nonetheless so much agreed with papal doctrine that they belong to an "Image of the Beast."

> Who then are they that worship his Image? The Image of the Beast . . . is all Nationall and Diocesan, and Provincial Churches; and they that rule them are the Image of the second Beast [of the Book of Revelations] So then they that worship the Image of the Beast, be such as are devoted to the Canons of Popish Churches.

Cotton was saying here that the Church of England and its supporters accepted so much of the heritage of the Church of Rome that they were, in effect, ecclesiastical "fellow travelers."

This posed a serious problem, since New England Puritans, hoping the king would leave them alone, refused to separate officially from the Church of England. Roger Williams demanded that New England churches formally deny their connection with an Anglican Church corrupted by Romish practices and governed by bishops. When the churches of Massachusetts refused to act on the clear implications of their conviction that the Church of England was an "Image of the Beast," Williams accused them of operating under papal influence.

The entire dispute between Roger Williams and the Massachusetts Bay ministers, led by John Cotton, was carried out in the terminology of antipapal rhetoric, with Williams hurling at Cotton the same complaint that Cotton flung at the Church of England. "The daughter New England," claimed Williams, "separating from her mother in Old England, yet maintaines and practices communion with Parishes in Old. Who sees not, then, but by the links of this mystical chaine, New English churches are still fastened to the Pope himself." Cotton denied that any such links could be discerned and charged that Williams' attempts to forge them ignored the basic fact that New England's churches, composed of the elect, did not in any manner resemble the parishes of the mother country. Practical politics, not mystical affinities, accounted for New England's refusal to break openly with the king's church.

Williams bolstered his contention that New England Puritans were uncomfortably close to popery with an accusation more difficult for Cotton to counter. The Massachusetts Bay authorities behaved exactly like states under papal domination or England under James I and Archbishop Laud—all oppressed genuine Puritans. The argument of Winthrop and Cotton that the magistrates must punish heretics because heresy threatens all social order and not just the purity of the churches was, Williams insisted, precisely the argument the Pope used to justify the Inquisition. "Mr. Cotton's Suppositions and the Papist's," Williams grimly announced, "come both out of the same Babylonian Quiver."

New England leaders justified the similarity of the state in New England, England, and the Continent by a continuous reiteration of Cotton's blunt declaration that "they that have been so busie in putting to death innocents . . . should also be put to death." Roger Williams, indeed, agreed that toleration could not embrace murderous and subversive Papists, and they were excepted from the toleration of Rhode

Island. He refused to see, however, the hand of the Pope in every deviant theological speculation and denied that departure from the Massachusetts way was a laxness produced by an intellectual pride that must inevitably lead the dissenter to Rome.

Williams' contention that New England, eager to combat conspiracy, had erected a grotesque parody of the European Antichrist must have bewildered other Puritans. They were convinced that they had avoided the source of the power of Antichrist: their churches were organically separate from the state, and the doctrine of the elect protected the churches from invasion by devilish power seekers who might use the secular power of the church to corrupt pure religion. In short, the very structure of the Commonwealth prevented that fatal mingling of secular power and spiritual authority that was the means by which Antichrist destroyed the primitive church. To Williams the argument was unconvincing: the state rushed in to stamp out heresy in the name of civil order, and that was unpleasantly reminiscent of Romish practices. Williams' strictures had little effect in New England, but they added to the shaping of a concept emerging in England.

The polemics of Cotton and Williams were published in England and must be seen as part of the debate over church structure and toleration that swirled through Parliament and the New Model Army in the 1640s. There were, after all, no Catholics in New England, and after the triumph of Cromwell and the ending of the Thirty Years' War on the continent, there was little prospect of a papally sponsored invasion. Yet the dire warnings of papal enmity continued; what was at stake was not just the security of New England, but the future of the Reformation.

The approach of Williams, however, appealed far more to Cromwell than that of the authorities of Massachusetts. Beset by Scotch Presbyterians on one side and extreme Independents on the other, and ruling an England filled with Anglicans, the leaders of the English Puritan Revolution had no choice but to adopt a position of relative toleration toward expressions of Protestantism. John Milton argued that in purely religious matters the use of the civil arm to compel adherence to doctrine was unwarranted. Indeed, as Milton pointed out, "chiefly for this do all true Protestants account the Pope Antichrist, for that he assume to himself this Infallibility over both the Conscience and the Scriptures." As a practical matter Cromwell's Puritan Commonwealth could not extend this toleration to Roman Catholicism, and Milton's reasoning was the same as that of Roger Williams: Catholicism had to be understood not as a religion, "but a Roman Principality rather, endeavoring to keep up her old Universal Dominion. . . . Justly therefore to be suspected, not tolerated by the Magistrates of another Country."

Missing from the writings of Milton is the conviction of imminent danger at the hands of the papacy, and equally absent is the militant note that inspired the Reformers. This calm tone reflects more than the acceptance of the political settlement of 1648 in Europe; more profoundly, it is testimony to the decline of the apocalyptic expectations that drove earlier generations of Reformers. The lurid episodes of the Restoration period obscure the degree to which the vision of England as a belligerent in a cosmic war had faded. The position of Milton, with its unwillingness to demand monolithic loyalty in matters of religion in the face of Antichrist, was a prophecy of the future. But before that future could be realized, England was summoned to one last battle against the "Beast."

The policies of Charles II and James II alarmed Protestants on both sides of the Atlantic. The dramatic revelations of Titus Oates in 1678 that a "Popish Plot" was brewing against England seemed credible in light of the known religious preferences of the monarch. Propaganda against Rome continued unabated; pamphlets, broadsides, and poems reminded Protestants of the history of conspiracy directed by Rome.

In 1683 Bostonians were regaled by an American edition of one of the most popular antipapal tracts, Benjamin Keach's *Sion in Distress or the Groans of the Protestant Church*. Claiming that the sinfulness of the people must lead to popery, Keach emphasized a theme prominent in all conspiracy rhetoric, the sexual depravity of the enemy. The papacy, he announced, "hast not only countenanced Stews and Brothel-Houses, where abominable Sodomy and Adulteries are practiced, but even [the] very Nunneries are become Habitations of Whoredome and Filthiness, the bottoms of whose Motes and Ponds have shewed the Murders of new born Babes."

The policies of Charles II and especially James II gave these outpourings a timeliness, a relevance reinforced by the traditional material that the polemics contained. They placed the Stuarts within a familiar historical framework. It was widely believed that James sought to return England to the Church of Rome. Although his secret treaty with Louis XIV, which promised to restore the ancient church, was not known, Englishmen observed that, in two Declarations of Indulgence, James permitted Catholics to hear Mass in private and removed other restrictions placed upon them. Papists joined the army, and rumors spread that troops loyal to the Pope had been stationed near London. In this atmosphere of tales of dire conspiracies against Protestant England, the king had an heir who would be baptized a Catholic.

Horrified Englishmen revolted, deposed James, and invited William and Mary to occupy the throne.

This Glorious Revolution had counterparts in America, with rebellions flaring up in Boston, New York, and Maryland. Historians have noted the local roots of these revolts and traced the social tensions in late seventeenth-century American society revealed by them. Significant as these social and economic grievances undoubtedly were, the catalyst that made men act was antipapal rhetoric. The Stuarts had sought to centralize the administration of the colonies, joining the New England colonies to New York and New Jersey in a dominion governed by Sir Edmund Andros. He arrived two years after New England's leading theologian, Samuel Willard, had delivered a sermon explaining that the Pope was striving to destroy the Puritan Commonwealth. While God "hath wonderfully disappointed" the Pope to date, Willard warned, it was no time for Protestants to relax vigilance. New England was confronted with "a plot which is ever on foot, and unto which contribution is constantly made. . . . It is the Master Plot of the World." This vision of an untiring, scheming Antichrist, using every means from colorful ceremonies to revolting licentiousness to undermine the sturdy faith of New England, was basic to the Puritan perception of the troubles that befell them in the 1680s and 1690s. These disasters, ranging from the establishment of the Dominion of New England to Indian wars, from fires that swept Boston to witches, surely were the acts of an angry God reminding his people that they stood in covenant with him. The ministers bewailed the sins of the people and prophesied that God would forsake an apostate New England, afflicting it with "judgments" of his aroused wrath. Edmund Andros was a judgment; abandonment of New England by God in the face of Antichrist's juggernaut was the consequence of sin.

The administration of Andros was marked by actions that New Englanders found tyrannical: confiscation of land titles, banning of town meetings, and provision of Congregational churches for the use of the Church of England. These actions were seen as typical not merely of despotism, but specifically of papal despotism. As in the Popish Plot, "Wherein," stated Cotton Mather, "the Bloody Devotoes of Rome had in their Design and Prospect no less than the Extinction of the Protestant Religion," so it was in Andros' plans.

Not the least of those plans was a secret understanding with the Indians. When Indian wars began to rage along the frontiers in the 1680s, they were promptly placed in the context of the struggle against Antichrist. The Declaration of the Protestant Associates of Maryland, justifying rebellion against their proprietor, the Catholic Lord Baltimore, flatly accused French Jesuits of leading the Indians. In Boston the accusations were directed at Andros. Cotton Mather claimed that an army of New England militia, "under Popish Commanders" appointed by the governor, had deliberately failed to stop Indian attacks. "We cannot but suspect in it a Branch of the Plot to bring us low." Exasperated, Bostonians rose up and jailed Andros. A broadside celebrated the overthrow of the governor by pointing out that

> We, by Papistick wiles, may well believe
> Were mark't a lingering Ruin to receive
> They grudged that we should harmlessly possess
> With ease and freedom this our Wilderness . . .
> Knaves, Beggers, *Papists* form'd a triple League
> Which carry'd on the ruinous Intreague.

The Glorious Revolution became a landmark in the literature of anti-Catholicism; clearly and firmly a terrible papal plot, seeking to impose arbitrary government and religious despotism on the English-speaking world, had been defeated. Jonathan Edwards, in a series of sermons published as *A History of the Work of Redemption,* later said of the Stuart period,

> There was at that time a strong conspiracy between the king of England and Louis XIV of France, who were both Papists, to extinguish . . . the protestant religion, not only out of England, but out of all Europe; and they had so laid their scheme that they seemed to be almost sure of their purpose. . . . And just as their matters came to a head, God, in His providence, suddenly dashed all their schemes in pieces by the revolution.

The rescue of Protestantism once again from the strings of the dying "Beast of Rome" was celebrated in terms radically different from earlier paens on the defeat of the Armada. The theme of the arbitrariness of government, of political despotism, dominates the literature about the Glorious Revolution.

To be sure, the great theme of a struggle between Christ and Satan, between the people of God and the antichristian papacy, continued to resound through the rhetoric. But the prophecies of the imminent downfall of the papacy declined; ministers became more hesitant to predict the time of the killing of the "Beast." This removed from the rhetoric much of its urgency; the old chiliastic vision was fading. Among other things, this slow retreat from the grand confidence of the Reformers that the destruction of Antichrist could be expected in the near future gave to the language a tiredness, a formal, stereotyped quality that turned from a description of reality into a metaphor.

Antipapal rhetoric underwent a secularization in the eighteenth century. Where both Puritans and Anglicans in the seventeenth century used it to justify official intolerance and governmental suppression of heresy, it now became a weapon in the arsenal of the Enlightenment. The papacy came to stand for cruelty, barbarism, ignorance, control over the press, and religious bigotry. The familiar rhetoric became a vehicle for the importation of new ideas. William Livingston, whose *Independent Reflector* (1754) urged freedom of press and conscience, saw the Stuart regime as "the late horrid and impious Attack on our happy Constitution."

> Had our unrelenting Enemies succeeded in their detestable Designs; instead of enjoying our invaluable Liberties, we had long e'er now beheld Persecution brandishing her Sword and felt the insulting Victor loading us with Chains: In a word, we had seen Tyranny like a ravenous Harpy devouring the fruits of our Industry; and Popery, with her malignant spirit, plunging us into the Depths of Misery.

To Livingston, and to most commentators, popery and the government of France were two sides of the same coin. The French and Indian Wars were indeed seen as part of the age-old conflict between Rome and Protestantism. When the New England militia captured the mighty French fortress of Louisbourg, the Congregational minister from York, Maine, completed the triumph by demolishing the high altar of the Catholic Church with an axe.

The rhetoric of conspiracy lost none of its ability to evoke the terrible nature of the struggle. In 1760 the Rev. William Adams of New London asked:

> And from such horrid confederacies, and combinations of the powers of darkness; what various designs have been set on foot against the Lord's people? What subtil stratagems have been invented? What deep and artful plots have been laid up for their ruin? Yea, what barbarities and massacres have been perpertrated? The sacred records abound with accounts of the artful and mischievous devices, the black and cruel attempts of the worldly powers against Israel of God.

Benjamin Franklin, seeking to arm Quaker Pennsylvania against the enemy, argued that the danger was not merely external, not merely a matter of Indians skulking in the western forests. "Are there no Priests among us, think you, that might . . . give an Enemy . . . good Encouragement?"

For all this, however, the rhetoric reveals a distinct change in the language by which the combatants in the war between the Lord's people and Antichrist's minions were characterized. The description of the American Israel became increasingly secular, and the threat of Antichrist was defined in more mundane terms than was previously the case. "If popish power had prevailed," declared a sermon celebrating the fall of Montreal, "we must have bid adieu to our Rights and Privileges, Liberties and Properties, our dear Country, and what is more, our holy Religion, we had been made slaves in our native as in some distant land." Religion had become one of a number of advantages enjoyed by the English colonies, rather than the heart and soul of the settlement.

The flood of antipapal rhetoric called forth by the French and Indian Wars had little effect on Catholics in the colonies. The Rev. James Sterling, preaching in 1755 before the governor of Maryland, urged that "without Cruelty to their Persons, or overstraining of the laws, let us muzzle the Bear, or cut the Tyger's Fangs, and take all speedy, Parliamentary, and Christian Methods for Self-Security." No Puritan magistrate would have balked at cruelty or overstraining the law in the face of domestic papists. But in Maryland, Sterling noted, there were "Roman Catholic Gentlemen of Fortune and Family . . . who do not swallow implicitly all the Impositions of that Church, though they hold external Communion with it." Religious loyalty, he declared, did not determine or undermine patriotism. Although Catholics were denied the right to vote and hold office in Maryland, they not only were no further molested, they played an influential informal role in politics. In Pennsylvania, too, Catholics were free to worship openly, and a number of Catholics lived in New York without difficulty—despite the conviction of some New Yorkers that the slave revolt of 1741 had been instigated by papal agents.

The fear of conspiracy, in short, was becoming abstract; the idea of an international struggle against Antichrist was replaced by a series of patriotic wars against France and, incidentally, the papacy. Sterling himself was sufficiently alarmed by the danger of subversion to suggest that Catholics, "when these tend to the Destruction of the State, and their Toleration becomes incompatible with its Safety, then it is incumbent on the civil Establishment . . . either to totally suppress them or keep them under . . . Restrictions." The restrictions were not forthcoming. On the contrary, antipapal rhetoric was a major constituent in the demand for toleration.

A traditional fear of American colonists, going back to the early seventeenth century, was the possibility of an American establishment of the Church of England. In the South and in the lower four counties of New York the Anglican church was a state church, governed by the Bishop of London, but it had no official position within the colonial political structure, as did English bishops who sat in the House of Lords. Moreover, by 1760 it had arrived at a *modus vivendi* with dissenting sects. History revealed, however, that a theologically aroused king, like James I, or a zealous prelate, like Archbishop Laud, would seek to stamp out dissent. Jonathan Mayhew, in his *Discourse on Unlimited Submission* (1750) had James and Laud in mind when he warned that bishops and kings have a dangerous tendency "to be willing that the clergy should do what they would—set up a monstrous hierarchy like that of Rome—a monstrous inquisition like that of Spain or Portugal. . . ." From the standpoint of a Congregational clergyman like Mayhew the great danger was the possibility that the English Church might send a resident bishop to America to govern the colonial church. This fear, invariably presented in terms of the "popishness" of Anglican bishops, persisted throughout the eighteenth century and forms part of the generalized alarm over British policy after 1763.

Within the colonies the battle for toleration usually pitted Baptists, Presbyterians, and Quakers against Congregationalists or Anglicans. The issue focused around the mandatory payment of taxes to support the salaries of ministers of established churches. One dissenter traced the whole system to

> . . . Ancient Ages, when the English Realm
> And Popish zealots, placed at the Helm
> To stablish that Religion, Tythes were fixed
> By Common Laws, with civil intermix'd
> Which formed the English Constitution so
> That after Ages can't the Tythes forego.

The old complaint that the papacy drained the treasuries of Western Europe was now applied by dissenters to the dominant Congregationalists in New England and Anglicans elsewhere.

Another line of argument for toleration couched in traditional anti-Catholic rhetoric can be traced to John Trenchard, Thomas Gordon, John Locke, and ultimately John Milton. These writers, strongly opposed to the divine right of kings and favoring toleration as a matter of human right, were severely and sometimes savagely anticlerical. They saw established churches as the result of a back-room plot among the clergy to seize power and wealth. Trenchard and Gordon, whose

Independent Whig (1720) went through many editions, including two in America, echoed Roger Williams' accusation that all established churches have popish inclinations. When defenders of the Church of England

> . . . debate with the Papists, they praise the Scriptures, inveigh against the imposing of Opinions, and speak in the Stile of Dissenters: But when they are pleased to rebuke Non-conformists, they borrow the Language of Papists, and urge the Authority of our Apostolick Church, and her divine Right to judge for others; and deal hard Language, and worse Usage, to all that take the same Privilege which they do.

Their objections to popery were not based on the Book of Revelations or on traditional theological grounds. The papacy, they complained, attempted to compel men's minds, engross their wealth, and destroy their liberties. The papacy was conceived of as an ultimate version of all religious bodies that used the power of the state to enforce doctrine. Hence, it was most at home in a despotic monarchy like France. The arbitrary Vatican was the antithesis of constitutional England.

The danger to England, then, came only partly from France, Stuart pretenders, or the papacy. The greatest threat to the constitution came not from the "Beast," but from his image, now divested of theological trappings. Politicians and clergymen, who out of avarice and a lust for domination sought to bridle the rights of others, increase taxes, and put disabilities on dissenting sects, all imitated the methods of the Pope and his supporters.

The most famous American exponent of these views was William Livingston's short-lived newspaper, *The Independent Reflector*. As English libertarians had accused the Church of England of aping the papal desire for spiritual and political hegemony, so Livingston assailed the clergy of the Calvinist sects of America: "Rome is just as far from Geneva, as Geneva from Rome. For Orthodoxy, as it is commonly used, is a meer levitical Engine, that has done more Mischief to Mankind, than all the Tyrants that ever ravag'd the Globe."

Eighteenth-century Americans were convinced that the papacy maintained its power by keeping people in mental bondage; Catholicism was the anti-Enlightenment. Jonathan Edwards observed that:

> The holy Scriptures by degrees were taken out of the hands of the laity, the better to promote the unscriptural and wicked designs of the Pope and clergy; and instead of promoting knowledge among the people, they industriously promoted ignorance. It was a received maxim among them that ignorance is the mother of devotion: and so great was the darkness of those times, that learning was almost extinct in the world.

John Adams ascribed the ability of the Roman Church to persuade men that the Church both mediated grace and had the right to depose princes by "reducing their minds to a state of sordid ignorance and staring timidity, and by infusing into them a religious horror of letters and knowledge." If the papacy worked in this fashion, it could not be defeated by armies, penal laws, and intolerance. The battle against Antichrist would be won by widely diffusing education.

Strangulation of the press was another old theme of antipapal rhetoric. "The admirable art of Printing," said *A Plaine Description of the Barmudas* (1613), promoted "the restoration of learning, diffusion of knowledge, and consequently the discoverie and destruction of Poperie, that the Pope and Popish Politicians wish it had never beene, and have bestowed many a secret curse upon him that first received it. . . ." It was not until the eighteenth century that the implications of this antipapal rhetoric became commonplace. Freedom of the press was an essential condition for the exposure of the enemy, Livingston argued, since, "Popery and Slavery could not stand before true Religion and Liberty, and as the Press was the Instrument of both, the Rights of St. Peter's Chair were no sooner publically contested, than despised and diminished." Governments that would restrain the criticism of the press were as arbitrary as France, imitated the papacy, and might even be serving papal ends.

Intolerance, ignorance, and censorship were the methods by which the papacy secured domination and the policies adopted by arbitrary Catholic governments. The eighteenth-century arguments against the papacy emphasized the danger of any government adopting similar means to destroy liberty. The papacy was not particularly dangerous in and of itself, the literature rarely argued that the Pope continued to organize armadas. Rather, the papacy was a bad example, an incontestably evil power whose actions must be the opposite of what sound Englishmen and Americans desired.

Fear of popery, then, was a familiar rhetoric by which political dangers could be measured; actions of government could be lambasted on the grounds that they smacked of popery. Livingston regarded the papacy as the most extreme form of a government dominated or unhealthily influenced by the clergy. Political tyranny and an established church went hand in hand. The danger was no longer that Jesuits would by artful persuasion convert Protestants or that papal agents would sabotage Protestant states; it was that Protestant governments themselves would become the image of the "Beast."

The American revolutionaries inherited, then, two mutually reinforcing traditions of antipapal rhetoric. The older view, which continued to find expression, disposed them to see events in terms of conspiracies of international and, indeed, cosmic scope. The Enlightenment version of antipapal polemic made the conspiracies more mundane. Both shaped an American conviction that liberty and Manifest Destiny were God's answer to Antichrist. The defeat of France revived the great millennial hopes for America. As the Rev. Nathaniel Appleton, rejoicing over the conquest of Canada, expressed it:

> As the Romish, antichristian Power, that was set up in a corner of this Land is now brought under, what may we hope for? . . . May we not hope that under the Divine Favor we shall grow a much greater and mightier people than we now are; and the true and pure Religion of Our Lord Jesus Christ shall spread itself through the land to the distant parts thereof?

The dashing of these dreams accounts in no small part of the frustration of Americans and their willingness to read conspiratorial designs into the actions of the British government.

The reorganization of the empire, contemplated and partly carried out by British ministries after 1760, aroused a people who automatically sought to discern malevolent plots in political events. Samuel Adams claimed that the Stamp Act "was contrived with a design only to inure people to the habit of contemplating themselves as the slaves of men; and the transition from thence to subjection to Satan is mighty easy." The President of Harvard, looking back over the years from the perspective of 1775, asked, "Have we not great reason to suspect that all the late measures respecting the colonies have originated from popish schemes of men who would gladly restore the race of Stuart and who look on Popery as a religion most favorable to arbitrary power?" Alexander Hamilton feared that as a result of the Quebec Art, "priestly tyranny may hereafter find as propitious soil in America as it ever had in Spain or Portugal."

While the Quebec Act evoked a flood of pamphlets and letters to newspapers insisting that the "Beast" was again on the prowl, the Revolutionary literature, in general, did not especially emphasize the theme nor did it display serious fear of internal subversion by Catholics. When, for example, Daniel Dulany of Maryland attacked Charles Carroll of Carrollton for espousing the Revolutionary cause, he declared that Carroll's Catholicism should make him suspect in the eyes of all Marylanders. But the issue fell flat—the rhetoric had long since ceased to refer to a specific danger posed by individual Catholics—and Carroll was ultimately to represent Maryland in Congress and sign the Declaration of Independence.

The anti-Catholic rhetoric had a more important effect than its applicability to the actions of the ministers of George III. It helped define the nature of the governments Americans must establish. John Adams praised the Puritans, who "saw clearly that popular powers must be placed as a guard, a control, a balance, to the powers of the monarch and the priest, in every government, or else it would soon become the man of sin, the whore of Babylon, the mystery of iniquity, a great and detestable system of fraud and violence." Separation of church and state, freedom of the press, the encouragement of education—a catalogue of republican virtues—were one legacy of antipapal rhetoric.

A darker heritage of this rhetoric was a mind shaped to regard conspiracy, directed by foreign powers eager to lay waste the land and revoke the liberties and traditions of the citizens, as a normal feature of politics. Over 150 years of reiteration of the master plot of the Antichrist there had been molded a mind that almost instinctively looked behind the turmoil of current politics to discern the maneuvers of the Devil.

2

The Logic of Rebellion: Conspiracy Fears and the American Revolution

Bernard Bailyn

Bernard Bailyn argues that many American revolutionaries feared that ministers of the British government had formed a conspiracy to destroy the liberties of Americans. This fear of a plot in the highest levels of imperial government was a basic ingredient of American revolutionary ideology. He traces the conviction that government is dominated by malign conspirators to early eighteenth-century opposition writers in British politics. Hatred of political corruption, fear of standing armies, and suspicion of the established church fostered a profound fear of the misuse of governmental power. The selection printed below, from Bailyn's Pulitzer Prize winning The Ideological Origins of the American Revolution, *shows how Americans adapted these ideas to their own situation.*

The colonists believed they saw emerging from the welter of events during the decade after the Stamp Act a pattern whose meaning was

---

Excerpted by permission of the publishers from pp. 94–143 of Bernard Bailyn, The Ideological Origins of the American Revolution, *Cambridge, Mass.: the Belknap Press of Harvard University, copyright, 1967, by the President and Fellows of Harvard College.*

unmistakable. They saw in the measures taken by the British government and in the actions of officials in the colonies something for which their peculiar inheritance of thought had prepared them only too well, something they had long conceived to be a possibility in view of the known tendencies of history and of the present state of affairs in England. They saw about them, with increasing clarity, not merely mistaken, or even evil, policies violating the principles upon which freedom rested, but what appeared to be evidence of nothing less than a deliberate assault launched surreptitiously by plotters against liberty both in England and in America. The danger to America, it was believed, was in fact only the small, immediately visible part of the greater whole whose ultimate manifestation would be the destruction of the English constitution, with all the rights and privileges embedded in it.

This belief transformed the meaning of the colonists' struggle, and it added an inner accelerator to the movement of opposition. For, once assumed, it could not be easily dispelled: denial only confirmed it, since what conspirators profess is not what they believe; the ostensible is not the real; and the real is deliberately malign.

It was this—the overwhelming evidence, as they saw it, that they were faced with conspirators against liberty determined at all costs to gain ends which their words dissembled—that was signaled to the colonists after 1763, and it was this above all else that in the end propelled them into Revolution.

Suspicion that the ever-present, latent danger of an active conspiracy of power against liberty was becoming manifest within the British Empire, assuming specific form and developing in coordinated phases, rose in the consciousness of a large segment of the American population before any of the famous political events of the struggle with England took place. No adherent of a nonconformist church or sect in the eighteenth century was free from suspicion that the Church of England, an arm of the English state, was working to bring all subjects of the crown into the community of the Church; and since toleration was official and nonconformist influence in English politics formidable, it was doing so by stealth, disguising its efforts, turning to improper uses devices that had been created for benign purposes. In particular, the Society for the Propagation of the Gospel in Foreign Parts, an arm of the Church created in 1701 to aid in bringing the Gospel to the pagan Indians, was said by 1763 to have "long had a formal design to root out Presbyterianism, etc., and to establishing both episcopacy and bishops."

This suspicion, which had smoldered in the breasts of New Englanders and nonconformists throughout the colonies for half a century or more, had burst into flame repeatedly, but never so violently as in 1763, in the Mayhew-Apthorp controversy which climaxed years of growing anxiety that plans were being made secretly to establish an American episcopate. To Mayhew, as to Presbyterian and Congregational leaders throughout the colonies, there could be little doubt that the threat was real. Many of the facts were known, facts concerning maneuvers in London and in America. Angelican leaders in New York and New Jersey had met almost publicly to petition England for an American episcopate, and there could be little doubt also of the role of the Society for the Propagation of the Gospel in this undercover operation. For if the ostensible goal of the Society was the gospelizing of the pagan Indians and Negroes, its true goal was manifestly revealed when it established missions in places like Cambridge, Massachusetts, which had not had a resident Indian since the seventeenth century and was well-equipped with "orthodox" preachers. Such missions, Mayhew wrote, have "all the appearance of entering wedges . . . carrying on the crusade, or spiritual siege of our churches, with the hope that they will one day submit to an episcopal sovereign." Bishops, he wrote unblinkingly in reply to the Archbishop of Canterbury, have commonly been instruments in arbitrary reigns of "establishing a tyranny over the bodies and souls of men," and their establishment in America would mark the end of liberty in Massachusetts and elsewhere. By 1765, when the final exchanges in this pamphlet war were published, it was commonly understood in New England and elsewhere that "the stamping and episcopizing [of] our colonies were . . . *only different branches of the same plan of power.*"

Fear of an ecclesiastical conspiracy against American liberties, latent among nonconformists through all of colonial history, thus erupted into public controversy at the very same time that the first impact of new British policies in civil affairs was being felt. And though it was, in an obvious sense, a limited fear (for large parts of the population identified themselves with the Anglican Church and were not easily convinced that liberty was being threatened by a plot of Churchmen) it nevertheless had a profound indirect effect everywhere, for it drew into public discussion—evoked in specific form—the general conviction of eighteenth-century Englishmen that the conjoining of "temporal and spiritual tyranny" was, in John Adams' words, an event totally "calamitous to human liberty," yet an event that in the mere nature of things perpetually threatened.

For, as David Hume had explained, "in all ages of the world priests have been enemies to liberty . . . Liberty of thinking and of expressing our thoughts is always fatal to priestly power . . . and, by an infallible connection which prevails among all kinds of liberty, this privilege can never be enjoyed . . . but in a free government. Hence . . . all princes that have aimed at despotic power have known of what importance it was to gain the established clergy; as the clergy, on their part, have shown a great facility in entering into the views of such princes." Fear of the imposition of an Anglican episcopate thus brought into focus a cluster of ideas, attitudes, and responses alive with century-old Popish-Stuart-Jacobite associations that would enter directly into the Revolutionary controversy in such writings as John Adams' *Dissertation on the Canon and Feudal Law* (1765) and Samuel Adams' "A Puritan" pieces published in the *Boston Gazatte* in 1768. And more than that, it stimulated among highly articulate leaders of public opinion, who would soon be called upon to interpret the tendency of civil affairs, a general sense that they lived in a conspiratorial world in which what the highest officials professed was not what they in fact intended, and that their words masked a malevolent design.

Reinforcement for this belief came quickly. Even for those who had in no way been concerned with the threat of an episcopal establishment, the passage of the Stamp Act was not merely an impolitic and unjust law that threatened the priceless right of the individual to retain possession of his property until he or his chosen representative voluntarily gave it up to another; it was to many, also, a danger signal indicating that a more general threat existed. For though it could be argued, and in a sense proved by the swift repeal of the act, that nothing more was involved than ignorance or confusion on the part of people in power who really knew better and who, once warned by the reaction of the colonists, would not repeat the mistake—though this could be, and by many was, concluded, there nevertheless appeared to be good reason to suspect that more was involved. For from whom had the false information and evil advice come that had so misled the English government? From officials in the colonies, said John Adams, said Oxenbridge Thacher, James Otis, and Stephen Hopkins—from officials bent on overthrowing the constituted forms of government in order to satisfy their own lust for power, and not likely to relent in their passion. Some of these local plotters were easily identified. To John Adams, Josiah Quincy, and others the key figure in Massachusetts from the beginning to the end was Thomas Hutchinson who by "serpentine wiles" was befuddling and victimizing the weak, the avaricious, and the incautious in order to increase his notorious engrossment of public office. In Rhode Island it was, to James Otis, that "little, dirty, drinking, drabbing, contaminated knot of thieves, beggars, and transports . . . made up of Turks, Jews, and other infidels, with a few renegado Christians and Catholics"—the Newport junto, led by Martin Howard, Jr., which had already been accused by Stephen Hopkins and others in Providence of "conspiring against the liberties of the colony."

But even if local leaders associated with power elements in England had not been so suspect, there were grounds for seeing more behind the Stamp Act than its ostensible purpose. The official aim of the act was, of course, to bring in revenue to the English treasury. But the sums involved were in fact quite small, and "some persons . . . may be inclined to acquiesce under it." But that would be to fall directly into the trap, for the smaller the taxes, John Dickinson wrote in the most influential pamphlet published in America before 1776, the more dangerous they were, since they would the more easily be found acceptable by the incautious, with the result that a precedent would be established for making still greater inroads on liberty and property.

> Nothing is wanted at home but a PRECEDENT, the force of which shall be established by the tacit submission of the colonies . . . If the Parliament succeeds in this attempt, other statutes will impose other duties . . . and thus the Parliament will levy upon us such sums of money as they choose to take, *without any other* LIMITATION *than their* PLEASURE.

Others saw more drastic hidden meanings and implications in the passage of the Stamp Act. "If the real and only motive of the minister was to raise money from the colonies," Joseph Warren wrote in 1766, "that method should undoubtedly have been adopted which was least grievous to the people." Choice of so blatantly obnoxious a measure as the Stamp Act, consequently, "has induced some to imagine that the minister designed by this act to force the colonies into a rebellion, and from thence to take occasion to treat them with severity, and, by military power, to reduce them to servitude." Such a supposition was perhaps excessive: "charity forbids us to conclude [the ministry] guilty of so black a villainy. But . . . it is known that tyrannical ministers have, at some time, embraced even this hellish measure to accomplish their cursed designs," and speculation based on "admitting this to have been his aim" seemed well worth pursuing. To John Adams it seemed "very manifest" that the ultimate design behind the Stamp Act was an effort to forge the fatal link between ecclesiastical and civil despotism, the first by stripping the colonists "in a great measure of the means of knowledge, by loading the press, the colleges, and even an almanac and a newspaper with restraints and duties," the second, by recreating the inequalities and dependencies of feudalism "by taking from the poorer sort of people all their little subsistence, and conferring it on a set of stamp officers, distributors, and their deputies." This last point was the most obvious: "as the influence of money and places generally procures to the minister a majority in Parliament," Arthur Lee wrote, so an income from unchecked taxation would lead to a total corruption of free government in America, with the result that the colonies would "experience the fate of the *Roman* people in the deplorable times of their slavery."

But by then, in 1768, more explicit evidence of a wide-ranging plot was accumulating rapidly. Not only had the Townshend Duties, another revenue act, been passed by Parliament despite all the violence of the colonists' reaction to the Stamp Act, but it was a measure that enhanced the influence of the customs administration, which for other reasons had already come under suspicion. There had been, it was realized by the late 1760s, a sudden expansion in the number of "posts in the [colonial] 'government' . . . worth the attention of persons of influence in Great Britain"—posts, Franklin explained, like the governorships, filled by persons who were

> generally strangers to the provinces they are sent to govern, have no estate, natural connection, or relation there to give them an affection for the country . . . they come only to make money as fast as they can; are sometimes men of vicious characters and broken fortunes, sent by a minister merely to get them out of the way.

By the late 1760s, in the perspective of recent events, one could see that the invasion of customs officers "born with long claws like eagles," had begun as far back as the last years of the Seven Years' War and was now being reinforced by the new tax measures. The wartime Orders in Council demanding stricter enforcement of the Navigation Laws; the Sugar Act of 1764, which had multiplied the customs personnel; and the American Board of Customs Commissioners created in 1767 with "power," Americans said, "to constitute as many under officers as they please"—all of these developments could be seen to have provided for an "almost incredible number of inferior officers," most of whom the colonists believed to be "wretches . . . of such infamous characters that the merchants cannot possibly think their interest safe under their care." More important by far, however, was their influence on government.

For there was an obvious political and constitutional danger in having such "a set of *idle drones*," such "lazy, proud, worthless *pensioners* and *placemen*," in one's midst. . . .

Parasitic officeholders, thoroughly corrupted by their obligations to those who had appointed them, would strive to "*distinguish themselves* by their sordid zeal in defending and promoting measures which *they know beyond all question* to be *destructive* to the *just rights* and *true interests* of their country." Seeking to "*serve the ambitious purposes of great men* at home" these "*base-spirited wretches*" would urge—were already urging—as they logically had to, the specious attractions of "SUBMISSIVE behavior." . . .

In the end, this extension of executive patronage, based on a limitless support of government through colonial taxation, would make the whole of government "merely a ministerial engine"; by throwing off the balance of its parts, it would destroy the protective machinery of the constitution.

But even this did not exhaust the evidence that a design against liberty was unfolding. During the same years the independence of the judiciary, so crucial a part of the constitution, was suddenly seen to be under heavy attack, and by the mid-1760s to have succumbed in many places.

This too was not a new problem. The status of the colonial judiciary had been a controversial question throughout the century. The Parliamentary statute of 1701 which guaranteed judges in England life tenure in their posts had been denied to the colonies, in part because properly trained lawyers were scarce in the colonies, especially in the early years, and appointments for life would prevent the replacement of ill-qualified judges by their betters, when they appeared; and in part because, judicial salaries being provided for by temporary legislative appropriations, the removal of all executive control from the judiciary, it was feared, would result in the hopeless subordination of the courts to popular influences. The status of the judiciary in the eighteenth century was therefore left open to political maneuvering in which, more often than not, the home government managed to carry its point and to make the tenure of judges as temporary as their salaries. Then suddenly, in the early 1760s, the whole issue exploded. In 1759 the Pennsylvania Assembly declared that the judges of that province would thereafter hold their offices by the same permanence of tenure that had been guaranteed English judges after the Glorious Revolution. But the law was disallowed forthwith by the crown. Opposition newspapers boiled with resentment; angry speeches were made in the Assembly; and a pamphlet appeared explaining in the fullest detail the bearing of judicial independence on constitutional freedom. . . .

All the colonies were affected. In some, like New Jersey, where the governor's incautious violation of the new royal order led to his removal from office, or like North Carolina, where opposition forces refused to concede and managed to keep up the fight for permanent judicial tenure throughout the entire period from 1760 to 1776, the issue was directly joined. In others, as in Massachusetts, where specific Supreme Court appointments were vehemently opposed by antiadministration interests, the force of the policy was indirect. But everywhere there was bitterness at the decree and fear of its implications, for everywhere it was known that judicial tenure "at the will of the crown" was "dangerous to the liberty and property of the subject," and that if the bench were occupied by "men who depended upon the smiles of the crown for their daily bread," the possibility of having an independent judiciary as an effective check upon executive power would be wholly lost.

This fear was magnified by the rumor, which was circulating vigorously as early as 1768, that it was part of the administration's policy to have the salaries of the colonial judges "appointed for them by the crown, independent of the people." If this ever happened, the Boston Town Meeting asserted when the rumor was becoming actuality, it would "complete our slavery." The reasoning was simple and straightforward:

> if taxes are to be raised from us by the Parliament of Great Britain without our consent, and the men on whose opinions and decisions our properties, liberties, and lives in a great measure depend receive their support from the revenues arising from these taxes, we cannot, when we think of the depravity of mankind, avoid looking with horror on the danger to which we are exposed!

"More and more," as the people contemplated the significance of crown salaries for a judiciary that served "at pleasure," was it clear that "the designs of administration [were] totally to subvert the constitution." Any judge, the House in Massachusetts ultimately stated, who accepted such salaries would thereby declare "that he has not a due sense of the importance of an impartial administration of justice, that he is an enemy to the constitution, and has it in his heart to promote the establishment of an arbitrary government in the province."

Long before this, however, another aspect of the judicial system was believed also to have come under deliberate attack. The jury system, it was said, in New York particularly but elsewhere as well, was being systematically undermined. In New York the same executive who had fought the permanent tenure of judges insisted on the legality of allowing jury decisions, on matters of fact as well as of law, to be appealed to the governor and Council. This effort, though defeated within a year by action of the Board of Trade in England, had a lasting impact on the political consciousness of New Yorkers. It was publicly assailed, in the year of the Stamp Act, as "arbitrary" and "scandalous" in its deliberate subversion of the British constitution.

Associated with this but more important because more widespread in its effect was the extension and enforcement of the jurisdiction of the vice-admiralty courts—"prerogative" courts composed not of juries but of single judges whose posts were "political offices in the hands of the royal governors, to be bestowed upon deserving friends and supporters." Since these courts had jurisdiction over the enforcement of all laws of trade and navigation as well as over ordinary marine matters, they had always been potentially threatening to the interests of the colonists. But in the past, by one means or another, they had been curtailed in their effect, and much of their business had been shunted off to common law courts dominated by juries. Suddenly in the 1760s they acquired a great new importance, for it was into their hands that the burden of judicial enforcement of the new Parliamentary legislation fell. It was upon them, consequently, and upon the whole principle of "prerogative" courts that abuse was hurled as the effect of their enhanced power was felt. "What has America done," victims of the decisions of these courts asked, "to be thus particularized, to be disfranchised and stripped of so invaluable a privilege as the trial by jury?" The operations of the vice-admiralty courts, it was felt, especially after their administrative reorganization in 1767, denied Americans a crucial measure of the protection of the British constitution. . . .

The more one looked the more one found evidences of deliberate malevolence. In Massachusetts, Thomas Hutchinson's elaborate patronage machine, long in existence but fully organized only after the arrival of Governor Francis Bernard in 1760, appeared to suspicious tribunes like Oxenbridge Thacher and John Adams to constitute a serious threat to liberty. The Hutchinsons and the Olivers and their ambitious allies, it was said (and the view was widely circulated through the colonies), had managed, by accumulating a massive plurality of offices, to engross the power of all branches of the Massachusetts government thereby building a "foundation sufficient on which to erect a tyranny." . . .

Meanwhile an event even more sinister in its implications had taken place in the colonies themselves. On October 1, 1768, two regiments of regular infantry, with artillery, disembarked in Boston. For many months the harassed Governor Bernard had sought some legal means or excuse for summoning military help in his vain efforts to maintain if not an effective administration then at least order in the face of Stamp Act riots, circular letters, tumultuous town meetings, and assaults on customs officials. But the arrival of troops in Boston increased rather than decreased his troubles. For to a populace steeped in the literature of eighteenth-century English politics the presence of troops in a peaceful town had such portentous meaning that resistance instantly stiffened. It was not so much the physical threat of the troops that affected the attitudes of the Bostonians; it was the bearing their arrival had on the likely tendency of events. Viewed in the perspective of Trenchard's famous tracts on standing armies and of the vast derivative literature on the subject that flowed from the English debates of the 1690s, these were not simply soldiers assembled for police duties; they were precisely what history had proved over and over again to be prime movers of the process by which unwary nations lose "that precious jewel *liberty*." The mere rumor of possible troop arrivals had evoked the age-old apprehensions. "The raising or keeping a standing army within the kingdom in time of peace, unless it be with the consent of Parliament, is against the law," the alarmed Boston Town Meeting had resolved. It is, they said,

> the indefeasible right of [British] subjects to be *consulted* and to give their *free consent in person* or by representatives of their own free election to the raising and keeping a standing army among them; and the inhabitants of this town, being free subjects, have the same right derived from nature and confirmed by the British constitution as well as the said royal charter; and therefore the raising or keeping a standing army without their consent in person or by representatives of their own free election would be an infringement of their natural, constitutional, and charter rights; and the employing such army for the enforcing of laws made without the consent of the people, in person or by their representatives, would be a grievance.

But the troops arrived, four regiments in all: in bold, stark actuality a standing army—just such a standing army as had snuffed out freedom in Denmark, classically, and elsewhere throughout the world. True, British regulars had been introduced into the colonies on a permanent basis at the end of the Seven Years' War; that in itself had been disquieting. But it had then been argued that troops were needed to police the newly acquired territories, and that they were not in any case to be regularly garrisoned in peaceful, populous towns. No such defense could be made of the troops sent to Boston in 1768. No simple, ingenuous explanation would suffice. The true motive was only too apparent for those with eyes to see. One of the classic stages in the process of destroying free constitutions of government had been reached.

To those most sensitive to the ideological currents of the day, the danger could scarcely have been greater. "To have a standing army!" Andrew Eliot wrote from Boston to Thomas Hollis in September 1768, "Good God! What can be worse to a people who have tasted the sweets of liberty! Things are come to an unhappy crisis; there will never be that harmony between Great Britain and her colonies that there hath been; all confidence is at an end; and the moment there is any blood shed all affection will cease." He was convinced, he wrote, that if the English government "had not had their hands full at home they would have crushed the colonies." As it was, England's most recent actions tended only "to hasten that independency which at present the warmest among us deprecate." "I fear for the nation," he concluded, and his fears were shared not only by all liberty-minded Bostonians but also, through the stimulation of the "Journal of the Times," a day-by-day account of Boston "under military rule" that was, in effect, syndicated throughout the colonies, it was shared by politically and ideologically sensitive Americans everywhere. Time did not ease these anxieties; it merely complicated them. Fear and hatred became edged with contempt. "Our people begin to despise a military force," Eliot observed a year after the troops had first appeared; they coolly woo away the soldiers and drag offending officers before the courts—which, he grimly added, continue to function "notwithstanding all their efforts." But "things cannot long remain in the state they are now in; they are hastening to a crisis. What will be the event, God knows." . . .

And then, a few weeks later, came the Boston Massacre. Doubts that the troops in Boston constituted a standing army and that it was the purpose of standing armies to terrify a populace into compliance with tyrannical wills were silenced by that event, which, Eliot assured Hollis, had obviously been coming. It "serves to show the impossibility of our living in peace with a standing army. A free people will sometimes carry things too far, but this remedy will always be found worse than the disease. Trenchard's *History of Standing Armies,* with which you formerly obliged me, is excellent . . . Unless there is some great alteration in the state of things the era of the independence of the colonies is much nearer than I once thought it, or now wish it." The same response was generally broadcast in the narrative of the Massacre, written by James Bowdoin and others for the Boston Town Meeting, which was distributed everywhere in the English-speaking world. This famous pamphlet stressed the deliberateness of the shooting and the clarity of the design that lay behind the lurid event; nor was the parallel to the St. George's Fields murders neglected. The acquittal of the indicted soldiers did not alter the conviction that the Massacre was the logical work of a standing army, for it accentuated the parallel with the English case which also had concluded with acquittal; and in Boston, too, there was suspicion of judicial irregularities. How the murderers managed to escape was known to some, it was said, but was "too dark to explain."

Unconstitutional taxing, the invasion of placemen, the weakening of the judiciary, plural officeholding, Wilkes, standing armies—these were major evidences of a deliberate assault of power upon liberty. Lesser testimonies were also accumulating at the same time: small episodes in themselves, they took on a large significance in the context in which they were received. Writs of assistance in support of customs officials were working their expected evil: "our houses, and even our bedchambers, are exposed to be ransacked, our boxes, trunks, and chests broke open, ravaged, and plundered by wretches whom no prudent man would venture to employ even as menial servants." Legally convened legislatures had been "adjourned . . . to a place highly inconvenient to the members and greatly disadvantageous to the interest of the province"; they had been prorogued and dissolved at executive whim. Even the boundaries of colonies had been tampered with, whereby *"rights of soil"* had been eliminated at a stroke. When in 1772 the Boston Town Meeting met to draw up a full catalogue of the "infringements and violations" of the "rights of the colonists, and of this province in particular, as men, as Christians, and as subjects," it approved a list of twelve items, which took seventeen pamphlet pages to describe.

But then, for a two-year period, there was a détente of sorts created by the repeal of the Townshend Duties, the withdrawal of troops from Boston, and the failure of other provocative measures to be taken. It ended abruptly, however, in the fall and winter of 1773, when, with a rush, the tendencies earlier noted were brought to fulfillment. In the space of a few weeks, all the dark, twisted roots of malevolence were finally revealed, plainly, for all to see.

The turning point was the passage of the Tea Act and the resulting Tea Party in Boston in December 1773. Faced with this defiant resistance to intimidation, the powers at work in England, it was believed, gave up all pretense of legality—"threw off the mask," John Adams said in a phrase that for a century had been used to describe just such climactic disclosures—and moved swiftly to complete their design. In a period of two months in the spring of 1774 Parliament took its revenge in a series of coercive actions no liberty-loving people could tolerate: the Boston Port Act, intended, it was believed, to snuff out the economic life of the Massachusetts metropolis; the Administration of Justice Act, aimed at crippling judicial processes once and for all by permitting trials to be held in England for offenses committed in Massachusetts; the Massachusetts Government Act, which stripped from the people of Massachusetts the protection of the British constitution by giving over all the "democratic" elements of the province's government—even popularly elected juries and town meetings—into the hands of the executive power; the Quebec Act, which, while not devised as a part of the coercive program, fitted it nicely, in the eyes of the colonists, by extending the boundaries of a "papist" province, and one governed wholly by prerogative, south into territory claimed by Virginia, Connecticut, and Massachusetts; finally, the Quartering Act, to take effect in all colonies, which permitted the seizure for the use of troops of all buildings, public and private, deserted and occupied.

Once these coercive acts were passed there could be little doubt that "the system of slavery fabricated against America . . . is the offspring of mature deliberation." To the leaders of the Revolutionary movement there was, beyond question, "a settled, fixed plan for *enslaving* the colonies, or bringing them under arbitrary government, and indeed the nation too." By 1774 the idea "that the British government—the *King, Lords,* and *Commons*— have laid a regular plan to enslave America, and that they are now deliberately putting it in execution" had been asserted, Samuel Seabury wrote wearily but accurately, "over, and over, and over again." The less inhibited of the colonial orators were quick to point out that "the MONSTER of a standing ARMY" had sprung directly from "a PLAN . . . *systematically* laid, and pursued by the British *ministry,* near twelve years, for enslaving America"; the Boston Massacre, it was claimed, had been "planned by Hillsborough and a knot of treacherous knaves in Boston." Careful analysts like Jefferson agreed on the major point; in one of the most closely reasoned of the pamphlets of 1774 the Virginian stated unambiguously that though "single acts of tyranny may be ascribed to the accidental opinion of a day . . . a series of oppressions, begun at a distinguished period and pursued unalterably through every change of ministers, too plainly prove a deliberate and systematical plan of reducing us to slavery." So, too, the fastidious and scholarly John Dickinson, though in 1774 he still clung to the hope that inadvertence, at least on the part of the King, was involved, believed that "a plan had been deliberately framed and pertinaciously adhered to, unchanged even by frequent changes of ministers, unchecked by any intervening gleam of humanity, to sacrifice to a passion for arbitrary dominion the universal property, liberty, safety, honor, happiness, and prosperity of us unoffending yet devoted Americans." So, too, Washington, collaborating with George Mason in writing the Fairfax Resolves of 1774, agreed that the trouble had arisen from a "regular, systematic plan" of oppression, the English government "endeavoring by every piece of art and despotism to fix the shackles of slavery upon us"; he was convinced "beyond the smallest doubt," he wrote privately, "that these measures are the result of deliberation . . . I am as fully convinced as I am of my own existence that there has been a regular, systematic plan formed to enforce them." The more sensitive observers were to ideological issues—the more practiced in theoretical discourse—the more likely they were to find irrefutable evidence of what Richard Henry Lee called "designs for destroying our constitutional liberties." In 1766 Andrew Eliot had been unsure; the Stamp Act, he wrote, had been "calculated (I do not say designed) to enslave the colonies." By 1768 things had worsened, and the distinction between "calculation" and "design" disappeared from his correspondence. "We have everything to fear and scarce any room to hope," he then wrote to Hollis; "I am sure this will put you in mind of 1641." He was convinced that the English government "had a design to new-model our constitution, at least in this province," and they would already have succeeded had they not been so occupied with other business at home. His friends in Boston concurred, and, beginning in 1770, wrote out in a series of town resolutions, instructions to representatives, and House declarations their conviction that

> a deep-laid and desperate plan of imperial despotism has been laid, and partly executed, for the extinction of all civil liberty . . . The august and once revered fortress of English freedom—the admirable work of ages—the BRITISH CONSTITUTION seems fast tottering into fatal and inevitable ruin. . . .

But who, specifically, were these enemies, and what were their goals? Josiah Quincy, at the center of affairs in London in the winter of 1774–75, was convinced "that all the measures against America were planned and pushed on by Bernard and Hutchinson." But most observers believed that local plotters like Hutchinson were only "creatures" of greater figures in England coordinating and impelling forward the whole effort. There were a number of specific identifications of these master influences. One of the most common was the claim that at the root of the evil stood the venerable John Stuart, Lord Bute, whose apparent absence from politics since 1763 could be seen as one of his more successful dissimulations: "he has been aiming for years . . . to destroy the ancient right of the subjects," and now was finally taking steps to "overthrow both . . . King and state; to bring on a revolution, and to place another whom he [is] more nearly allied to upon the throne." Believing the people to "have too much liberty," he intended to reduce them to the "spiritless SLAVES" they had been "in the reign of the *Stuarts*." . . . A more general version of this view was that a Stuart-Tory party, the "corrupt, Frenchified party in the nation," as it was described in 1766—"evil-minded individuals," Jonathan Mayhew believed, "not improbably in the interests of the houses of Bourbon and the Pretender"—was at work seeking to reverse the consequences of the Glorious Revolution. It was a similar notion that in all probability accounts for the republication of Rapin's *Dissertation on . . . the Whigs and Tories* in Boston in 1773; and it was this notion that furnished Jefferson with his ultimate understanding of the "system" that sought to destroy liberty in America. Still another explanation, drawing no less directly on fears that had lain at the root of opposition ideology in England since the turn of the century, emphasized the greed of a "monied interest" created by the crown's financial necessities and the power of a newly risen, arrogant, and irresponsible capitalist group, that battened on wars and stock manipulation. The creation of this group was accompanied "by levying of taxes, by a host of tax gatherers, and a long train of dependents of the crown. The practice grew into system, till at length the crown found means to break down those barriers which the constitution had assigned to each branch of the legislature, and effectually destroyed the independence of both Lords and Commons."

The most common explanation, however—an explanation that rose from the deepest sources of British political culture, that was a part of the very structure of British political thought—located "the spring and cause of all the distresses and complaints of the people in England or in America" in "a kind of fourth power that the constitution knows nothing of, or has not provided against." This "overruling arbitrary power, which absolutely controls the King, Lords, and Commons," was composed, it was said, of the "ministers and favorites" of the King, who, in defiance of God and man alike, "extend their usurped authority infinitely too far," and, throwing off the balance of the constitution, make their "despotic will" the authority of the nation.

> For their power and interest is so great that they can and do procure whatever laws they please, having (by power, interest, and the application of the people's money to *placemen* and *pensioners*) the whole legislative authority at their command. So that it is plain (not to say a word of a particular reigning arbitrary *Stuarchal* power among them) that the rights of the people are ruined and destroyed by ministerial *tyrannical* authority, and thereby . . . become a kind of slaves to the ministers of state.

This "junto of courtiers and state-jobbers," these "court-locusts," whispering in the royal ear, "instill in the King's mind a divine right of authority to command his subjects" at the same time as they advance their "detestable scheme" by misinforming and misleading the people. . . .

But why were not these manipulators of prerogative satisfied with amassing power at home? Why the attention to faraway provinces in America? Several answers were offered, besides the general one that power naturally seeks to drive itself everywhere, into every pocket of freedom. One explanation was that the court, having reached a limit in the possibilities of patronage and spoils in the British Isles, sought a quarrel with the colonies as an excuse for confiscating their wealth. "The long and scandalous list of placemen and pensioners and the general profligacy and prodigality of the present reign exceed the annual supplies. England is drained by taxes, and Ireland impoverished to almost the last farthing . . . America was the only remaining spot to which their oppression and extortion had not fully reached, and they considered her as a fallow field from which a large income might be drawn." When the colonists' reaction to the Stamp Act proved that "raising a revenue in America quietly" was out of the question, it was decided to destroy their power to resist: the colonies were to be "politically broken up." And so the Tea Act was passed, not to gain a revenue but, as in the case of the Massacre, to provoke a quarrel. The ministry wished "to see America in arms . . . because it furnished them with a pretense for declaring us rebels; and persons conquered under that character forfeit their all, be it where it will or what it will, to the crown." England did not desire an accommodation of any sort, Lord North's conciliatory plan notwithstanding. "From motives of political avarice," she sought an excuse for conquest: "it is on this ground only that the continued obstinacy of her conduct can be accounted for." Not that the crown was necessarily implicated. Most commentators, until 1776, considered the crown equally the victim of ministerial machinations, one writer reporting to London from Philadelphia late in 1774 that "it is suspected here that a design is regularly prosecuted by the ministry to make His Majesty dethrone himself by the calamities and convulsions his reign is likely to bring on his whole people. Please to inform me what is thought on this point in England." . . .

That by 1774 the final crisis of the constitution, brought on by political and social corruption, had been reached was, to most informed colonists, evident; but if they had not realized it themselves they would soon have discovered it from the flood of newspapers, pamphlets, and letters that poured in on them from opposition sources in England. Again and again reports from the home country proclaimed that the English nation had departed, once and for all and completely, from the true principles of liberty: the principles not of "certain modern Whigs," as one English pamphlet of 1774, reprinted in the colonies no less than seven times within a year of its first appearance, explained, but of "Whigs before the [Glorious] Revolution and at the time of it; I mean the principles which such men as Mr. Locke, Lord Molesworth, and Mr. Trenchard maintained with their pens, Mr. Hampden and Lord [William] Russell with their blood, and Mr. Algernon Sidney with both." To those Englishmen who in the 1770s most directly inherited and most forcefully propagated these principles—Richard Price, Joseph Priestley, James Burgh—the situation at home if not abroad justified, even exaggerated, the worst fears for the future of liberty that their predecessors had expressed. For these latter-day radicals had witnessed personally the threatening rise of prerogative influence in the English government and its dramatic manifestation in the Wilkes affair; and they had seen revealed the rapacity and bankruptcy of the swollen East India Company, a revelation which illuminated to them the corruption of their era as dramatically as the collapse of the South Sea Company had revealed the rottenness of the era of George I to Trenchard and Gordon. Everywhere there was cynicism and gluttonous self-seeking. What more was needed to convince one that affairs in Britain were plummeting toward complete and irrecoverable collapse? The long-awaited signs of the total degeneration of the moral qualities necessary to preserve liberty were unmistakable, and these English radicals said so, vigorously, convincingly, in a series of increasingly shrill pamphlets and letters that were read avidly, circulated, published, and republished, in America.

But it was not only the radicals. A wide range of public figures and pamphleteers, known and read in America, carried forward the cries of corruption that had been heard in earlier years and directed them to the specific political issues of the day. William Bollan, the former agent and advocate-general of Massachusetts, still well-known in America and experienced in analyzing colonial affairs, produced in London in 1768 two pamphlets of blasting condemnation, one "wherein the great mischief and danger of corruption are set forth and proved from its operations in *Greece* and *Rome*," the other covering, as the title indicated, the whole range of *Continued Corruption, Standing Armies, and Popular Discontents.* In the same vein the prominent London printer and publicist (and political conservative) William Strahan wondered, in letters to the Philadelphian David Hall, publisher of the *Pennsylvania Gazette,* whether England had "virtue enough to be saved from that deluge of corruption with which we have been so long overwhelmed"—a concern that gnawed at him as he contemplated the "immense sums [that] are daily given to secure seats in Parliament" and that resulted in the selection of "men who in the east, by rapine and plunder, in most cases attended with the most shocking instances of barbarity, have suddenly acquired immense wealth. Such you will perhaps think not the most proper guardians of our constitution and liberties." He could only hope, he wrote, that "before matters come to extremity the nation . . . the happiest nation this world ever contained . . . will come to their senses, and not suffer a fabric, the work of ages and the envy of the rest of the world, to be materially injured."

But far greater voices than these were heard, some in the highest reaches of the English government. In the year of Burke's *Thoughts on the Present Discontents,* the most famous of all the attacks on the plots of "a certain set of intriguing men . . . *to secure to the court the unlimited and uncontrolled use of its own vast influence under the sole direction of its own private favor* . . . [pursuing] a scheme for undermining all the foundations of our freedom," Burke's patron, the Marquis of Rockingham, explained in a speech in the House of Lords the "total change in the old system of English government" which could be traced to the accession of George III and which alone could explain the secret motivations behind the Stamp Act. But it was left for the colonists' Olympian champion, William Pitt, now Earl of Chatham, to probe the ultimate sources of English corruption. The reason "the constitution at this moment stands violated," this grandson of "Diamond Pitt," East India merchant and governor of Madras, declared, is perfectly clear:

> For some years past there has been an influx of wealth into this country which has been attended with many fatal consequences, because it has not been the regular, natural produce of labor and industry. The riches of Asia have been poured in upon us, and have brought with them not only Asiatic luxury but, I fear, Asiatic principles of government. Without connections, without any natural

> interest in the soil, the importers of foreign gold have forced their way into Parliament by such a torrent of private corruption as no private hereditary fortune could resist. My Lords, I say nothing but what is within the knowledge of us all; the corruption of the people is the great original cause of the discontents of the people themselves, of the enterprise of the crown, and the notorious decay of the internal vigor of the constitution.

Something, he said, must be done, immediately, "to stop the rapid progress of corruption"; he advocated strengthening the health of Parliament as a representative body by increasing the number of representatives from the still independent, unbought constituencies, the counties and the great and growing cities, at the expense of the rotten, purchasable, boroughs.

All of this was borne to America, and there carried conviction to a far larger part of the population, and bore more dramatic implications than it did in England. "Liberty," John Adams wrote, "can no more exist without virtue and independence than the body can live and move without a soul," and what liberty can be expected to flow from England where "luxury, effeminacy, and venality are arrived at such a shocking pitch" and where "both electors and elected are become one mass of corruption"? It was not hard to see where England stood: it was, Adams declared, precisely at the point "where the Roman republic was when Jugurtha left it, and pronounced it 'a venal city, ripe for destruction, if it can only find a purchaser.' " The analogy to the decline and fall of Rome and its empire was intriguing and informative; others carried it further and became more specific. Like Rome in its decline, England, "from being the nursery of heroes, became the residence of musicians, pimps, panders, and catamites." The swift decline of her empire, which, it was observed, had reached its peak only between 1758 and the Stamp Act, resulted from the same poison that had proved so fatal to free states in classical antiquity: the corruption, effeminacy, and languor that came from "the riches and luxuries of the East" and led to a calamitous "decay of virtue" and the collapse of the constitution. Even Franklin, his old caution and careful optimism gone, agreed, writing in 1775 to his one-time political ally Joseph Galloway, that he would himself, reluctantly, have to oppose Galloway's plan for reconciliation.

> . . . when I consider the extreme corruption prevalent among all orders of men in this old rotten state, and the glorious public virtue so predominant in our rising country, I cannot but apprehend more mischief than benefit from a closer union. I fear they will drag us

after them in all the plundering wars which their desperate circumstances, injustice, and rapacity may prompt them to undertake; and their wide-wasting prodigality and profusion is a gulf that will swallow up every aid we may distress ourselves to afford them. Here numberless and needless places, enormous salaries, pensions, perquisites, bribes, groundless quarrels, foolish expeditions, false accounts or no accounts, contracts and jobs, devour all revenue and produce continual necessity in the midst of natural plenty. I apprehend, therefore, that to unite us intimately will only be to corrupt and poison us also.

Patrick Henry used a variation of the same argument in discussing Galloway's proposal in Congress: "We shall liberate our constituents from a corrupt House of Commons but throw them into the arms of an American legislature that may be bribed by that nation which avows, in the face of the world, that bribery is a part of her system of government." Even Galloway himself had to agree that "Parliament and ministry is wicked and corrupt." So often, so stridently, and so convincingly was it said in the colonies that in England "luxury has arrived to a great pitch; and it is a universal maxim that luxury indicates the declension of a state"—so often was it argued that vigor was gone, exhaustion and poverty approaching, that those who would defend British policy were obliged to debate the point: to assert the health and strength of English society, arguing, as Samuel Seabury did, that England was a "vigorous matron, just approaching a green old age; and with spirit and strength sufficient to chastise her undutiful and rebellious children" and not at all, as his adversary Alexander Hamilton had pictured her, "an old, wrinkled, withered, worn-out hag."

The fact that the ministerial conspiracy against liberty had risen from corruption was of the utmost importance to the colonists. It gave a radical new meaning to their claims: it transformed them from constitutional arguments to expressions of a world regenerative creed. For they had long known—it had been known everywhere in the English-speaking world in the eighteenth century—that England was one of the last refuges of the ancient gothic constitution that had once flourished everywhere in the civilized world. And now, in the outpourings of colonial protest, it was again repeated, but with new point and urgency, that by far "the greatest part of the human race" already lies in "total subjection to their rulers." . . . And if now, in this deepening gloom, the light of liberty went out in Britain too—in Britain, where next to "self-preservation, political liberty is the main aim and end of her constitution"—if, as events clearly portended and as "senators and historians are repeatedly predicting . . . continued corruption and standing armies will prove mortal distempers in her constitution"—what then? What refuge will liberty find?

"To our own country," it was answered, "must we look for the biggest part of that liberty and freedom that yet remains, or is to be expected, among mankind . . . For while the greatest part of the nations of the earth are held together under the yoke of universal slavery, the North American provinces yet remain *the country of free men:* the *asylum,* and the last, to which such may yet flee from the common deluge." More than that:"our native country . . . bids the fairest of any to promote *the perfection and happiness of mankind."* . . . No one, therefore, can conceive of the cause of America as "the cause of a mob, of a party, or a faction." The cause of America "is the cause of *self-defense,* of *public faith,* and of the *liberties of mankind* . . . 'In our destruction, liberty itself expires, and human nature will despair of evermore regaining its first and original dignity.' "

3

The Federalist Era as an Age of Passion

Marshall Smelser

After the Revolution the new American government was confronted by difficult problems: opening the West to settlement, steering a neutral course during the wars following the French Revolution, and determining the economic policies for the young republic. Above all, the Founding Fathers felt a need to preserve the precarious unity of a nation spread over a vast extent of territory and containing such different social systems as those in the free and slave states. Attempts to solve these problems posed a dilemma for American leaders, who, as Bailyn's article demonstrates, were convinced that the exercise of power could endanger liberty. Marshall Smelser, a specialist on fear of conspiracy during the 1790s, discusses the deep suspicions that wracked American politics in the first decade of the nation's existence.

The years of the administrations of Presidents Washington and Adams are usually regarded by the educated layman—although not by

---

From Marshall Smelser, "The Federalist Period as an Age of Passion," American Quarterly, *X (1958), pp. 301–419. Reprinted without footnotes by permission of the author and the publishers.*

the few specialists in the era—as years in which public life was marked by statesmanlike decorum and a reliance on logic. This view has been encouraged by the overcompression of short popular accounts and the remarks of enthusiastic amateurs. While not wholly inaccurate, such a conception neglects to notice that the political activity of the Federalist period was strongly influenced by the passions of hate, anger, and fear. It is possible to tell the story of this politically-conscious age so as to make it the narrative of a series of great statutes and treaties, enacted and ratified by heroes who set precedents which still serve us as guides. That is the way the tale is usually told. Yet the story can be organized quite differently by writing it as "emotional history," with the effect of emphasizing some almost forgotten motivations of the principal builders of the federal republic.

The ruling faction in the national politics of the United States, the group which controlled the three branches of government for the first twelve years of the federal republic (some months of congressional history excepted) were known as the Federalists—later, the Federalist Party. This group did not accept equalitarian principles. Their rejection was based on a theory of human nature which emphasized differences of individual abilities and the inherent depravity of passionate, self-interested human nature. When translated into the political jargon of the day this psychological analysis was much coarsened. For example, Edmund Burke's unfortunate epithet applied to the French people at large, "a swinish multitude," was widely used by the opposition party in America, the Republicans, to illustrate the contempt in which aristocracy held the people everywhere. And the Republicans were not misusing the phrase.

To select illustrations of this attitude toward the populace is almost to call the roll of the best minds of Federalism. Alexander Hamilton, Fisher Ames, George Cabot, Timothy Dwight, John Quincy Adams, James Iredell—all have left ample literary evidence of their real fear of equalitarianism. Some of them explained themselves psychologically, some theologically, and in others—evidence is clear—snobbery was sufficient ground. About the only notable exception to the demophobia of Federalism was the political theory of the most able of Federalist constitutional historians, John Adams. Adams did not fear democracy more than other forms of government. It was absolute power that he feared, whether despotic, oligarchic, or democratic. But few of his collaborators were so dispassionate.

Whether a republic could be made to work, even with promising human material, was a question which was complicated by American geography. The vast area of the United States discouraged many, both

Republicans and Federalists. It seemed very likely that the interstate and intersectional jealousies which had vexed the old Confederation would prove too strong for the union. The difficulties seemed so great that at every particular crisis there were fears of disunion and threats of secession. At the time of the congressional debates over Hamilton's proposal that the federal government assume the state debts—the "Assumption" controversy—there was a hint that New England and South Carolina might secede if Assumption did not carry. In 1792 George Washington was urged to accept a second term as President by Attorney General Edmund Randolph and by Secretary of the Treasury Alexander Hamilton because his presence would help to preserve the union, and this was no new idea to the President. Northern senators were again speaking privately of secession in the Third Congress. During the hullaballoo over the Jay Treaty, Virginians threatened secession if the treaty were ratified, and northerners threatened the same if southerners did not behave more responsibly. In the presidential campaign of 1796 some Yankees hoped that New England would secede if Thomas Jefferson were elected to the presidency. During the uproar over the X.Y.Z. Affair, Jefferson thought that the Federalist outcry was aimed in part at justifying a secession which might soon occur, but he himself opposed secession when John Taylor of Caroline seriously suggested that Virginia and North Carolina leave the union.

The leaders of the nation were dealing with hard facts when they contemplated the interstate and intersectional rivalries and jealousies. These were differences rooted in the psychology, the culture, and the economy of the Americans. The weakness of the government under the Articles of Confederation had been its inability to harmonize local interests and to enforce a common will against stubborn sectionalism. With the ratification of the new constitution, national solutions of national problems might for the first time be possible. One national solution just *might* be the abolition of the states. Hamilton is well-remembered as an extreme "consolidationist" who would have been pleased to see the states abolished. What is less well-remembered is that he was not alone. Men of such views were disappointed when sectionalism did not quickly die. They did not think of sectionalism as the effect of deep and permanent causes but as the product of selfishness or envy, sectional opposition became malicious opposition, or, at best, a quarrel of the "outs" and the "ins." . . .

With their pessimistic view of human nature, their fear of localism, and their almost universally held doubts of the permanence of the union, it is little wonder that the Federalists took an intolerant position regarding the opposition party, which seemed to be a race of marplots characterized by excessive ambition, unwholesome partisanship, and a dangerous reliance upon the judgment of the voters. At best the Republicans often seemed governed by obstinacy, envy, malice, or ambition. At worst they were seditious and treasonable. Federalist private correspondence was peppered with references to Republican disloyalty, insincerity, intrigue, and demagoguery, and similar allegations were made in the pamphleteering war. To Federalists it was obvious that Republican opposition was malicious mischief. The conclusion almost forced upon the reader of these and hundreds more of Federalist condemnations is that the two-party system is immoral. Since both parties could not be correct, one must be the foe of order. Protestations of the loyalty of an opposition party were insincere. It became almost normal to consider opposition as seditious and, in extraordinary cases, as treasonable.

The appearance of the Democratic-Republican societies in 1793 seemed sufficient proof of an organized conspiracy against the liberty of the nation. These political clubs were formed by city workers and western farmers and, as we now see, were the nuclei of the Republican Party. Called "demoniacal" as a pun on the word "democratical," their seditious character was assumed and their legality denied. They needed only to take up arms to be a revolutionary army.

Another evidence of the bad intentions of the Republicans was that they went to some trouble to gain popularity, and disgraced themselves by seeking votes. To run for office was plainly beneath the dignity of the wellborn. Man must not seek office; office must seek the man. It was bad enough to canvass the opinions of the vulgar on the qualifications of men. It was worse to ask the mob to pass on questions of public policy. Young John Quincy Adams thought a victorious majority in a Boston Town Meeting "looked as if they had been collected from all the jails of the continent," and a Federalist Secretary of State once stated it as a principle that the larger the attendance at a public meeting the less weight should be given to its resolutions. It is hard now to imagine that an administration which was at once fearful and contemptuous of the people could expect to stay long in power. But the Federalists saw no weakness in their political theory. Weakness, they admitted, but it was a weakness of disposition and organization in their own followers whereby rich men evaded responsibility and thereby helped their natural enemies. Such renegades feared to make government strong enough to be workable and opposed a spirit of determination in government because they were too timid to risk the loss of public favor. One would gather that the American republic was dying of senility while still in its cradle.

Once the newspapers had found their normal level of stridency, which had been pretty well established by the last year of Washington's first term, many Federalists felt that they lived permanently on the edge of doom. The harshness of partisanship made it seem unlikely that government could be administered or the union preserved. Nevertheless, although they might claim to despise popularity-seeking and electioneering, Federalists worked hard to influence public opinion by means of the press. Hardly a Federalist leader can be named who did not at some time or other, over his own name or a pseudonym, engage in newspaper controversy. A reading of the polemics shows that a good deal of the writing was much less concerned with informing the intellect than it was with whipping up those same passions which the Republicans were accused of trying to arouse. The result was the publication of some of the ripest vituperation in American literary history.

Before 1798 and the enactment of the Sedition Act, the Federalists had few remedies for the acute infection of the body politic. About the only constructive suggestions were those for the conduct of local political campaigns. But it seemed probable that the malevolence of the Republicans could be explained and counter-attacked by moral theology. In their discussions of the infidelity and immorality of their opponents, the Federalists owed much in their thinking to foreign writers, particularly to Edmund Burke who, in his *Reflections on the Revolution in France,* had described a systematic plan of literary men to destroy Christianity. The same trend was noticed by some commentators in America, and in the course of identifying infidelity in religion with democracy in politics, Jefferson's private life was slanderously attacked in prose and verse—an attack which established a false tradition that is still alive.

It was strongly suspected that the turbulent demagogues and their depraved followers were untrustworthy on the subject of the rights of property. There seemed to be many evidences for this, but the unreliability of the Republicans was sufficiently shown by their consistent opposition to the Hamiltonian design for safeguarding property and establishing the national credit.

If the opposition to administration measures had been limited to words and votes, the Federalists, in time, might have come to accept partisanship as the normal state of American politics, but in 1794 and 1795 opposition erupted into violence which appeared to justify the worst fears of the ruling group. Violence was used to prevent the enforcement of the federal excise law in western Pennsylvania, and large crowds, perhaps mobs, demonstrated in many places to show their disapproval of the Jay Treaty.

The news of the Whiskey Rebellion sent a shock wave of alarm through the country. The appearance of rebellion and anarchy was what Federalists had been predicting and fearing. After the rioters dispersed before the approach of troops sent by the President, a great deal of talk and writing, both public and private, of Federalist leaders in the next few months was devoted to the motives, causes, and dangers of the whiskey disturbance. Washington's opinions on the subject are valuable, because he had the responsibility for suppressing the insurrection and he also had the most widespread network of correspondents. He was convinced that the troubles were the work of a conspiracy organized by the Democratic-Republican clubs but set in motion prematurely. He was gratified by the popular support of the government. His views were formally summarized in his annual message to the Congress in November 1794. (The true view of responsible Republicans was glumly expressed by James Madison who thought the leaders of the rebellion did a service to despotism. Insurrections "increase the momentum of power" as had been shown by Shays's Rebellion in the 1780s.)

The Whiskey Rebellion had been quieted only briefly when sporadic violence broke out in many towns as part of the opposition to the Jay Treaty. Jay's character was symbolically and systematically defamed. A Philadelphia crowd demonstrated before the house of the British Minister and smashed windows elsewhere. Hamilton was stoned by a hostile mob in New York. Several disturbances in Boston led to a charge that Governor Samuel Adams evaded responsibility for keeping public order. Anti-Jay rioting extended as far north as Portsmouth, New Hampshire. It was very hard for Federalists to believe that these outbursts, these lawless proceedings so uncomfortably reminiscent of the French Revolution, were spontaneous. There simply had to be a plot.

The partisan press appeared to be a principal tool of organized malevolence. And as early as the end of Washington's first term it was a settled conviction of the Federalists that the *National Gazette,* edited by the poet Philip Freneau, was the trumpet of treason. Hamilton detected subversion in it as early as the summer of 1792, and he often appeared in print (over pseudonyms) in John Fenno's *Gazette of the United States* in controversy with Freneau's paper, questioning Freneau's integrity, and blaming Jefferson for the foundation of a paper which existed only to calumniate and blacken the reputations of responsible administrators. Others—Fisher Ames, Timothy Dwight, even Washington—questioned the honesty of the editor's purposes. . . .

The Federalists were quite willing to get down to individual cases. Not only did they damn the Republican Party en bloc as subversive but, in private letters, they named the traitors personally. Aaron Burr, George Clinton, Albert Gallatin, Thomas Mifflin, John Langdon, James Madison, and many lesser men were tagged as intriguing, vile, mischievous, disloyal, overly ambitious, or intellectually dishonest. Thomas Jefferson, of course, was the arch-anarch. A socially conscious intellectual, both his learning and his morals were mocked. Possessed of such an unpromising character, the author of the Declaration of Independence could hardly help being a conspirator against his country, in short, a traitor. This point was persistently developed over the years, both in letters and in print, by Hamilton, but Hamilton was not alone in the matter.

The extravagance and ferocity of Federalist assaults on the motives, character, and reputations of Republicans, collectively and singly, can be partly explained as the tactics of resentful self-defense. They were responding to pain, suffered directly or vicariously in sympathy with men they admired. Washington was reasonably sure that Republican malignity would destroy the union. Oliver Wolcott, Senior, could hardly praise Hamilton enough for the immense national benefits of his economic program and regretted that he was subject to attacks because of that "basest and vilest of human affections, envy." He was also convinced of a plot to drive the President to resign "by giving him constant disturbance." Hamilton had the expanded theory that "an unprincipled and daring combination" was trying to destroy Washington's popularity as the first step to the destruction of national independence. As for Hamilton himself, his letters to Washington and to some others show a constant feeling of being persecuted. But a plea of self-defense would go down better if the private records of the Federalists did not so plainly reveal their arrogant prior assumption of a monopoly of patriotism.

Just as the Republicans accused the Federalists of being the tools of a foreign power, so the Federalists charged the Republicans with being instruments of France. But there were differences. For one thing, the Federalists circulated their slurs much more frequently than did their opponents. Surviving records show three or four denunciations of alleged disloyalty by the Federalists for every one by the Republicans. Secondly, unlike the followers of Jefferson, the Federalists were in a position to act on their convictions, to use the engine of the state to defend the people against the subversive conspiracy they claimed to recognize.

The French Revolution provided the occasion for the imputation. At its beginning probably most Americans were sympathetic, but some were skeptical and regarded the enthusiasm for France as unbecoming (and dangerous to) the citizens of a sovereign republic. A prerevolutionary suspicion of French political philosophy had invaded the minds of many thoughtful men long before the stirring events in Paris. A politically minded people soon introduced the issue into politics. Charges of dangerous attachment to France and to Britain were exchanged in the campaign of 1792, and the Republicans were permanently tagged as "Jacobins" in that year at the same time as Thomas Jefferson was singled out as the head Gallican of the country.

The internal conflict over the French Revolution and its influence in the United States is not only an episode of our political history; it is also a chapter in the history of the American intellect, in the course of which, to the satisfaction of most conservatives, the Jeffersonians were temporarily but completely identified as revolutionary corruptors of morality. Each side fired salvos of books. The first pair of combatants were imports: Thomas Paine's *Rights of Man* and the book to which it was a reply, Edmund Burke's *Reflections on the Revolution in France.* In America Paine's work was also considered an answer to John Adams' *Discourses on Davila,* a constitutional treatise which had been read by Republicans as a royalist tract. Twenty-four-year-old John Quincy Adams contradicted Paine with his eleven *Publicola Letters,* which were attributed to his father and with that attribution reprinted in London, and pseudonymously in Glasgow and Dublin. All of this by the end of 1791. Thereafter the French Revolution and its controlling ideas remained the chief topic of journalistic and literary controversy, with special reference to the loyalty of American admirers.

More oil was poured on the flames by the arrival of Paine's contemptuous attack on revelation, the *Age of Reason.* Another frightening book was *Ruins; or, A Survey of the Revolutions of Empires,* by the history professor Constantin Volney, a work strongly anticlerical which concluded that there could be no certain determination of the true religion—with easily imagined effects on the conservative clergy in America. Even more shocking was the translation of Paul Dieterich, Baron Holbach's *Christianity Unveiled,* avowedly hedonistic and anti-Christian.

Worse than words were deeds, such as the founding of Deistical

Societies in the United States, and of the synthetic (and short-lived) religion called Theophilanthropy, which—it was rumored—was to be exported to the United States from France.

The defenders sallied vigorously from the citadel of New England orthodoxy, led by clergymen and the legal profession. The world view most influential in shaping arguments against France and French ideas was that of Edmund Burke. Apart from theoretical generalizations there is a remarkable coincidence of Burke and the Federalists in most points of applied political science. Burke's ideas were adopted and expanded for domestic consumption by able controversialists, among them Fisher Ames and Noah Webster.

Burke had recommended looking into the workings of a group which has been blamed or credited with full responsibility for starting the French Revolution, the Society of Illuminati, of Bavaria. This society, it was said, aimed to control the world by corrupting its morals. The notion captured the imaginations of Federalists everywhere when they read John Robison's *Proof of a Conspiracy* and Abbé Barruel's *Memoirs, Illustrating the History of Jacobinism,* both on the same subject, which were reprinted in the United States. Abigail Adams circulated Barruel, Phi Beta Kappa was suspected of illuminism, the President of Yale, Timothy Dwight, denounced Jacobinism in America. Gallophobia had become an obsession which confined the minds and colored the rhetoric of Federalists, blinding the leaders to American political realities and distracting them from the kind of practical politics necessary to keep them in power. The provincializing effect of the mania was shown by the rejection of the metric system in 1795 because it was too French.

The war between France and Britain brought to a peak the excitement previously stimulated by the overthrow of the monarchy and the proclamation of the French Republic. Successive military victories won by the French so heated the blood of their American well-wishers that in at least eighteen American cities and towns such French events were the occasions of civic celebrations. To the Federalists war against Britain was war against the chief bastion of civilization, and the excesses of Republican enthusiasm for France seemed hardly credible unless—unless, it was all a great plot to involve the United States in the war on the side of France. A nationwide plot requires a highly placed plotter, so leadership was accorded to Citizen Charles Edmond Genêt, the newly arrived Minister of France, aided, no doubt, or even directed by that same Thomas Jefferson who had probably helped to start the French Revolution when he represented the United States in Paris during the first days of the uprising. Whether the Republicans had been bought off or flattered by the French, leading Federalists were sure they saw evidence on all sides that they were plant agents of France.

Western expansionist projects were taken up and promoted by Genêt (who was condemned for originating more of them than he actually did). Where they involved the use of armies against British or Spanish colonies in the new world it was feared that the armies were really to be used against the United States. The decline and dismissal of Genêt eased Federalist nervous tension somewhat, but it appeared that he had left a legacy—the network of Democratic-Republican societies which coincided with the term of his mission. "Gallic Jackals" were carrying on the bad work in these seditious societies. The analogy with the Jacobin Clubs of France and her satellites was only too apparent (actually the Jacobin Clubs owed more to American examples than vice versa). A first fruit of the founding of the Democratic-Republican societies appeared to be the Whiskey Rebellion. The alarm of the administration was shown by the size of the force sent into the west. As Bernard De Voto put it, thirteen thousand men were more than were needed "to collect an excise."

It was charged that an important element of Jacobin tactics was to attempt to destroy the Hamiltonian system of public finance, thus protecting southern planter-debtors, and making it difficult for a then impoverished administration to govern at home or to war abroad. Another Jacobin operation was a smear campaign against President Washington, to destroy his popular reputation which was the chief obstacle against French domination. When a clumsy French spy visited the western country, one of his purposes was to campaign for Jefferson for the office of president; Gallatin, it was said, drafted the instructions and itinerary. The heat of the Republican attack on the Jay Treaty convinced some of the Federalists that the Republican rancor was inspired by France, an inspiration which extended into the House of Representatives. Outside the Congress, French influence over the enemies of the Treaty was equally visible, whether in the press or, more alarming, in the riotous demonstrations against the administration. . . .

Before the heat generated by the Jay Treaty contest had cooled, the election of 1796 occurred. Put in an elementary and almost over-simple way, the Anglo-French war was the central issue. On the one hand, the nation was threatened with Jefferson and a French alliance to bring war on Britain, and, on the other, it was Adams and a continuation of the Jay Treaty spirit of appeasement to involve us in a war with France. It is reasonably certain that the French government actively interested itself in the result of the presidential election, through interference in the United States by its Minister, Adet. John Adams, heir presumptive to Washington, had predicted French opposition, and his fellow Federalists said the same. For once they were right about French activity. As a reprisal against the Jay Treaty, in a note of very menacing tone, Adet announced that the French would treat American shipping in the same manner in which the United States allowed Britain to treat American shipping. The note was simultaneously given to the Republican press. Infuriated Federalists cried that this was an electioneering trick arranged by the Republicans. Except that it was not arranged by the Republicans, the conjecture was reasonable, even obvious, since the note was published on the Monday before the Friday when Pennsylvanians were to choose their presidential electors. Federalist anger was almost boundless.

Meanwhile, back in the American legation in Paris, more trouble. Charles Cotesworth Pinckney had been sent to succeed Monroe but his presence was ignored by the Directory. Eventually he withdrew to the Netherlands. The rejection of Pinckney could only be part of the American Jacobin plot, and Monroe was suspected of having arranged the humiliation.

A good deal of the responsibility for the Federalist obsession with the American Jacobin plot must be attributed to the Adams family. Practically every time one of their letters touched on Franco-American relations it revealed an explicit or implicit conviction of the existence of a pro-French American faction which was a grave threat to the nation. John Quincy Adams, abroad in the foreign service, was their main source of information. For several years the younger Adams stated flatly in almost every one of his letters to the United States from his successive legations that a conspiracy existed between the French government and certain Americans. This correspondence flowed in a steady stream to two Secretaries of State, to Vice-President and President Adams, to his mother, Abigail Adams, and to neighboring Americans in the foreign service. The high regard in which he was held made his reports the more credible, and gained him the unofficial position of being the Department of State's chief expert on the French Revolution. The tone of his letters can be illustrated by his conclusion that a third of the members of the House of Representatives loved France and French doctrines more than their own country; no greater calumniation of the Congress has been put in writing by an American official since that time.

The Federalists kept up their high clamor, both publicly and privately. In his newspaper Noah Webster printed eleven of his own pieces on the French revival of the Roman institution of vassal states and graphically described the coming partition of the United States. Hamilton wrote a series of newspaper articles entitled "The Warning," in which he cautioned against Americans who were heated enough to try to provoke war with Great Britain although they could excuse anything French. In private letters he supported the idea of sending another mission to France to succeed Pinckney, because the French might soon have an idle army which could be employed in America, assisted by an "INTERNAL INVASION. . ." [capitals his]. President Adams in his Inaugural Address expressed his fear for the freedom of American elections. To the first session of the Fifth Congress he said the French Directory revealed a hope of separating the American people from their government. Minister John Quincy Adams, in letters to his father, continued to sniff treason in the breezes and told how French policy was the joint product of the French government and the American Jacobins. But signals were sometimes confused. When President Adams decided to send a three-man mission to France, Hamilton suggested that Madison be appointed, but Oliver Wolcott, Jr. wrote to Hamilton to tell him that Madison's name had been put in nomination by the French. Washington wrote of France "encouraged . . . by a party among ourselves." Secretary of War McHenry told Washington that France planned to dismember the American union, and himself received the identical news some months later from William Vans Murray, United States Minister at the Hague. Murray also blamed Vice-President Jefferson's personal charm for much of the moral deterioration of the Senate. Writing to the younger Adams he confided—"His influence . . . does I am convinced immense mischief in the Senate." He invited senators to "philosophising dinners," and blended "theories of universal benevolence and philanthropy . . . easily with the politics of the day." William Henry Harrison, Captain, First Infantry Regiment, the same who was to be called "Tippecanoe," advised the Secretary of War that it was the duty of all to expose traitors. But Fisher Ames had good news for his friends: Jacobinism was declining in Dedham.

While the President, the ex-President, cabinet officers, and diplomatists were aggravating each other's quasi-paranoia, the judiciary did not remain silent. Supreme Court Justice James Iredell warned the Philadelphia Grand Jury against those Americans who had foreign attachments, and his colleague of the same bench, Samuel Chase, fretted about "a licentious press."

Thus was an unstable compound balanced for detonation. The concussion which set it off has become memorable as the "X.Y.Z. Affair." Its touches of comic relief went unnoticed in the 1790s as, in the tension of the time, it produced an explosion which almost blew away the First Amendment. Put briefly the story was this. In 1797 the President sent a three-man mission to France, which was not received by the French Foreign Minister, Talleyrand. Instead the Americans were approached by several unofficial characters who told them that unless a private bribe and a public loan were offered there could be no negotiation. The Americans refused to be parties to this kind of diplomacy (which was standing procedure with the French Directory) and two of them, Charles Cotesworth Pinckney and John Marshall, withdrew. The third, Elbridge Gerry, stayed in Paris, apparently because he feared that a total severance would inevitably bring on war. In the United States the dispatches from the commissioners were published with the names of the French extortionists deleted and the letters "X," "Y," and "Z" substituted. The public reaction was, one might say, *bouleversé*. Forceful addresses from civic groups poured in upon the President and were answered with equal ardor. That remarkable woman his wife, Abigail, in letters to her sister and to the historian Mercy Warren showed great excitement; she saw conspirators everywhere.

Federalist reaction in the Congress was equally intense. A pamphlet by Harrison Gray Otis, successor to the seat of Fisher Ames, warned of a French plan to establish Trans-Appalachian and Cis-Appalachian Republics. The Speaker of the House announced to the representatives that an army had been assembling on the coast of France, not to invade Britain as previously believed, but for the invasion of the United States ("confirmed" in the *Gazette of the United States* a month later). Representative Robert G. Harper gave out tantalizing hints of treasonable correspondence between Americans and Frenchmen. Harper it was who also apologized to the House for attacking an opponent only verbally; the opposition Congressman was too old to be physically beaten.

John Quincy Adams, now stationed in Berlin, expressed himself in his usual vein in several letters on the subject. William Vans Murray, Minister at the Hague, suggested a security measure to the President—organized counterespionage. Rufus King, Minister at London, wrote to an English correspondent that much of the trouble in America was owing to the ease with which lower-class Irish immigrants could be organized for mischievous purposes. Governor John Jay of New York was convinced that American "Jacobins" were "numerous," "desperate," "active."

These public officials were heartily supported by leading private citizens, the most influential and articulate being Hamilton, Ames, and ex-President Washington. Hamilton returned to the press with sulphuric phrases—"Gallic faction," "subaltern mercenaries"—and an oblique reference to Vice-President Jefferson as "so prostitute a character." Fisher Ames thought the Federalist leadership should take care to rouse the public. The government needed more force, more revenue, a more warlike use of ships, repudiation of the French treaties of 1778, presidential authority to embargo trade with the French West Indies, a sedition law, "more decision and dispatch." Half measures were weak. The country must wage full but undeclared war. Ex-President Washington, in letters to eminent friends, showed himself in general agreement with the Federalist world view. . . .

One question remains to be examined. Just how spontaneous was the combustion of 1798? Almost everything that happens in practical politics is arranged to happen. Both John C. Miller and Gilbert Chinard have suspected that the hysteria was induced. Events and opinions of 1797 can be marshaled to support a conclusion that the sentiment was whipped up by men who were themselves cool and calculating. The Bank of England was in distress and some were alarmed by the thought that Britain might therefore make peace with France. The hypothesis can be advanced that the British financial strains encouraged the American Federalists to use violence against France and terror against the Democratic-Republicans as a support of Britain, for economic reasons and for moral reasons that were equally if not more weighty in their minds. Letters of George Cabot, Alexander Hamilton, Chauncey Goodrich, and Oliver Wolcott, Jr. in the first quarter of 1797, rumble and mutter with hopes and fears of the attitude of the Fourth Congress toward military matters. Certainly the enactments of that Congress were unsatisfactorily parsimonious to this group. Military and naval appropriations were cut, not raised. There had been hopes for enlargement of the army and the navy, for a policy of arming and convoying merchant shipping, for the fortification of ports, and for a firm line with the French, but they were not fulfilled before the X.Y.Z. Affair. Certainly the emotional turbulence of 1798 could have been seen as a very opportune circumstance for the promotion of the military measures of 1797—that is, military measures and "some others" as Hamilton cryptically put it.

But whether the passions were spontaneous or caused deliberately, they existed. The United States in the year 1798 was a scene of fear and hate, warmed by seven or eight years of heating. Then, subject to these temperatures and surrounded by political commotion, the

Congress of the United States sat to enact laws for the internal security of the nation.

The year 1798 was a year of crisis in the history of constitutional liberty. It was a year in which fear of a foreign ideology and of its effects on fellow citizens goaded a party in power to attempt by statute to destroy free speech and a free press. In the same year there was legislation severely restricting the privileges of aliens but the Alien Laws are not our chief concern. Although harsh and probably impolitic, the Alien Laws were undoubtedly constitutional. But the Sedition Law of 1798 attempted to achieve what the First Amendment was written to prohibit. It is not necessary here to analyze the passage, provisions, and enforcement of the Sedition Act. The story of that law, and of the three acts applicable to aliens, has been definitively written by James Morton Smith in his *Freedom's Fetters*. It is sufficient to observe of the prosecutions under the Sedition Act that every defendant was a Republican, every judge and practically all jurors were Federalists. The results of the prosecutions support the historical generalization that in state trials, courts and juries have generally thought it a mark of patriotism to find the defendants guilty.

Although a few Federalists favored conciliation and moderation, the public mood was too excitable for them to prevail. Outside the courtrooms there was widespread social paranoia. A motion to censure Representative John Randolph of Roanoke for denouncing the manners of the military lost in the House by only two votes. Minister Rufus King warned the Secretary of State that several suspicious French characters were leaving Hamburg for Charleston, with dispatches from the Directory concealed in tubs with false bottoms, which report was widely printed as a "diabolical plot" to incite a slave insurrection. The passengers went on from Charleston to Guadeloupe as they had intended, but no Federalist newspaper printed a correction of the story of the great Tub Plot. In an outburst of personal passions, Federalist Representative Rufus Griswold and Republican Representative Matthew Lyon exchanged insults and twice fought on the floor of the House. There was armed resistance—the Hot Water Riots, or Fries Rebellion—to direct federal taxation in Pennsylvania, led by one John Fries who was convicted of treason but pardoned by President Adams.

Alexander Hamilton was zealous to change the nature of the federal republic in the interest of national security. Perhaps because of his money troubles, more likely out of a genuine fear of impending anarchy and civil war, he proposed a vast extension of federal power. He also seems to have been in the center of a scheme to conquer

South America. It is not impossible that the failure of Hamilton's political career prevented the prussianizing of the American state.

At this point in their grand ascent John Adams tripped the Federalists and cast them down from the pinnacle by nominating William Vans Murray to negotiate with France. This was shocking news to the Hamiltonian wing of his party. If peace with France were formally made, the Federalist position on domestic sedition and foreign foes was untenable. But from public officers and from private citizens the President had good reasons to think the French were ready to be conciliatory. The best that outraged extremists of his own party could accomplish was to get the nomination of a commission of three instead of Murray alone. In the Hamiltonian group all was execration. Their bitterness almost passes belief. Frantic, almost hysterical, they used the strongest polemic language yet heard or read in that decade. . . .

Despite delays deliberately arranged by several in the Cabinet, delays equivalent to contumacy, the mission went to France. The political reaction, and the phrase is used literally, opened the eyes of the Adams family to the warlike and frenzied spirit of that part of the Federalist group which looked to Hamilton for inspiration. Peace was made with France in the "Convention of 1800" but Federalist Senatorial diehards unsuccessfully fought it to the last ditch. It began to appear that Federalism was irreparably split. Adams regarded the French peace as his greatest achievement, which, perhaps, it was.

We can better understand the bitterness of the Hamiltonian Federalists when we realize how high they sat after the X.Y.Z. Affair. It seemed that everyone was anti-Gallican. The composition of the new Sixth Congress, elected in 1798, caused exultation in Federalist hearts, and the elections in the spring of 1799 brought further cheer. But all this was merely the last flare of the ember before it turned black. As Adams proved adamant on the question of his mission to France, the Federalist correspondence lost its buoyancy and sank, until by the end of 1799 it began to show querulousness and irritation. The drama played to its almost inevitable climax, an open break between Adams and the Hamiltonians, which began with a purge of two of his Cabinet who were more loyal to Hamilton than to him. His patience exhausted, in May 1800, Adams rid himself of his Secretaries of State and War, Pickering and McHenry. Thus in the year of a national election the angry President shook the pillars of the Federalist house. His political career was to perish in the wreckage of his party.

Thus far we have seen how the faction which administered the government attempted to discredit and suppress the other faction, and simultaneously suffered a serious internal cleavage. The national political events leading to the election of 1800—the publication of the Kentucky and Virginia Resolutions, the case of "Jonathan Robbins," the continued existence of endemic Anglophobia, the dislike of the tax load, the relevant local elections—all these things have been well-studied and need no repetition. Only an emphasis on certain occurrences as part of the national emotional storm is here necessary to complete the picture of an age of passion. . . .

Republican industry and confidence in this period made a sharp contrast with Federalist defeatism. An economic downturn caused a certain loss of confidence among the followers, and the Adams mission to France had certainly shaken the Federalist leaders. One can only repeat the conclusion that their obsession with the French danger had blinded these men to their own excesses and to Republican tactics. While the Federalists stamped out a nonexistant treasonable conspiracy their opponents built a good political machine. Face-to-face with that machine the Federalists were quitters. There is plenty of evidence of defeatism, while all felt a consciousness of impending climax—the presidential election of 1800. Psychologically the Federalists were at a disadvantage in any election; for that kind of work they were too fastidious. . . .

The Federalist press worked hard to influence the legislators who chose presidential electors, the presidential electors and the small body of voters at large. The *Columbian Centinel* of Boston had a department devoted solely to attacking Jefferson's morals, opinions, and public record. Several newspapers carried a serial feature called "The Jeffersoniad" and intended to destroy his reputation. The *Connecticut Courant* and the *Gazette of the United States* were especially ferocious. The Philadelphia *Monthly Magazine* in November reviewed four pamphlets on Jefferson's atheism.

But it was hate's labor lost. The final electoral count was Jefferson seventy-three, Burr seventy-three, Adams sixty-five, Pinckney sixty-four and Jay one. Burr's superb management in New York had been decisive. Outside of New York, Adams ran as well or better, than he did in 1796 when he carried this state. Losing New York in 1800 he lost the presidency. Of course the electoral vote did not settle the presidential contest, for Jefferson and Burr were tied (in a manner later made impossible by the Twelfth Amendment). The decision now had to be made in the House of Representatives—a "lame duck" House be it noted—where each state had one vote only.

The Federalists were going out of power, and nothing in their term of office so ill became them as the manner of their leaving it, for many congressional Federalists now decided to support Burr, who had been intended by the Republicans to be Vice-President. Neither party in New York approved of this course, but even Hamilton's expostulations (legend to the contrary notwithstanding) had little weight. As for Burr, he held his tongue and pen and waited it out. The votes of nine states were needed to elect. On the first ballot and on the next thirty-four ballots, Jefferson received eight and Burr six. At length Representative Bayard, sole member from Delaware, managed to learn indirectly that Jefferson had no thought of undoing every Federalist legislative work, and arrangements were made by Bayard and friends to elect Jefferson on the thirty-sixth ballot. And so was completed the "Revolution of 1800."

The Federalist period of American history can thus be presented as a span of twelve years in which every great public decision, every national political act, was somehow governed by fierce passions, by hatred, fear, and anger. Although this view must not be stretched beyond proportion, certain it is that the Founding Fathers had less confidence in each other and in the Constitution than our generation has in both. From suspicion of each other it was a short step to fear and hate.

The Democratic-Republicans feared a centralization which would lead to monarchy. Their fear caused them to make angry and fantastic charges against men now venerated. They thought of their opponents as tools of the British crown, turned against republicanism and the rights of man. Their accusations wounded contemporaries but did no particular damage to posterity because they were not in control of the state; they could only write, speak, and, occasionally, riot.

The Federalists feared democracy as mobocracy. They hated the French Revolution and its sympathizers. They could do much harm because they were in charge of the government and could make their enemies feel its force. They jailed and fined in a manner which the First Amendment was intended to prohibit, and they fired off accusations of treason or sedition like birdshot. The most extreme among them justified suspicions of a plot to new-model the government as a unitary, militarized state. They honestly believed that political opposition was founded on sloth, envy, senseless rage, or treason. Fear of the "mob," and fear of subversives, made it impossible for them to build a real political engine capable of keeping them "in" and the Republicans "out." Their tragedy was that they were the prisoners of their own propaganda.

These verbal blows were not just "campaign oratory," but were delivered, on both sides, in dead earnest. The evidence is in their private letters to friends, close collaborators, and relatives, and in memoranda noted privately for their own guidance. These private documents used the same passionate rhetoric as did the public literature. Some believed so intensely that—blinded by emotion—they willingly destroyed their party rather than admit to errors or excesses.

4

Some Themes of Countersubversion: An Analysis of Anti-Masonic, Anti-Catholic, and Anti-Mormon Literature

David Brion Davis

David Brion Davis has written extensively on the theme of anti-conspiracy fears in the antebellum period. Exploring the ideological significance of attacks on subversives, Davis finds that for Americans "the subversive group was essentially an inverted image of Jacksonian democracy." The lack of institutional controls in the United States left many Americans rootless and confused, groping toward social unity and ideological identity. In part, this need was met by rallying the country to defeat secret societies and churches they believed to be antidemocratic. In this respect the antebellum crusades played a similar role to that of the colonial antipapal literature: it "served to clarify national values" and "to establish the legitimacy and just authority of American institutions."

From David Brion Davis, "Some Themes of Countersubversion: An Analysis of Anti-Masonic, Anti-Catholic, and Anti-Mormon Literature," The Mississippi Valley Historical Review, *XLVII (September 1960), 205–224. Reprinted with most of the footnotes omitted by permission of the author and the publisher.*

During the second quarter of the nineteenth century, when danger of foreign invasion appeared increasingly remote, Americans were told by various respected leaders that Freemasons had infiltrated the government and had seized control of the courts, that Mormons were undermining political and economic freedom in the West, and that Roman Catholic priests, receiving instructions from Rome, had made frightening progress in a plot to subject the nation to popish despotism. This fear of internal subversion was channeled into a number of powerful countermovements which attracted wide public support. The literature produced by these movements evoked images of a great American enemy that closely resembled traditional European stereotypes of conspiracy and subversion. In Europe, however, the idea of subversion implied a threat to the established order—to the king, the church, or the ruling aristocracy—rather than to ideals or a way of life. If free Americans borrowed their images of subversion from frightened kings and uneasy aristocrats, these images had to be shaped and blended to fit American conditions. The movements would have to come from the people, and the themes of countersubversion would be likely to reflect their fears, prejudices, hopes, and perhaps even unconscious desires.

There are obvious dangers in treating such reactions against imagined subversion as part of a single tendency or spirit of an age.[1] Anti-Catholicism was nourished by ethnic conflict and uneasiness over immigration in the expanding cities of the Northeast; anti-Mormonism arose largely from a contest for economic and political power between western settlers and a group that voluntarily withdrew from society and claimed the undivided allegiance of its members. Anti-Masonry, on the other hand, was directed against a group thoroughly integrated in American society and did not reflect a clear division of economic, religious, or political interests. Moreover, anti-Masonry gained power in the late 1820s and soon spent its energies as it became absorbed in national politics; anti-Catholicism reached its maximum force in na-

---

[1] For an alternative to the method followed in this article, see John Higham's perceptive essay, "Another Look at Nativism," *Catholic Historical Review* (Washington), XLIV (July 1958), 147–158. Higham rejects the ideological approach to nativism and stresses the importance of concrete ethnic tensions, "status rivalries," and face-to-face conflicts in explaining prejudice. Though much can be said for this sociological emphasis, as opposed to a search for irrational myths and stereotypes, the method suggested by Higham can easily lead to a simple "stimulus-response" view of prejudice. Awareness of actual conflicts in status and self-interest should not obscure the social and psychological functions of nativism, nor distract attention from themes that may reflect fundamental tensions within a culture.

tional politics a full generation later; anti-Mormonism, though increasing in intensity in the 1850s, became an important national issue only after the Civil War. These movements seem even more widely separated when we note that Freemasonry was traditionally associated with anti-Catholicism and that Mormonism itself absorbed considerable anti-Masonic and anti-Catholic sentiment.

Despite such obvious differences, there were certain similarities in these campaigns against subversion. All three gained widespread support in the northeastern states within the space of a generation; anti-Masonry and anti-Catholicism resulted in the sudden emergence of separate political parties; and in 1856 the new Republican party explicitly condemned the Mormons' most controversial institution. The movements of countersubversion differed markedly in historical origin, but as the image of an un-American conspiracy took form in the nativist press, in sensational exposés, in the countless fantasies of treason and mysterious criminality, the lines separating Mason, Catholic, and Mormon became almost indistinguishable.

The similar pattern of Masonic, Catholic, and Mormon subversion was frequently noticed by alarmist writers. The *Anti-Masonic Review* informed its readers in 1829 that whether one looked at Jesuitism or Freemasonry, "the organization, the power, and the secret operation, are the same; except that Freemasonry is much the more secret and complicated of the two." William Hogan, an ex-priest and vitriolic anti-Catholic, compared the menace of Catholicism with that of Mormonism. And many later anti-Mormon writers agreed with Josiah Strong that Brigham Young "out-popes the Roman" and described the Mormon hierarchy as being similar to the Catholic. It was probably not accidental that Samuel F. B. Morse analyzed the Catholic conspiracy in essentially the same terms his father had used in exposing the Society of the Illuminati, supposedly a radical branch of Freemasonry, or that writers of sensational fiction in the 1840s and 1850s depicted an atheistic and unprincipled Catholic Church obviously modeled on Charles Brockden Brown's earlier fictional version of the Illuminati.[2]

---

[2] In Ned Buntline's *The G'hals of New York* (New York, 1850) the Jesuits seem to be connected with all secret conspiracies, and their American leader, Father Kerwin, is probably modeled on Brown's Carwin. George Lippard admired Brown, dedicated a novel to him, and was also fascinated by secret societies and diabolical plots to enslave America. In *New York: Its Upper Ten and Lower Million* (New York, 1853), the Catholic leaders are Illuminati-like atheists who plan revolutions, manipulate public opinion, and stop at no crime in their lust for wealth and power. These amoral supermen were clearly inspired by such characters as Brown's Ormond, as well as by the anti-Catholic writings of Eugène Sue and others.

If Masons, Catholics, and Mormons bore little resemblance to one another in actuality, as imagined enemies they merged into a nearly common stereotype. Behind specious professions of philanthropy or religious sentiment, nativists[3] discerned a group of unscrupulous leaders plotting to subvert the American social order. Though rank-and-file members were not individually evil, they were blinded and corrupted by a persuasive ideology that justified treason and gross immorality in the interest of the subversive group. Trapped in the meshes of a machine-like organization, deluded by a false sense of loyalty and moral obligation, these dupes followed orders like professional soldiers and labored unknowingly to abolish free society, to enslave their fellow men, and to overthrow divine principles of law and justice. Should an occasional member free himself from bondage to superstition and fraudulent authority, he could still be disciplined by the threat of death or dreadful tortures. There were no limits to the ambitious designs of leaders equipped with such organizations. According to nativist prophets, they chose to subvert American society because control of America meant control of the world's destiny.

Some of these beliefs were common in earlier and later European interpretations of conspiracy. American images of Masonic, Catholic, and Mormon subversion were no doubt a compound of traditional myths concerning Jacobite agents, scheming Jesuits, and fanatical heretics, and of dark legends involving the Holy Vehm and Rosicrucians. What distinguished the stereotypes of Mason, Catholic, and Mormon was the way in which they were seen to embody those traits that were precise antitheses of American ideals. The subversive group was essentially an inverted image of Jacksonian democracy and the cult of the common man; as such it not only challenged the dominant values but stimulated those suppressed needs and yearnings that are unfulfilled in a mobile, rootless, and individualistic society. It was therefore both frightening and fascinating.

It is well known that expansion and material progress in the Jacksonian era evoked a fervid optimism and that nationalists became intoxicated with visions of America's millennial glory. The simultaneous growth of prosperity and social democracy seemed to prove that Providence would bless a nation that allowed her citizens maxi-

---

[3] — Though the term "nativist" is usually limited to opponents of immigration, it is used here to include anti-Masons and anti-Mormons. This seems justified in view of the fact that these alarmists saw themselves as defenders of native traditions and identified Masonry and Mormonism with forces alien to American life.

mum liberty. When each individual was left free to pursue happiness in his own way, unhampered by the tyranny of custom or special privilege, justice and well-being would inevitably emerge. But if a doctrine of laissez-faire individualism seemed to promise material expansion and prosperity, it also raised disturbing problems. As one early anti-Mormon writer expressed it: What was to prevent liberty and popular sovereignty from sweeping away "the old landmarks of Christendom, and the glorious old common law of our fathers"? How was the individual to preserve a sense of continuity with the past, or identify himself with a given cause or tradition? What, indeed, was to insure a common loyalty and a fundamental unity among the people?

Such questions acquired a special urgency as economic growth intensified mobility, destroyed old ways of life, and transformed traditional symbols of status and prestige. Though most Americans took pride in their material progress, they also expressed a yearning for reassurance and security, for unity in some cause transcending individual self-interest. This need for meaningful group activity was filled in part by religious revivals, reform movements, and a proliferation of fraternal orders and associations. In politics Americans tended to assume the posture of what Marvin Meyers has termed "venturesome conservatives," mitigating their acquisitive impulses by an appeal for unity against extraneous forces that allegedly threatened a noble heritage of republican ideals. Without abandoning a belief in progress through laissez-faire individualism, the Jacksonians achieved a sense of unity and righteousness by styling themselves as restorers of tradition. Perhaps no theme is so evident in the Jacksonian era as the strained attempt to provide America with a glorious heritage and a noble destiny. With only a loose and often ephemeral attachment to places and institutions, many Americans felt a compelling need to articulate their loyalties, to prove their faith, and to demonstrate their allegiance to certain ideals and institutions. By so doing they acquired a sense of self-identity and personal direction in an otherwise rootless and shifting environment.

But was abstract nationalism sufficient to reassure a nation strained by sectional conflict, divided by an increasing number of sects and associations, and perplexed by the unexpected consequences of rapid growth? One might desire to protect the Republic against her enemies, to preserve the glorious traditions of the Founders, and to help insure continued expansion and prosperity, but first it was necessary to discover an enemy by distinguishing subversion from simple diversity. If Freemasons seemed to predominate in the economic and political life of a given area, was one's joining them shrewd business judgment or a betrayal of republican tradition? Should Maryland citizens heed the warnings of anti-Masonic itinerants, or conclude that anti-Masonry was itself a conspiracy hatched by scheming Yankees? Were Roman Catholics plotting to destroy public schools and a free press, the twin guardians of American democracy, or were they exercising democratic rights of self-expression and self-protection? Did equality of opportunity and equality before the law mean that Americans should accept the land claims of Mormons or tolerate as jurors men who "swear that they have wrought miracles and supernatural cures"? Or should one agree with the Reverend Finis Ewing that "the 'Mormons' are the common enemies of mankind and ought to be destroyed"?

Few men questioned traditional beliefs in freedom of conscience and the right of association. Yet what was to prevent "all the errors and worn out theories of the Old World, of schisms in the early Church, the monkish age and the rationalistic period," from flourishing in such salubrious air? Nativists often praised the work of benevolent societies, but they were disturbed by the thought that monstrous conspiracies might also "show kindness and patriotism, when it is necessary for their better concealment; and oftentimes do much good for the sole purpose of getting a better opportunity to do evil." When confronted by so many sects and associations, how was the patriot to distinguish the loyal from the disloyal? It was clear that mere disagreement over theology or economic policy was invalid as a test, since honest men disputed over the significance of baptism or the wisdom of protective tariffs. But neither could one rely on expressions of allegiance to common democratic principles, since subversives would cunningly profess to believe in freedom and toleration of dissent as long as they remained a powerless minority.

As nativists studied this troubling question, they discovered that most groups and denominations claimed only a partial loyalty from their members, freely subordinating themselves to the higher and more abstract demands of the Constitution, Christianity, and American public opinion. Moreover, they openly exposed their objects and activities to public scrutiny and exercised little discrimination in enlisting members. Some groups, however, dominated a larger portion of their members' lives, demanded unlimited allegiance as a condition of membership, and excluded certain activities from the gaze of a curious public.

Of all governments, said Richard Rush, ours was the one with most to fear from secret societies, since popular sovereignty by its very nature required perfect freedom of public inquiry and judgment. In a virtuous republic why should anyone fear publicity or desire to conceal activities, unless those activities were somehow contrary to the public interest? When no one could be quite sure what the public interest was, and when no one could take for granted a secure and well-defined place in the social order, it was most difficult to acknowledge legitimate spheres of privacy. Most Americans of the Jacksonian era appeared willing to tolerate diversity and even eccentricity, but when they saw themselves excluded and even barred from witnessing certain proceedings, they imagined a "mystic power" conspiring to enslave them.

Readers might be amused by the first exposures of Masonic ritual, since they learned that pompous and dignified citizens, who had once impressed non-Masons with allusions to high degrees and elaborate ceremonies, had in actuality been forced to stand blindfolded and clad in ridiculous garb, with a long rope noosed around their necks. But genuine anti-Masons were not content with simple ridicule. Since intelligent and distinguished men had been members of the fraternity, "it must have in its interior something more than the usual revelations of its mysteries declare." Surely leading citizens would not meet at night and undergo degrading and humiliating initiations just for the sake of novelty. The alleged murder of William Morgan raised an astonishing public furor because it supposedly revealed the inner secret of Freemasonry. Perverted by a false ideology, Masons had renounced all obligations to the general public, to the laws of the land, and even to the command of God. Hence they threatened not a particular party's program or a denomination's creed, but stood opposed to all justice, democracy, and religion.

The distinguishing mark of Masonic, Catholic, and Mormon conspiracies was a secrecy that cloaked the members' unconditional loyalty to an autonomous body. Since the organizations had corrupted the private moral judgment of their members, Americans could not rely on the ordinary forces of progress to spread truth and enlightenment among their ranks. Yet the affairs of such organizations were not outside the jurisdiction of democratic government, for no body politic could be asked to tolerate a power that was designed to destroy it. Once the true nature of subversive groups was thoroughly understood, the alternatives were as clear as life and death. How could democracy and Catholicism coexist when, as Edward Beecher warned, "The systems are diametrically opposed: one must and will exterminate the other"? Because Freemasons had so deeply penetrated state and national governments, only drastic remedies could restore the nation to its democratic purity. And later, Americans faced an "irrepressible conflict" with Mormonism, for it was said that either free institutions or Mormon despotism must ultimately annihilate the other.

We may well ask why nativists magnified the division between unpopular minorities and the American public, so that Masons, Catholics, and Mormons seemed so menacing that they could not be accorded the usual rights and privileges of a free society. Obviously the literature of countersubversion reflected concrete rivalries and conflicts of interest between competing groups, but it is important to note that the subversive bore no racial or ethnic stigma and was not even accused of inherent depravity.[4] Since group membership was a matter of intellectual and emotional loyalty, no *physical* barrier prevented a Mason, Catholic, or Mormon from apostatizing and joining the dominant in-group, providing always that he escaped assassination from his previous masters. This suggests that countersubversion was more than a rationale for group rivalry and was related to the general problem of ideological unity and diversity in a free society. When a "system of delusion" insulated members of a group from the unifying and disciplining force of public opinion, there was no authority to command an allegiance to common principles. This was why oaths of loyalty assumed great importance for nativists. Though the ex-Catholic William Hogan stated repeatedly that Jesuit spies respected no oaths except those to the Church, he inconsistently told Masons and Odd Fellows that they could prevent infiltration by requiring new members to swear they were not Catholics. It was precisely the absence of distinguishing outward traits that made the enemy so dangerous, and true loyalty so difficult to prove.

When the images of different enemies conform to a similar pattern, it is highly probable that this pattern reflects important tensions within a given culture. The themes of nativist literature suggest that its authors simplified problems of personal insecurity and adjustment to bewildering social change by trying to unite Americans of diverse political, religious, and economic interests against a common enemy. Just as revivalists sought to stimulate Christian fellowship

---

[4] It is true that anti-Catholics sometimes stressed the inferiority of lower-class immigrants and that anti-Mormons occasionally claimed that Mormon converts were made among the most degraded and ignorant classes of Europe. This theme increased in importance toward the end of the century, but it seldom implied that Catholics and Mormons were physically incapable of being liberated and joined to the dominant group. Racism was not an original or an essential part of the countersubversive's ideology. Even when Mormons were attacked for coarseness, credulity, and vulgarity, these traits were usually thought to be the product of their beliefs and institutions.

by awakening men to the horrors of sin, so nativists used apocalyptic images to ignite human passions, destroy selfish indifference, and join patriots in a cohesive brotherhood. Such themes were only faintly secularized. When God saw his "lov'd Columbia" imperiled by the hideous monster of Freemasonry, he realized that only a martyr's blood could rouse the hearts of the people and save them from bondage to the Prince of Darkness. By having God will Morgan's death, this anti-Mason showed he was more concerned with national virtue and unity than with Freemasonry, which was only a providential instrument for testing republican strength.

Similarly, for the anti-Catholic "this brilliant new world" was once "young and beautiful; it abounded in all the luxuries of nature; it promised all that was desirable to man." But the Roman Church, seeing "these irresistible temptations, thirsting with avarice and yearning for the reestablishment of her falling greatness, soon commenced pouring in among its unsuspecting people hoardes of Jesuits and other friars." If Americans were to continue their narrow pursuit of self-interest, oblivious to the "popish colleges, and nunneries, and monastic institutions," indifferent to manifold signs of corruption and decay, how could the nation expect "that the moral breezes of heaven should breathe upon her, and restore to her again that strong and healthy constitution, which her ancestors have left to her sons"? The theme of an Adamic fall from paradise was horrifying, but it was used to inspire determined action and thus unity. If Methodists were "criminally indifferent" to the Mormon question, and if "avaricious merchants, soulless corporations, and a subsidized press" ignored Mormon iniquities, there was all the more reason that the "*will of the people* must prevail."

Without explicitly rejecting the philosophy of laissez-faire individualism, with its toleration of dissent and innovation, nativist literature conveyed a sense of common dedication to a noble cause and sacred tradition. Though the nation had begun with the blessings of God and with the noblest institutions known to man, the people had somehow become selfish and complacent, divided by petty disputes, and insensitive to signs of danger. In his sermons attacking such self-interest, such indifference to public concerns, and such a lack of devotion to common ideals and sentiments, the nativist revealed the true source of his anguish. Indeed, he seemed at times to recognize an almost beneficent side to subversive organizations, since they joined the nation in a glorious crusade and thus kept it from moral and social disintegration.

The exposure of subversion was a means of promoting unity, but it also served to clarify national values and provide the individual ego with a sense of high moral sanction and imputed righteousness. Nativists identified themselves repeatedly with a strangely incoherent tradition in which images of Pilgrims, Minute Men, Founding Fathers, and true Christians appeared in a confusing montage. Opposed to this heritage of stability and perfect integrity, to this society founded on the highest principles of divine and natural law were organizations formed by the grossest frauds and impostures, and based on the wickedest impulses of human nature. Bitterly refuting Masonic claims to ancient tradition and Christian sanction, anti-Masons charged that the Order was of recent origin, that it was shaped by Jews, Jesuits, and French atheists as an engine for spreading infidelity, and that it was employed by kings and aristocrats to undermine republican institutions.[5] If the illustrious Franklin and Washington had been duped by Masonry, this only proved how treacherous was its appeal and how subtly persuasive were its pretensions.[6] Though the Catholic Church had an undeniable claim to tradition, nativists argued that it had originated in stupendous frauds and forgeries "in comparison with which the forgeries of Mormonism are completely thrown into the shade." Yet anti-Mormons saw an even more sinister conspiracy based on the "shrewd cunning" of Joseph Smith, who convinced gullible souls that he conversed with angels and received direct revelations from the Lord.

By emphasizing the fraudulent character of their opponents' claims, nativists sought to establish the legitimacy and just authority of American institutions. Masonic rituals, Roman Catholic sacraments, and Mormon revelations were preposterous hoaxes used to delude naïve or superstitious minds; but public schools, a free press, and jury trials were eternally valid prerequisites for a free and virtuous society.

Moreover, the finest values of an enlightened nation stood out in

---

[5] The charge was often repeated that higher degrees of Freemasonry were created by the "school of Voltaire" and introduced to America by Jewish immigrants. Masonry was also seen as an "auxiliary to British foreign policy."

[6] This question was most troubling to anti-Masons. Though some tried to side-step the issue by quoting Washington against "self-created societies," as if he had been referring to the Masons, others flatly declared that Washington had been hoodwinked, just as distinguished jurists had once been deluded by a belief in witchcraft. Of course Washington had been unaware of Masonic iniquities, but he had lent his name to the cause and had thus served as a decoy for the ensnarement of others.

bold relief when contrasted with the corrupting tendencies of subversive groups. Perversion of the sexual instinct seemed inevitably to accompany religious error.[7] Deprived of the tender affections of normal married love, shut off from the elevating sentiments of fatherhood, Catholic priests looked on women only as insensitive objects for the gratification of their frustrated desires. In similar fashion polygamy struck at the heart of a morality based on the inspiring influence of woman's affections: "It renders man coarse, tyrannical, brutal, and heartless. It deals death to all sentiments of true manhood. It enslaves and ruins woman. It crucifies every God-given feeling of her nature." Some anti-Mormons concluded that plural marriage could only have been established among foreigners who had never learned to respect women. But the more common explanation was that the false ideology of Mormonism had deadened the moral sense and liberated man's wild sexual impulse from the normal restraints of civilization. Such degradation of women and corruption of man served to highlight the importance of democratic marriage, a respect for women, and careful cultivation of the finer sensibilities.[8]

But if nativist literature was a medium for articulating common values and exhorting individuals to transcend self-interest and join in a dedicated union against evil, it also performed a more subtle function. Why, we may ask, did nativist literature dwell so persistently on themes of brutal sadism and sexual immorality? Why did its authors describe sin in such minute details, endowing even the worst offenses of their enemies with a certain fascinating appeal?

Freemasons, it was said, could commit any crime and indulge any passion when "upon the square," and Catholics and Mormons were even less inhibited by internal moral restraints. Nativists expressed horror over this freedom from conscience and conventional morality, but they could not conceal a throbbing note of envy. What was it like to be a member of a cohesive brotherhood that casually abrogated the laws of God and man, enforcing unity and obedience with dark and mysterious powers? As nativists speculated on this ques-

---

[7] According to Beadle, religious error and sexual perversion were related "because the same constitution of mind and temperament which gives rise to one, powerfully predisposes toward the other."

[8] Though Horace Greeley was moderate in his judgment of Mormonism, he wrote: "I joyfully trust that the genius of the Nineteenth Century tends to a solution of the problem of Woman's sphere and destiny radically different from this."

tion, they projected their own fears and desires into a fantasy of licentious orgies and fearful punishments.

Such a projection of forbidden desires can be seen in the exaggeneration of the stereotyped enemy's powers, which made him appear at times as a virtual superman. Catholic and Mormon leaders, never hindered by conscience or respect for traditional morality, were curiously superior to ordinary Americans in cunning, in exercising power over others, and especially in captivating gullible women.[9] It was an ancient theme of anti-Catholic literature that friars and priests were somehow more potent and sexually attractive than married laymen and were thus astonishingly successful at seducing supposedly virtuous wives. Americans were cautioned repeatedly that no priest recognized Protestant marriages as valid and might consider any wife legitimate prey. Furthermore, priests had access to the pornographic teachings of Dens and Liguori, sinister names that aroused the curiosity of anti-Catholics, and hence learned subtle techniques of seduction perfected over the centuries. Speaking with the authority of an ex-priest, William Hogan described the shocking result: "I have seen husbands unsuspiciously and hospitably entertaining the very priest who seduced their wives in the confessional, and was the parent of some of the children who sat at the same table with them, each of the wives unconscious of the other's guilt, and the husbands of both, not even suspecting them." Such blatant immorality was horrifying, but everyone was apparently happy in this domestic scene, and we may suspect that the image was not entirely repugnant to husbands who, despite their respect for the Lord's Commandments, occasionally coveted their neighbors' wives.

The literature of countersubversion could also embody the somewhat different projective fantasies of women. Ann Eliza Young dramatized her seduction by the Prophet Brigham, whose almost superhuman powers enchanted her and paralyzed her will. Though she submitted finally only because her parents were in danger of being ruined by the Church, she clearly indicated that it was an exciting privilege to be pursued by a Great Man. When anti-Mormons

[9] It should be noted that Freemasons were rarely accused of sexual crimes, owing perhaps to their greater degree of integration within American society, and to their conformity to the dominant pattern of monogamy. They were sometimes attacked, however, for excluding women from their Order, and for swearing not to violate the chastity of wives, sisters, and daughters of fellow Masons. Why, anti-Masons asked, was such an oath not extended to include *all* women?

claimed that Joseph Smith and other prominent Saints knew the mysteries of animal magnetism, or were endowed with the highest degree of "amativeness" in their phrenological makeup, this did not detract from their covert appeal. In a ridiculous fantasy written by Maria Ward, such alluring qualities were extended even to Mormon women. Many bold-hearted girls could doubtless identify themselves with Anna Bradish, a fearless Amazon of a creature, who rode like a man, killed without compunction, and had no pity for weak women who failed to look out for themselves. Tall, elegant, and "intellectual," Anna was attractive enough to arouse the insatiable desires of Brigham Young, though she ultimately rejected him and renounced Mormonism.

While nativists affirmed their faith in Protestant monogamy, they obviously took pleasure in imagining the variety of sexual experience supposedly available to their enemies. By picturing themselves exposed to similar temptations, they assumed they could know how priests and Mormons actually sinned.[10] Imagine, said innumerable anti-Catholic writers, a beautiful young woman kneeling before an ardent young priest in a deserted room. As she confesses, he leans over, looking into her eyes, until their heads are nearly touching. Day after day she reveals to him her innermost secrets, secrets she would not think of unveiling to her parents, her dearest friends, or even her suitor. By skillful questioning the priest fills her mind with immodest and even sensual ideas, "until this wretch has worked up her passions to a tension almost snapping, and then becomes his easy prey." How could any man resist such provocative temptations, and how could any girl's virtue withstand such a test?

We should recall that this literature was written in a period of increasing anxiety and uncertainty over sexual values and the proper role of woman. As ministers and journalists pointed with alarm at the spread of prostitution, the incidence of divorce, and the lax and hypocritical morality of the growing cities, a discussion of licentious subversives offered a convenient means for the projection of guilt as well as desire. The sins of individuals, or of the nation as a whole, could be pushed off upon the shoulders of the enemy and there punished in righteous anger.

Specific instances of such projection are not difficult to find. John C. Bennett, whom the Mormons expelled from the Church as a re-

[10] The Mormons, for instance, were imagined to engage in the most licentious practices in the Endowment House ceremonies.

sult of his flagrant sexual immorality, invented the fantasy of "The Mormon Seraglio" which persisted in later anti-Mormon writings. According to Bennett, the Mormons maintained secret orders of beautiful prostitutes who were mostly reserved for various officials of the Church. He claimed, moreover, that any wife refusing to accept polygamy might be forced to join the lowest order and thus become available to any Mormon who desired her.

Another example of projection can be seen in the letters of a young lieutenant who stopped in Utah in 1854 on his way to California. Convinced that Mormon women could be easily seduced, the lieutenant wrote frankly of his amorous adventures with a married woman. "Everybody has got one," he wrote with obvious pride, "except the Colonel and Major. The Doctor has got three—mother and two daughters. The mother cooks for him and the daughters sleep with him." But though he described Utah as "a great country," the lieutenant waxed indignant over polygamy, which he condemned as self-righteously as any anti-Mormon minister: "To see one man openly parading half a dozen or more women to church . . . is the devil according to my ideas of morality virtue and decency."

If the consciences of many Americans were troubled by the growth of red light districts in major cities, they could divert their attention to the "legalized brothels" called nunneries, for which no one was responsible but lecherous Catholic priests. If others were disturbed by the moral implications of divorce, they could point in horror at the Mormon elder who took his quota of wives all at once. The literature of countersubversion could thus serve the double purpose of vicariously fulfilling repressed desires, and of releasing the tension and guilt arising from rapid social change and conflicting values.

Though the enemy's sexual freedom might at first seem enticing, it was always made repugnant in the end by associations with perversion or brutal cruelty. Both Catholics and Mormons were accused of practicing nearly every form of incest. The persistent emphasis on this theme might indicate deep-rooted feelings of fear and guilt, but it also helped demonstrate, on a more objective level, the loathsome consequences of unrestrained lust. Sheer brutality and a delight in human suffering were supposed to be the even more horrible results of sexual depravity. Masons disemboweled or slit the throats of their victims; Catholics cut unborn infants from their mothers' wombs and threw them to the dogs before their parents' eyes; Mormons raped and lashed recalcitrant women, or seared their mouths with red-hot irons. This obsession with details of sadism, which reached pathological proportions in much of the literature, showed a furious determination to purge the enemy of every admirable quality. The imagined enemy might serve at first as an outlet for forbidden desires, but nativist authors escaped from guilt by finally making him an agent of unmitigated aggression. In such a role the subversive seemed to deserve both righteous anger and the most terrible punishments.

The nativist escape from guilt was more clearly revealed in the themes of confession and conversion. For most American Protestants the crucial step in anyone's life was a profession of true faith resulting from a genuine religious experience. Only when a man became conscious of his inner guilt, when he struggled against the temptations of Satan, could he prepare his soul for the infusion of the regenerative spirit. Those most deeply involved in sin often made the most dramatic conversions. It is not surprising that conversion to nativism followed the same pattern, since nativists sought unity and moral certainty in the regenerative spirit of nationalism. Men who had been associated in some way with un-American conspiracies were not only capable of spectacular confessions of guilt, but were best equipped to expose the insidious work of supposedly harmless organizations. Even those who lacked such an exciting history of corruption usually made some confession of guilt, though it might involve only a previous indifference to subversive groups. Like ardent Christians, nativists searched in their own experiences for the meanings of sin, delusion, awakening to truth, and liberation from spiritual bondage. These personal confessions proved that one had recognized and conquered evil, and also served as ritual cleansings preparatory to full acceptance in a group of dedicated patriots.

Anti-Masons were perhaps the ones most given to confessions of guilt and most alert to subtle distinctions of loyalty and disloyalty. Many leaders of this movement, expressing guilt over their own "shameful experience and knowledge" of Masonry, felt a compelling obligation to exhort their former associates to "come out, and be separate from masonic abominations." Even when an anti-Mason could say with John Quincy Adams that "I am not, never was, and never shall be a Freemason," he would often admit that he had once admired the Order, or had even considered applying for admission.

Since a willingness to sacrifice oneself was an unmistakable sign of loyalty and virtue, ex-Masons gloried in exaggerating the dangers they faced and the harm that their revelations supposedly inflicted on the enemy. In contrast to hardened Freemasons, who refused to answer questions in court concerning their fraternal associations, the seceders claimed to reveal the inmost secrets of the

Order, and by so doing to risk property, reputation, and life. Once the ex-Mason had dared to speak the truth, his character would surely be maligned, his motives impugned, and his life threatened. But, he declared, even if he shared the fate of the illustrious Morgan, he would die knowing that he had done his duty.

Such self-dramatization reached extravagant heights in the ranting confessions of many apostate Catholics and Mormons. Maria Monk and her various imitators told of shocking encounters with sin in its most sensational forms, of bondage to vice and superstition, and of melodramatic escapes from popish despotism. A host of "ex-Mormon wives" described their gradual recognition of Mormon frauds and iniquities, the anguish and misery of plural marriage, and their breath-taking flights over deserts or mountains. The female apostate was especially vulnerable to vengeful retaliation, since she could easily be kidnapped by crafty priests and nuns, or dreadfully punished by Brigham Young's Destroying Angels. At the very least, her reputation could be smirched by foul lies and insinuations. But her willingness to risk honor and life for the sake of her country and for the dignity of all womankind was eloquent proof of her redemption. What man could be assured of so noble a role?

The apostate's pose sometimes assumed paranoid dimensions. William Hogan warned that only the former priest could properly gauge the Catholic threat to American liberties and saw himself as providentially appointed to save his Protestant countrymen. "For twenty years," he wrote, "I have warned them of approaching danger, but their politicians were deaf, and their Protestant theologians remained religiously coiled up in fancied security, overrating their own powers and undervaluing that of Papists." Pursued by vengeful Jesuits, denounced and calumniated for alleged crimes, Hogan pictured himself single-handedly defending American freedom: "No one, before me, dared to encounter their scurrilous abuse. I resolved to silence them; and I have done so. The very mention of my name is a terror to them now." After surviving the worst of Catholic persecution, Hogan claimed to have at last aroused his countrymen and to have reduced the hierarchy to abject terror.

As the nativist searched for participation in a noble cause, for unity in a group sanctioned by tradition and authority, he professed a belief in democracy and equal rights. Yet in his very zeal for freedom he curiously assumed many of the characteristics of the imagined enemy. By condemning the subversive's fanatical allegiance to an ideology, he affirmed a similarly uncritical acceptance of a different ideology; by attacking the subversive's intolerance of dissent, he worked to eliminate dissent and diversity of opinion; by censuring the subversive for alleged licentiousness, he engaged in sensual fantasies; by criticizing the subversive's loyalty to an organization, he sought to prove his unconditional loyalty to the established order. The nativist moved even farther in the direction of his enemies when he formed tightly knit societies and parties which were often secret and which subordinated the individual to the single purpose of the group. Though the nativists generally agreed that the worst evil of subversives was their subordination of means to ends, they themselves recommended the most radical means to purge the nation of troublesome groups and to enforce unquestioned loyalty to the state.

In his image of an evil group conspiring against the nation's welfare, and in his vision of a glorious millennium that was to dawn after the enemy's defeat, the nativist found satisfaction for many desires. His own interests became legitimate and dignified by fusion with the national interest, and various opponents became loosely associated with the un-American conspiracy. Thus Freemasonry in New York State was linked in the nativist mind with economic and political interests that were thought to discriminate against certain groups and regions; southerners imagined a union of abolitionists and Catholics to promote unrest and rebellion among slaves; gentile businessmen in Utah merged anti-Mormonism with plans for exploiting mines and lands.

Then too the nativist could style himself as a restorer of the past, as a defender of a stable order against disturbing changes, and at the same time proclaim his faith in future progress. By focusing his attention on the imaginary threat of a secret conspiracy, he found an outlet for many irrational impulses, yet professed his loyalty to the ideals of equal rights and government by law. He paid lip service to the doctrine of laissez-faire individualism, but preached selfless dedication to a transcendent cause. The imposing threat of subversion justified a group loyalty and subordination of the individual that would otherwise have been unacceptable. In a rootless environment shaken by bewildering social change the nativist found unity and meaning by conspiring against imaginary conspiracies.

5

The Slave Power Conspiracy: 1830–1860

Russel B. Nye

Historians have attempted to explain the origins of the American Civil War primarily in terms of economic conflict, moral outrage, and blundering statesmanship. Another factor that influenced antebellum politics was the acceptance of conspiratorial stereotypes by both northern and southern spokesmen. In this selection Russel B. Nye describes the abolitionist's conviction that a slave power conspiracy threatened to spread slavery throughout the Union and destroy civil liberties in the North. The fears Nye depicts reflect the inability of Americans to resolve their sectional differences by peaceable means.

The keynote of the abolitionist histories of the antebellum period, and of the literature produced by the abolitionist movement, was the thesis that the fight against slavery was not only a struggle to free the Negro from bondage, but one to remove as a dominant force in American life the threat of a well-organized, aggressive, threatening "Slave Power conspiracy," or what is called "Slaveocracy."

Russel B. Nye, "The Slave Power Conspiracy: 1830–1860," Science and Society, *X (Summer 1946), 262–274. Reprinted without footnotes by permission of the publishers.*

For the abolitionists, who remained a minority in the North throughout the entire prewar period, the "Slave Power threat" served as an invaluable device in gaining public support. There was, they charged, a tacit secret agreement among southern slaveholders not only to maintain undisturbed their "peculiar institution," but to foist it on the nation by extending it to the territories and free states (possibly to whites), to destroy civil liberties, control the policies of the Federal government, and complete the formation of a nationwide ruling aristocracy based on a slave economy.

To many in the North who were relatively uninterested in the Negro's freedom, the appeal of the charge was strong. Mechanics, immigrant laborers, farmers, and lower- and middle-class workmen, prone to suspect the motives of the rich and powerful, found in the abolitionist contention more logic than is usually supposed. During the thirties the abolitionists warned constantly of the existence of such a conspiratorial movement to crush liberty, though the term "Slave Power" did not come into wide use until the fifties. In 1839 the National Convention of Abolitionists, meeting at Albany, resolved that "the events of the last five or six years leave no room for doubt that the SLAVE POWER is now waging a deliberate and determined war against the liberties of the free states," and by 1845 repetitions of the charge became common. From that date on northern opinion was subjected to an increasing barrage of proof and began to be colored appreciably by acceptance of it. As the fear of "black Republicanism" and miscegenation was used by the proslavery element to unify southern opinion, so the genuine threat of the Slave Power became an important factor in consolidating antislavery sentiment in the North.

What was the Slave Power of which the abolitionist warned, and from what conditions did it arise? A typical definition called it "that control in and over the government which is exercised by a comparatively small number of persons . . . bound together in a common interest, by being owners of slaves"; all definitions agreed that it was fundamentally "an aristocracy constituted and organized on the basis of ownership of slaves." Its origins lay in the institution of slavery, which "developed and gratified the most intense spirit of personal pride, a love of class distinctions, and the lust of dominion. Hence arose a commanding power, ever sensitive, jealous, proscriptive, dominating, and aggressive. . . ." The threat of Slave Power domination was intensified, said the abolitionists, by the danger of a coalition of southern slaveholder and northern capitalist to form a ruling oligarchy. The two had certain moral affinities and a clear identity of interest, it was pointed out, and concerted action was logical and imminent. The tendency to include in the term "Slave Power" not only slaveholders but also northern industrialists grew, until by 1850 the term meant, as Wendell Phillips strikingly phrased it, an alliance of "the Lords of the Lash and the Lords of the Loom." "The wealth of the North and the wealth of the South," cried *The Antislavery Bugle,* "are combined to crush the liberal, free, progressive spirit of the age," and the fight against the Slave Power became a battle against conservatism, reaction, aristocracy, and the power of capital—in Ohio and Massachusetts as well as in South Carolina.

It was not difficult for the abolitionists to recruit evidence to prove that there actually was a Slave Power conspiracy. After 1850, when they began to publicize the charge in earnest, they interpreted the drift of recent events in the light of its existence. Joshua Giddings of Ohio, writing in the forties, listed ten proofs from history to substantiate the belief that a well-organized southern slaveholding cabal had operated in the past, and might again: the fugitive slave law of 1793, the Creek-Negro troubles in Florida in 1815, the Seminole War, the maintenance of slavery in the District of Columbia, the controversy over the mails and petitions in Congress in 1836, attacks on free speech and press, and demands for extension of the slavery to the Southwest and for the reopening of the slave trade. Seward in 1855 added the Missouri Compromise, the annexation of Texas, the Mexican War, the Kansas struggle, and the 1850 Compromise to the list of Slave Power victories. The Dred Scott case clinched the evidence, and by 1858 a substantial number of northerners were ready to believe, as did the nonabolitionist Cincinnati *Dial Commercial* of March 12, 1857, that "There is such a thing as the SLAVE POWER. It has marched over and annihilated the boundaries of the states. We are now one great homogeneous slaveholding community." The aim of this conspiracy, whose existence was thus established, was threefold: to reopen the slave trade; to extend slavery throughout the entire nation and beyond; and, most dangerous threat of all, to make the free white man a virtual slave to a privileged aristocracy of southern slaveholder and northern capitalist.

Southern agitation after 1850 for the renewal of the slave trade lent rather convincing proof to the first claim. The failing slave economy led many soutnerners to advocate a revival of slave importations as the only remedy for the South's economic difficulties, and abolitionists seized upon the argument as evidence that the Slave Power intended to entrench itself even more firmly by thus bolstering the institution upon which it rested. In the years following, southern demands became more insistent and frequent (a marked illustration of how completely the South had become committed to the defense and maintenance of slavery) while the abolitionist press kept careful watch of ruses, such as proposals to import "indentured" Negroes, Negro apprentices, or to form "African Labor Importation Associations." The loosening of the 1808 laws against the slave trade or their repeal, warned the abolitionists, would result without doubt in a new and doubly potent Slave Power.

Stressed more strongly by the abolitionists and supported by more substantial evidence was the claim that the Slave Power intended to establish slavery on a nationwide and possibly a hemispheric basis. Gamaliel Bailey in 1844 exposed "a deliberate plot . . . to sustain the slavery of this country . . . and to extend it over almost illimitable regions," and for more than a decade the press reported a boast by Toombs of Georgia that he would some day call the roll of his slaves on Bunker Hill. Furthermore, the abolitionist could cite the Kansas troubles, the attacks on antislavery men in the North, the Mexican War, Texas, the various Congressional compromises, the argument over slavery in the territories, and a host of other proofs. Nor was the Slave Power innocent of designs on Central America. It intended to make slave states of New Mexico and Utah, divide California into a free and a slave state, split Texas into four new slave states, take over at least Mexico, Cuba, San Domingo, Yucatan, and Nicaragua, "consolidating the whole into a vast slave empire." Toward the close of the fifties the accusation formed a major portion of almost every abolition argument, until antiextension became, by way of the Republican party, a cardinal political principle in the North.

More difficult to establish, but tremendously effective as a propaganda issue, was the accusation that the Slave Power aimed eventually to subvert the liberties of white men, and to introduce virtual white slavery as national policy. Since slavery, reasoned the abolitionists, was founded upon a violation of the principles of liberty and free government, it followed that by the simple fact of its existence slavery was a constant threat to those principles. Abolitionists had warned from the beginning that the Slave Power would some day crush white rights as it had black. . . .

It was not difficult to perceive the implications of the proslavery argument. If slavery were a positive good, superior to free society as an economic, political, and social system, it was reasonable to assume that the next step of its proponents would be to impose it upon the nation at large. Certain extreme statements from southern fire-eaters invited some such interpretation. The Richmond *Enquirer,* for example, declared editorially that "the laws of the slave states justify the holding of white men in bondage," while the Richmond *Examiner* thought that "the principle of slavery is itself right, and does not depend upon difference in complexion," and that "slavery black or white is necessary." Similar quotations were endlessly reprinted by the abolitionist press, which agreed that extension of slavery to white men was a definite objective of the Slave Power. And it could legally be done. The slave laws made no distinction in color; slavery was a matter of condition alone. If a person who was 99.9 percent white could, under the law, be claimed as a slave, the next step was a logical one. The only reason for the existence of pigmentation as a basis for slavery, warned the abolitionist, was simply that the Negro, who because of his helpless condition could be made a slave, happened to have a different color. The truth was that the institution did not rest upon a distinction of race at all; "Where is the man," asked William Goodell, "who may not at any moment become a slave?" that is, if slavery is founded not upon color, but upon the right of the strong to enslave the weak?

In making their charges, the abolitionists made a particular effort to point out to the immigrant and the laborer, the two groups most likely to respond, the great stake they held in the abolition of slavery and the consequent defeat of the Slave Power. "American slavery," resolved the Massachusetts Antislavery Society in 1843, "is the deadliest foe of the rights of labor, and ought, therefore, to be the object of special indignation and alarm to the hardworking Irish immigrant." "What security have the Germans and Irish that their children will not, within a hundred years, be reduced to slavery in this the land of their adoption?" asked the Cincinnati *Freeman.* Involuntary servitude, it was warned, could legally be made a prerequisite to citizenship, and by some such device the Slave Power might introduce white slavery for the foreign-born. As evidence, the abolitionists pointed to those provisions of the Nebraska bill which denied citizenship to territorial aliens for five years, and to the antiforeign riots attendant to the Know-Nothing movement. In general, the reaction of the foreign press, especially in the areas of German settlement, was sympathetic, while the influence of men such as C. C. Follen and Carl Schurz, both antislavery leaders, turned many immigrants toward the antislavery cause. Yet in the end it was not the Slave Power threat which enlisted the support of the foreign-born in abolitionism, but other factors, primarily economic and political, and after 1856 and the decline of the nativistic troubles, the abolitionist campaign to convince the immigrant of the threat of white slavery was largely written off.

More successful was the appeal to the laboring classes. The workman, though little interested in the humanitarian aspects of the slavery question, intuitively perceived that his own liberties were to some extent involved in the issue. The existence of a slave labor system threatened his own status, and he could readily see that the competition of skilled and unskilled slaves tended to depreciate the value of free labor. "Wage slavery" and chattel slavery were, in the opinion of the wisest labor leaders, closely connected, and the former could not be successfully attacked until the latter were abolished. For that matter, it was evident that wage slavery might conceivably turn into chattel slavery or something resembling it. . . .

Nearly the whole structure of the proslavery argument could be turned to support the abolitionist contention that the southern Slave Power intended to enslave white laborers. If slavery was the best possible system for labor and capital, was it not logical to assume that it would be an improvement over free labor in the northern factory system? If the laborer was unfitted for self-government, as the South argued, was it not implied that his employer should rule him? If slaves were much better off than the wage laborers, as Fitzhugh contended, the introduction of slavery into industry could be justified on the ground of bettering the free laborer's lot. Such, said the abolitionist, was the intent of the Slave Power, and, if it gained political control of the federal government, it could realize its aim. It was not difficult to find and publicize extremely significant statements from the South. The Republican party in 1856 distributed a reprint of a South Carolina paper's belief that "Slavery is the natural state and normal condition of the laboring man, black or white." The Charleston *Mercury* thought that the great evil of free society was "a servile class of mechanics and laborers, unfit for self-government, and yet clothed with the attributes and powers of citizens." These, and similar statements from prominent southerners, among them Leigh of Virginia, McDuffie of South Carolina, Calhoun, Dew, Fitzhugh, and others, made out a damaging case. . . . Neither were such sentiments restricted to the South. Solon Robinson of Indiana, a prominent agricultural authority, defended slavery as "a perfect labor system" and suggested its adoption on the nation's farms, a view that found some agreement in Ohio and Illinois. The Salem *Register*, the Pittsburgh *Post*, the New York *Herald* and the extremely southern New York *Day Book* thought slavery superior as a labor system, while in factory-conscious New England a debate was held on the question. The abolitionist claim that the extension of slavery to white labor was something more than an impossible chimera had a point and evidence to buttress it. If slavery were ever extended to include whites, the laborer, since his political and economic position was weakest, would be the first to be enslaved—a fact the abolitionists never allowed the laborer to forget. Thus, in 1839, *The Emancipator* summarized the issue: "The struggle is between the antagonist principles of free and slave labor. They cannot much longer coexist. One must prevail to the exclusion of the other. The laborers will either be free, or enslaved." Subsequent argument directed at northern labor by the abolitionists deviated but little from this line, and they continued their appeal to the labor interests for assistance against the Slave Power until the Civil War.

Although the laboring class was too disorganized and too politically immature during the period to exert much influence, nevertheless in the main the effect of the abolitionist warnings of the Slave Power threat to its liberties was relatively large. . . . But though laboring interests, divided as they were, could give the abolitionist movement little organized assistance, the long campaign to convince the laborer of the Slave Power threat brought individual support to the antislavery cause, and more material fruit when, in the form of the Republican party, it entered its political phase.

The abolitionist contention, that there existed a Slave Power conspiracy which threatened the continuation of liberty, was an important factor in enlisting support among certain northern elements for the antislavery movement. In some ways, and in some groups, the "great Slave Power plot" overshadowed in importance the religious, humanitarian, moral, and political issues of the controversy. The claim tended to discredit the proslavery argument, reading into it sinister implications; by carrying southern logic to its ultimate conclusion and by identifying the slaveholder with a conspiracy of infinitely dangerous designs, the abolitionists robbed the proslavery position of any possible appeal to the immigrant, the workman, and the lower middle class in the North. Then too, the Slave Power threat helped widen the rift between North and South by making it more difficult than ever to be neutral toward or tolerant of slavery or its extension. Neutrality or tolerance, said the abolitionist, implied lack of interest in or positive hostility to the preservation of the liberal, democratic tradition. The issue simply admitted of no compromise. Identifying their cause with the greater cause of liberty, with republican government, and with the interests of large relatively unorganized special groups such as laborers or immigrants, the abolitionists made theirs the cause of civil and political freedom. The Slave Power threat personified the proslavery argument, made it vivid and concrete, and dramatized the controversy into a contest between good and evil, freedom and oppression, democracy and aristocracy. When war came, it was justified by the abolitionists and others as the last phase of the contest, as the final defense against the assaults of the Slave Power on traditional American rights. The South waged war, it was said, ". . . not against Abolitionism or Republicanism *per se,* but against free institutions and the democratic theory of government," Had it not been for the abolitionists, who awakened the people to the "villainous purposes and character of the Slave Power," we should have had "a nation in which were only two classes, *masters* and *slaves.*"

Was there a Slave Power, and were the abolitionists correct in ascribing to it the evil designs which formed so large and important a part of the abolitionist propaganda? In the sense of the term as used by Wilson, Goodell, Bailey, Garrison, and others—a secret and highly organized group with conscious aims of imposing restrictions upon traditional liberties—the Slave Power conspiracy probably had no real existence. The South was never so completely unified as to warrant evidence of a definite "conspiracy." There was southern disagreement upon such vital issues as Texas annexation, the Mexican War, the Wilmot Proviso, the 1850 Compromise, and the Kansas question. However, it is clear that among southern leaders there was unity of belief that slavery was a good system, probably the best, and that it should be retained and extended; the events of the period from 1830 to 1860 showed that in preserving and extending it the South was willing to infringe upon basic civil and personal rights, free speech, free press, free thought, and constitutional liberty. The Calhoun-Fitzhugh school of thought, that slavery was a "positive good," was more than a defense of slavery; it was a counterattack upon free society, one which commanded excellent support in the South and, the abolitionist believed, significant support in the North. While the "conspiracy" of which the abolitionists warned was no doubt a natural alliance of common political and economic interests, its threat to liberty, North and South, was more than idle. There were too many public utterances of policy (emanating often, it is true, from extremists, but at the same time from southern leaders) for the times to disregard William Goodell's warning that "*the South is thoroughly in earnest*. She is no land of *shams*. There is reality, terrible reality there." The alliance itself was motivated by and founded upon the cardinal principle of slavery—the master principle—and the abolitionists were not so far wrong in believing that its existence seriously jeopardized, for the first time since the founding of the republic, the American tradition.

6

Lincoln's Loyal Opposition: The Problem of the "Copperheads"

Richard O. Curry

After the South seceded in the winter of 1860–1861, the Lincoln administration sought to maintain unity in the loyal states by emphasizing that the sole object of the war was the preservation of the Union. In 1862, when the war was transformed into a crusade to destroy slavery, unity was shattered beyond repair. Conservative northern Democrats bitterly attacked such Republican policies as the confiscation acts, the Emancipation Proclamation, and the enrollment of black soldiers in the Union Army. Republicans countered Democratic criticism by equating opposition to the war policies of the Lincoln administration with treason, a position accepted by most historians until the 1950s. In the analysis of Civil War historiography which follows, Richard O. Curry challenges the validity of the "Copperhead" stereotype, evaluates the interpretations of revisionist historians, and calls for new approaches in future research.

From Richard O. Curry, "The Union as It Was: A Critique of Recent Interpretations of the 'Copperheads,'" Civil War History, *XIII (March 1967), 25–39. Reprinted with most of the footnotes omitted by permission of the publishers.*

Americans like to think of themselves as rational, egalitarian, and God-fearing people whose generosity exceeds only their passion for individual liberty and freedom of conscience. Much of American history justifies this point of view. But a recurrent theme in our society, especially during periods of national crisis, is the sacrifice of democratic ideals to a devil theory of politics and history—whether in the form of Bavarian Illuminati, the "Great Beast" of Rome, the Anarchists, Radicals of the early 1920s, or communism.

Contemporary historians, as a rule, deal with the politics of hysteria in a detached and objective manner. One major exception has been the treatment accorded by many writers to those conservative opponents of the Lincoln administration commonly called "Copperheads," "Butternuts," or "Peace Democrats."

"Copperhead" was a loosely defined epithet coined by Republicans to characterize northern Democrats who criticized Lincoln's war policies. Copperheads condemned confiscation acts, arbitrary arrests, suspension of the writ of habeas corpus, the Emancipation Proclamation, the passage of federal conscription laws, and violations of freedom of the press. They wanted no part of what they termed "abolitionist fanaticism," and called for the restoration of "The Union As It Was" before the war began. In their view, the Radicals were subverting the Constitution, destroying civil liberties, and undermining the established social order by propagating poisonous theories of racial equality.

To Radicals, such a position was not only unenlightened and reactionary, but disloyal. Conservative rhetoric was little more than a diversionary tactic by which Copperheads tried to conceal treasonable motives. Failing in their attempt to seize political power in the North by peaceable means, so the story goes, traitors and rebel sympathizers turned to organizing secret societies—Knights of the Golden Circle, Sons of Liberty, Corps de Belgique, containing thousands of members, perhaps as many as 500,000—which discouraged enlistments aided desertion, circulated disloyal literature, recruited for the enemy, and eventually plotted revolution in the North itself.

Under the pressure of war, charges and countercharges leveled by Republican and Democratic partisans against each other are neither surprising nor unprecedented. Radicals and Copperheads occupied polar positions on slavery and the nature of the Union. War hysteria and the tendency of Republicans to equate opposition to the war policies of the Lincoln administration with treason produced an explosive, and at times, irrational political situation. Conservative northern Democrats, most of whom were not willing to acquiesce in Confederate independence as the *sine qua non* of peace, were on the defensive throughout most of the war, and "Waving the Bloody Shirt" remained a favorite Republican campaign device well into the 1880s.

What is surprising is the fact that a number of modern historians accept as valid many of the charges leveled by Radical Republicans against their conservative antagonists. . . . Gray's study *The Hidden Civil War* (1942) remains, however, the most extensive modern restatement of the traditional or "Radical" interpretation of Copperheadism, and is *the* book on which nearly all subsequent traditionalists draw heavily in their variations on themes of obstructionism, subversion, defeatism, and treason.

Copperheads began their obstructionist policies, Gray argues, even before the outbreak of war. Many Democratic "opponents of the war" favored "peaceable division" rather than the use of force to suppress rebellion. In fact, many "Peace Democrats" talked seriously of organizing a separate Northwest Confederacy, either allied with or having "very friendly connections" with the South. While making "full allowance for the individual nature of such statements," Gray concludes, "there remained a residue of true intent, ominous in import."

Gray admits that once Lincoln called for volunteers, Democrats as well as Republicans responded enthusiastically to the war effort; but he dismisses this apparent contradiction by arguing that many Democrats "had never been altogether sincere in their support of the war policy." According to Gray, Democrats, in all probability, had bowed temporarily "before the weight of public feeling and threats of mob action." Or perhaps they succumbed for the moment to the "influence of Douglas."

As the war progressed, Gray continues, Democrats defined their military and political objectives in Unionist terms; ". . . winning the war, stamping out fraud and graft in the purchase of military supplies, the checking of arbitrary arrests, and the legal punishment of the leaders of the rebellion, as contrasted with the Republican purpose of a sweeping and indiscriminate confiscation of the property of a whole section." But such protestations of loyalty undoubtedly were mere subterfuge. For example, the fact that the Illinois legislature voted "men and money" for the war in 1862 proved only that the Copperhead majority "lacked the nerve" not to do so.

After Clement L. Vallandigham's arrest, exile to the Confederacy, and unsuccessful bid for the governorship of Ohio in 1863, many Peace Democrats at last became convinced that "they must resort to revolution if they were to succeed in realizing their aims." Draft evaders, deserters, and "other desperate men constituted a nucleus for revolt." Thus it was, according to Gray, that in 1864, a secret semimilitary society, the Sons of Liberty, in combination with Confederate agents, conceived a fantastic plot, the "Great Northwest Conspiracy." Liberated Confederate prisoners, along with thousands of members of the Sons of Liberty, were scheduled to rise in armed rebellion, seize the governments of Ohio, Indiana, Illinois, and Missouri, and establish, if possible, a separate Northwest Confederacy. If this failed, an armed revolt would at least "undermine morale" and force the withdrawal of "troops from the South to crush it."

Somehow, the uprising failed to materialize. Gray is at a loss to explain why . . . except in terms of a lack of organization and leadership, and a loss of nerve by "revolutionary" leaders.

Evidence documenting the existence of such a conspiracy is limited, Gray writes, coming largely from accounts of two Canadian-based Confederate agents, Thomas H. Hines and John B. Castleman, "virtually the only sources of any value on the matter." But, "these men wrote of their experiences under conditions and at a time [1886–1887 and 1917] when they had no cause to distort what had occurred."

Far-reaching conclusions based on Confederate memoirs, however, are open to serious question. Castleman, in his book *Active Service* (1917), claims to have written both accounts,[1] and a careful examination of his evidence reveals little besides the fact that Confederate authorities were misled by Republican charges of widespread disaffection among northern Democrats. At Chicago, while the Democratic National Convention of 1864 was in session, Castleman and several other Confederate agents apparently made contact with a few southern sympathizers, reputed to be "commanders" of the Sons of Liberty, who, according to Castleman, "were appalled by the actual demand for overt action. . . ." Even so, there was "little reason to doubt that a large percent of the strangers in Chicago belonged to the semimilitary Order of the Sons of Liberty." The trouble, Castleman concludes, was that "they were distributed amongst a vast multitude and there was no organization." Disillusioned, about a third of the agents went back to the Confederacy, while the remainder returned to Canada. Confederate dreams of fomenting an armed uprising in the North thus came to an inglorious end.

---

[1] Castleman states that he, not Hines, wrote the articles that appeared in the *Southern Bivouac* in 1886–1887. "I wrote these to the joint credit of Hines or myself," says Castleman, "or in his name as I saw fit." *Active Service,* p. 138. See also, *Southern Bivouac: a Monthly Literary and Historical Magazine,* II (1886–1887), 437–455, 500–510, 567–574, and 669–704.

Concrete evidence substantiating other charges of subversion and treason is also lacking. Time and again, Gray and other traditionalists cite statements based on accounts in Republican newspapers of which the following are typical examples. In southern Illinois, the Knights of the Golden Circle "were thought to be" aiding men bound for the Confederacy. "It was asserted" that the KGC was burning homes of Union men. "Officials feared" that "dangerous, subversive forces were at work." Vallandigham was "understood to threaten war in the North." The "rumor circulated that. . . ." And so on. Such evidence clearly attests to bitter partisanship and war hysteria in the North; but that it constitutes proof of treason or treasonable intent may reasonably be doubted.

Other traditional interpretations of Copperheadism, in the Middle West and elsewhere—those of Richard C. Arena, John Niven, Samuel A. Pleasants, Leonard Kenworthy, and John Talmadge—are so similar to Gray's that detailed analysis would be repetitious. It is sufficient to say, for present purposes, that Niven and Talmadge view Connecticut conservatives as members of the "disloyal opposition"; Kenworthy characterizes Congressman Daniel Voorhees of Indiana as a "rebel sympathizer . . . tinged with Copperheadism"; Pleasants pictures Fernando Wood of New York as a corrupt politician who came "dangerously close to treason"; and Arena concludes that Copperheads in Iowa had two major objectives—"embarrasing . . . the Northern pro-Union government" and helping "the Confederacy . . . achieve its aims." Arena also argues that a number of "inactive people" harbored "treasonable thoughts." How such a conclusion about apparently anonymous and inarticulate individuals can be substantiated is not at all clear.

By no means, however, does the traditional point of view command universal support. Kenneth M. Stampp's *Indiana in the Civil War* (1949), was the first major study to challenge the validity of the Copperhead stereotype. In recent years, moreover, a number of revisionist books and articles have reached print, and it is now possible to place the aims and objectives of conservative northern Democrats in a more rational and meaningful perspective. In addition to Stampp, Frank L. Klement, Robert Rutland, David Lindsey, Justin E. Walsh, John D. Barnhart, and A. B. Beitzinger all analyze midwestern Democratic opposition to Lincoln's war policies in Unionist, if not entirely sympathetic terms. The same holds true for Charles L. Wagandt's study of emancipation in Maryland, Richard O. Curry's analysis of statehood politics in West Virginia, Nicholas B. Wainwright's treatment of Philadelphia conservatism, and Maurice Tandler's interpretation of politics in Civil War New Jersey.

Some of these writers raise as many questions as they answer; but before differentiating between revisionist viewpoints, it is necessary, first of all, to discuss common characteristics which set these historians apart from traditionalists.

First, they reject the idea of conspiracy, treason, or treasonable intent on the part of significant numbers of northern Democrats. Most revisionists also agree that Democrats were often as guilty as Republicans of employing partisan tactics to achieve their goals. Democratic editors and politicians tried to win votes by appealing to Negrophobia; and they attempted, during wartime, to rekindle old fears of class or sectional domination on such issues as the tariff, internal improvements, and banking legislation. Moreover, when Democrats were in control of midwestern legislatures, especially Indiana and Illinois, they tried to gerrymander opponents out of office; they interfered with the executive prerogatives of Republican governors; and even though they voted men and money for the war effort, they often appeared as much interested in gaining or retaining the spoils of political office as they were in winning the war itself.

But unenlightened partisanship is one thing; treason or "peace-at-any-price" something else again. Stampp's contention that "the triumph of Hoosier Democracy in 1862" represents "a repudiation of Republicanism," and not "a repudiation of the war for the Union" accurately reflects the views of other revisionists as regards Democratic victories at the polls in Indiana and elsewhere.

As Frank Klement observes, there was, in a sense, "a war within the war." The reaction of Republican governors like Yates of Illinois and Morton of Indiana; of Union generals like Frémont, Rosecrans, Burnside, and Milroy; and of newspapers like the Chicago *Tribune,* the Wheeling *Daily Intelligencer,* the Indianapolis *Daily Journal,* and the New York *Herald-Tribune* to Democratic opposition was even more partisan, vindictive, and extreme than that of the Democracy. What Stampp has called the "everlasting cry of treason" had meaning only in terms of Republican political strategy and war hysteria.

It was a highly successful strategy in most states. John D. Barnhart characterizes the Democratic party in Indiana as one of the "near casualties" of the war, while Robert Rutland writes that the "Copperhead label almost turned Iowa into a one-party state, and with few exceptions, wrecked the political future of the chief Iowa Democrats." New Jersey was the only northern state to retain both a Democratic governor and an annually elected Democratic legislature throughout the war. Even here, Republicans finally succeeded in "redeeming" the state in 1865.

If "rank partisanship" was one of the more obvious manifestations of Civil War party struggles, one must also recognize that partisanship, more often than not, is an expression of social, economic, or ideological differences, or a combination thereof, rather than a cause in itself. In the case of the Copperheads, charges of treason or of being proslavery serves only to obscure the real meaning to be derived by placing their major political and ideological tenets in historical perspective.

If the Republican party represented the wave of the future—that is, the triumph of nationalism, industrial capitalism, and the destruction of slavery—the inevitability of profound changes in the prevailing social and economic structure was neither obvious nor acceptable to all groups and individuals dedicated to the idea of Union in Civil War America. Considering the fact that a strict constructionist ideology has never been the private preserve of Southerners at any time in the American political experience, it is surprising that so many modern historians fail to recognize that both Radical Republicans and conservative northern Democrats could, during wartime, legitimately claim unwavering allegiance to the concept of Union, while disagreeing violently over the nature of that Union.

Only in terms of resistance to social change, of which partisanship was an essential part, and blind adherence to a vision of the past and a concept of Union that no longer existed can conservative Democratic opposition to Republican policies be understood. John J. Davis, a leading West Virginia conservative, expressed the Copperhead viewpoint well when he wrote to his fiancée:

> I look upon secession and abolition as twin brothers—I am no extremist—I condemn, abhor and detest the abolitionists and all their unconstitutional schemes. . . . I do not want the South subjugated, but I do want those citizens in rebellion subjected—I mean subjected to the laws and made obedient to them. The doctrine of "States' rights" as expounded by Yancey and Jeff Davis is a heresy, fatal to the existence of any government constructed upon such a theory—On the other hand the idea of "Centralization," or conferring upon the Federal Government unlimited power over the states is a heresy I do not countenance—Both dogmas are contrary to the spirit and letter of the Constitution. The present Congress in session at Washington is as much in rebellion against the government as far as words and legislation can constitute rebellion, as are the armed legions of Jeff Davis.

Yet Davis, and thousands of Democrats like him, who dedicated themselves to the task of reconstructing the old Federal Union, expounded a futile idea no longer acceptable either to Confederates, or the vast majority of Republicans. The war itself transformed rigid adherence to strict constructionist ideas into anathema and anachronism—a vision of the past lost beyond recall.

The bankruptcy of conservative thinking, considering the determination of Confederate states to maintain their independence, was nowhere better illustrated than by the position taken by Peace Democrats, a label attached to those Copperheads unrealistic enough to believe the Union could be restored if only North and South could be persuaded to come together at the conference table. In retrospect, such a position may seem foolish, and it was easily exploited by Republicans; but it did not indicate a willingness on the part of most Democrats to abandon the idea of Union. The controversial "peace plank" in the Democratic platform of 1864 did not, as charged by the Radicals, call for an immediate cessation of hostilities. Rather, it demanded that "immediate efforts be made" in this direction, in an attempt to restore peace "on the basis of the Federal Union of States" at "the earliest practicable moment." How such negotiations (already attempted by Horace Greeley, with Lincoln's consent) could resolve anything was never explained.

On the other hand, even if Republican leadership possessed the necessary vision to destroy slavery and preserve the Union, reconstruction was destined to become an uncompleted social revolution. And while it is true that Democrats, not Republicans, attempted to make political capital by exploiting Negrophobia during the war, unenlightened racial attitudes . . . were not monopolized by the Democratic party. Most Republicans did not fully comprehend either the forces they unleashed or opposed.

Thus far, this paper has challenged the accuracy of the Copperhead stereotype in three ways: by questioning the validity of evidence used by traditionalists to substantiate charges of treason or treasonable intent; by arguing that conspiratorial rhetoric had meaning only in terms of partisan politics; and by attempting to place Copperhead ideology within the framework of the history of conservative nationalism (or federalism) where it properly belongs.

Another angle of vision supporting the revisionist point of view is provided by careful examination of generalizations made by historians who locate major areas of disaffection in the less than fertile southern counties of Indiana, Illinois, Iowa, and Ohio, counties inhabited primarily by people of southern origin, or their descendents.[2]

---

[2] The revisionist historian Frank Klement accepts this view in part. He attributes the rise of Copperheadism, among many other factors, to the southern origins of large numbers of midwesterners.

In Iowa, however, as Robert Rutland observes, there "was no 'Copperhead' country" as such. Conservative strongholds reached from Sioux City in the north to Keokuk in the southeast, and followed "no geographic pattern whatever." Moreover, twelve of twenty counties which voted Democratic either in the elections of 1861, 1863, or 1864, were "located in the dark-colored silt loam region." In addition, the number of "newspapers, libraries, schools, and colleges in Iowa Democratic areas suggests that the literacy rate was comparable to that of other Midwestern communities. . . ." "Any attempt to fit the Iowa Copperhead into a die-stamped pattern is futile," Rutland concludes, as "statistics only show that the hard core of the Copperhead movement was located exactly where one would expect it, in the areas voting Democratic in prewar Iowa." Eugene H. Roseboom reaches similar conclusions for Ohio, pointing out that "the Peace Democrats of Ohio were the old-line, hard-shell Democrats, strongest in the areas, whether in north or south, that were rock-ribbed Democratic. Southern ancestry and economic ties with the South had little to do with their stand." Kenneth Stampp goes one step further by arguing that Hoosiers living in the southern part of the state, because of their dependence upon the river trade, had more to fear economically from a successful rebellion than people in any other section.

The implications of investigations like these far exceed the function of demolishing an earlier stereotype. They indicate the need, indeed, the necessity, for additional grass-roots research into the nature of Democratic party structure in northern and border states.

If the political objectives and major ideological tenets of the loyal opposition are clear, the forces that produced Copperheadism have not been precisely analyzed. No historian, including the present writer, has yet attempted an intensive quantitative analysis for any state, in an attempt to correlate ethnic, religious, social, and economic factors with Copperheadism. The idea that soil fertility or southern origins were major factors in determining Copperhead affinities are only two examples of generalizations that do not seem to withstand the challenge of critical revisionism. If, as Rutland observes, low soil fertility seems to be a major characteristic of eight Iowa Copperhead counties but not of twelve others, one may legitimately question whether soil fertility was at all important in shaping political loyalties. Further research might or might not uphold the validity of such a generalization for some areas; but if it did, one could analyze with greater certainty why this was so for some counties and not for others.

The use of quantitative data is not a panacea, however; historians have yet to discover any precise way of measuring the influence of an idea on the course of human events. In contrast to Gray, Klement, Barnhart, and Stampp, who place heavy emphasis on economic forces —especially midwestern opposition to tariff, banking, and railroad legislation—in accounting for the appeal of Copperheadism, Eugene Roseboom argues that one may "logically reverse the picture" of an Ohio Copperhead as an agrarian liberal, a forerunner of "later nineteenth-century agrarian reform movements" (a view supported by Klement), and

> describe him and his Ohio following as archconservative individualists, looking backward to a happier agrarian, state rights past, using the timeworn appeals of the Democrats of Jackson's day against banks, tariffs, and capitalists, and offering no solution for the nation's problems but "the Constitution as it is, the Union as it was, and the Negroes where they are."

Partial support for this point of view has appeared in Ronald P. Formisano's paper, "Copperheads, Grangers, and the Idea of Agrarian Radicalism," which challenges Klement's conclusion that "midwestern Copperheadism linked Jacksonian Democracy and Grangerism." A "substantial part of Klement's case," Formisano writes, "rests on his interpretation of the activities of the Illinois Constitutional Convention of 1862," where, according to Klement, "a Democratic majority ran the convention." The state's Copperheads, primarily "farmers from southern Illinois," dominated that majority, and used "the Convention for an attack on railroads." Klement's attempt to link Copperheadism to Grangerism thus depends largely on the argument that "Copperhead farmers" dominated the Illinois convention of 1862, and the assumption that "Granger farmers of the 1870s were responsible for railroad control."

Both contentions, according to Formisano, are erroneous. An attempt to apply the "agrarian radical" thesis to either movement overlooks, first of all, the findings of scholars like Chester M. Destler, Frederick Merk, Mildred Throne, George H. Miller, Lee Benson, and Harold D. Woodman, whose works show that mercantile and commercial, not farm groups, provided the major impetus behind Granger agitation in the 1870s. Secondly, Formisano's analysis of the significance of the railroad issue in the Illinois Constitutional Convention of 1862 clashes sharply with Klement's.

Delegate Daniel Reilly was the only Democrat from southern Illinois, the abode of Klement's "Copperhead and Granger farmers," to offer resolutions dealing with general railroad regulation, including rate control, the issue Formisano describes as the "great shibboleth" of the later Granger agitators. Three other Democrats offered resolutions similar to Reilly's, but two of the three represented counties in northern Illinois; the third came from the west-central part of the state. Two other delegates, both Republicans, also called for some form of regulation but were not concerned with rate control. Even more important, none of these resolutions was given serious consideration by the convention, and were easily shunted aside by the Democratic leadership, which included four prominent Copperheads from the southern part of the state. The only viable issue involving railroads at the convention, Formisano concludes, concerned the failure of the Illinois Central to meet the terms of its original charter by paying 7 percent of its annual profits to the state. Politics, an attempt to embarrass the administration of Republican Governor Yates, "not nascent Grangerism, lay behind the Illinois Central issue."

Questioning the validity of the "agrarian radical" thesis as applied to Copperheadism is one thing, however; arguing that Copperheads should be viewed as archconservative individualists having strong intellectual commitments to a vision of the past is quite another. Yet, the history of the Copperhead movement in West Virginia permits more careful differentiation here than elsewhere between economic, social, and ideological determinants. Generalizations cannot be made for the entire movement on the basis of findings in one state; but showing beyond reasonable doubt that ideological and social forces were major causative agents in producing Copperheadism in one state raises the question as to whether or not economic determinism and political partisanship *per se* can carry the weight assigned to them in the Middle West.

In West Virginia, three factors—political expediency, economic self-interest, and a desire to remain in the Union—were the major forces behind demands for the separation of this state from the Old Dominion. Sectional conflict had been one of the hallmarks of Virginia politics for more than fifty years. Future Copperheads like United States Senator John S. Carlile, who organized the resistance movement against secession in northwestern Virginia; ex-Congressman Sherrard Clemens; and John J. Davis, father of John W. Davis, led the "new state" movement in its early stages. Without Carlile's leadership and the active support of other Copperheads like Clemens, Davis, and state legislators John C. Vance and Andrew Wilson, it is doubtful that the adjourned session of the Second Wheeling Convention (August 6–20, 1861) could have passed a dismemberment ordinance, the first in a long series of acts leading to the creation of the state of West Virginia.

But in 1862, these men, and others like them, turned against separate statehood rather than accept what they termed "Congressional dictation" when the Willey Amendment, a gradual emancipation proviso, was attached to the West Virginia Bill by the Republican majority in Congress. Moreover, conservatives in West Virginia, as elsewhere, became frightened when the war for Union was transformed into a crusade to destroy slavery and subjugate the South. They conjured up visions of presidential or military dictatorship, unlimited Negro migration to the North, and disunion—all caused by the fanaticism of northern radicals. The slavery question, with its attendant ramifications, thus clouded all other issues, and Carlile and his associates in West Virginia set themselves down as critics and opponents of change. Yet, if any one idea had dominated the thinking of northwestern Virginia Unionists in 1861, including Carlile and most other conservatives, it was their recognition that after fifty years of sectional controversy the opportunity had presented itself to gain what they had always been denied by slaveholding agrarians: the right to legislate for themselves; the opportunity to develop their natural resources; and to expand and protect their infant industries in the Ohio, Kanawha, and Cheat River Valleys. The future of West Virginia, they reasoned, lay with the Northeast. For Carlile and his associates, the easiest path to follow, one dictated by economic self-interest and political expediency, was the one they did not take—the Willey Amendment.

In the process, Carlile, who previously had been the favorite of western Virginia Unionists, succeeded only in destroying his political career and consigning himself to oblivion. Yet he did so willingly, staunchly refusing to compromise in the face of heavy odds against him. Only in terms of exaggerated fears of social change—an intellectual commitment to a vision of a strict constructionist, Anglo-Saxon past—can Copperheadism in West Virginia be understood.

It may be argued that a socioideological interpretation applicable to Copperhead leadership in West Virginia is relevant only for an analysis of the motivating impulses of other Copperhead leaders, and not for the rank and file. The fact remains, however, that Carlile, Clemens, and others organized the movement, articulated its principles, and provided the driving force behind it. The fact remains also that the political and economic milieu that existed in West Virginia during the war provided arguments against, not favorable to, their cause. Moreover, conservative Unionism in border, middle Atlantic, and northeastern states, far stronger than most historians of midwestern Copperheadism have recognized, cannot be explained satisfactorily in terms of economic sectionalism; agrarian radicalism; southern birth;

soil fertility; illiteracy; or party loyalty. The assumption that Copperheadism flourished primarily in the Middle West is not a sound one. The sound and fury that characterized partisan politics in this area is not a measure of predominance. In New Jersey, Democratic control, not the absence of Copperhead attitudes, accounts for the comparative calm of wartime politics in this state. And recent studies show that conservative Unionism was a strong force in Pennsylvania, New York, and Connecticut, as well as in the border states of West Virginia, Maryland, Delaware, and Kentucky.

One may conclude, therefore, that if revisionist historians have demolished the traditional stereotype of the Copperhead as traitor, and if they have placed the political objectives and major ideological tenets of the movement in historical perspective, they have been less successful in analyzing the motivating impulses behind it. What then needs to be done? First, as mentioned earlier, basic research, using quantitative data, should permit historians to make more precise generalizations as to the nature of political party structure; secondly, comparative studies need to be made of conservative Unionism in midwestern, border, and northeastern states; and thirdly, an increased awareness that the sources of ideological commitment remain complex, obscure, and elusive should prevent the type of interpretive oversimplification that has characterized much of the previous writing on the subject. Calling attention, however, to the uncertain joys of interdisciplinary research, as contemporary historians are inclined to do when approaching the outer limits of their own training, research, or critical capacities, is not to belie its promise, or its importance. This comment applies not only to Copperheadism but to the entire range of American political experience involving exaggerated fears of foreign and domestic devils. Certainly, the "politics of hysteria" is one of the most challenging and potentially distinguished subjects to which American historians can address themselves; and if they can resolve some of the major sociopsychological problems connected with the politics of conspiracy, they will, at one and the same time, exorcise some of the "devils" involved in historical methodology itself.

7

The Folklore of Populism

Richard Hofstadter

During the 1880s and 1890s American farmers faced a severe economic crisis brought on by competition from foreign producers, overproduction, and a tight money supply. The Populist party, organized by farm leaders in 1892, advocated the free and unlimited coinage of silver and increased government intervention into the economy as a solution to their problems. In the selection that follows Richard Hofstadter argues that the Populists blamed their predicament on an international banking conspiracy and that their political rhetoric contained a strong dose of anti-Semitism.

There was something about the Populist imagination that loved the secret plot and the conspiratorial meeting. There was in fact a widespread Populist idea that all American history since the Civil War could be understood as a sustained conspiracy of the international money power.

The pervasiveness of this way of looking at things may be attributed to the common feeling that farmers and workers were not

---

simply oppressed but oppressed deliberately, consciously, continuously, and with wanton malice by "the interests." It would of course be misleading to imply that the Populists stand alone in thinking of the events of their time as the results of a conspiracy. This kind of thinking frequently occurs when political and social antagonisms are sharp. Certain audiences are especially susceptible to it—particularly, I believe, those who have attained only a low level of education, whose access to information is poor, and who are so completely shut out from access to the centers of power that they feel themselves completely deprived of self-defense and subjected to unlimited manipulation by those who wield power. There are, moreover, certain types of popular movements of dissent that offer special opportunities to agitators with paranoid tendencies, who are able to make a vocational asset out of their psychic disturbances. Such persons have an opportunity to impose their own style of thought upon the movements they lead. It would of course be misleading to imply that there are no such things as conspiracies in history. Anything that partakes of political strategy may need, for a time at least, an element of secrecy, and is thus vulnerable to being dubbed conspiratorial. Corruption itself has the character of conspiracy. In this sense the Crédit Mobilier was a conspiracy, as was the Teapot Dome affair. If we tend to be too condescending to the Populists at this point, it may be necessary to remind ourselves that they had seen so much bribery and corruption, particularly on the part of the railroads, that they had before them a convincing model of the management of affairs through conspiratorial behavior. Indeed, what makes conspiracy theories so widely acceptable is that they usually contain a germ of truth. But there is a great difference between locating conspiracies *in* history and saying that history *is,* in effect, a conspiracy, between singling out those conspiratorial acts that do on occasion occur and weaving a vast fabric of social explanation out of nothing but skeins of evil plots.

When conspiracies do not exist it is necessary for those who think in this fashion to invent them. Among the most celebrated instances in modern history are the forgery of the Protocols of the Elders of Zion and the grandiose fabrication under Stalin's regime of the Trotzkyite-Bukharinite-Zinovievite center. These inventions were cynical. In the history of American political controversy there is a tradition of conspiratorial accusations which seem to have been sincerely believed. Jefferson appears really to have believed, at one time, that the Federalists were conspiring to reestablish monarchy. Some Federalists believed that the Jeffersonians were conspiring to subvert Christianity. The movement to annex Texas and the war with Mexico were alleged by many northerners to be a slaveholders' conspiracy. The early Republican leaders, including Lincoln, charged that there was a conspiracy on the part of Stephen A. Douglas to make slavery a nationwide institution. Such pre-Civil War parties as the Know-Nothing and anti-Masonic movements were based almost entirely upon conspiratorial ideology. The Nye Committee, years ago, tried to prove that our entry into the first World War was the work of a conspiracy of bankers and munitions-makers. And now not only our entry into the second World War, but the entire history of the past twenty years or so is being given the color of conspiracy by the cranks and political fakirs of our own age.[1]

Nevertheless, when these qualifications have been taken into account, it remains true that Populist thought showed an unusually strong tendency to account for relatively impersonal events in highly personal terms. An overwhelming sense of grievance does not find satisfactory expression in impersonal explanations, except among those with a well-developed tradition of intellectualism. It is the city, after all, that is the home of intellectual complexity. The farmer lived in isolation from the great world in which his fate was actually de-

---

[1] One by-product of this conspiratorial mania is the myth that the recognition of Russia in 1933 was the result of a plot by the New Dealers. Paul Boller, Jr., in a highly amusing article, "The 'Great Conspiracy' of 1933: a Study in Short Memories," *Southwest Review*, Vol. XXXIX (Spring 1954), pp. 97–112, shows that some of the same persons who have indulged in the conspiracy cry were advocates of recognition before 1933.

In reading the excellent study by Leo Lowenthal and Norbert Guterman, *Prophets of Deceit* (New York, 1949), a study of recent authoritarian agitators, I am impressed by certain similarities in the style of thought displayed by their subjects and that of a certain type of Populist writer represented by Mrs. Emery, "Coin" Harvey, Donnelly, and Mrs. Lease. There seem to be certain persistent themes in popular agitation of this sort that transcend particular historical eras. Among the themes delineated by Lowenthal and Guterman that one finds in Populist literature as well as among their agitators are the following: the conception of history as conspiracy; an obsessive concern with the fabulous enjoyments deemed to be the lot of the plutocrats; cynicism about the two-party system; the notion that the world is moving toward an immense apocalypse; the exclusive attention to the greed and other personal vices of bankers and other selected plutocrats, as opposed to a structural analysis of the social system; anti-Semitism and xenophobia; the appeal to the native simplicity and virtue of the folk. There are, of course, other themes singled out by Lowenthal and Guterman that seem more peculiar to the conditions of our own time and lack cognates in the literature of Populism.

cided. He was accused of being unusually suspicious, and certainly his situation, trying as it was, made thinking in impersonal terms difficult. Perhaps the rural middle-class leaders of Populism (this was a movement of farmers, but it was not led by farmers) had more to do than the farmer himself with the cast of Populist thinking. At any rate, Populist thought often carries one into a world in which the simple virtues and unmitigated villainies of a rural melodrama have been projected on a national and even an international scale. In Populist thought the farmer is not a speculating businessman, victimized by the risk economy of which he is a part, but rather a wounded yeoman, preyed upon by those who are alien to the life of folkish virtue. A villain was needed, marked with the unmistakable stigmata of the villains of melodrama, and the more remote he was from the familiar scene, the more plausibly his villainies could be exaggerated.

It was not enough to say that a conspiracy of the money power against the common people was going on. It had been going on ever since the Civil War. It was not enough to say that it stemmed from Wall Street. It was international: it stemmed from Lombard Street. In his preamble to the People's Party platform of 1892, a succinct, official expression of Populist views, Ignatius Donnelly asserted: "A vast conspiracy against mankind has been organized on two continents, and it is rapidly taking possession of the world. If not met and overthrown at once it forebodes terrible social convulsions, the destruction of civilization, or the establishment of an absolute despotism." A manifesto of 1895, signed by fifteen outstanding leaders of the People's Party, declared:

> As early as 1865–1866 a conspiracy was entered into between the gold gamblers of Europe and America. . . . For nearly thirty years these conspirators have kept the people quarreling over less important matters while they have pursued with unrelenting zeal their one central purpose. . . . Every device of treachery, every resource of statecraft, and every artifice known to the secret cabals of the international gold ring are being made use of to deal a blow to the prosperity of the people and the financial and commerical independence of the country.

The financial argument behind the conspiracy theory was simple enough. Those who owned bonds wanted to be paid not in a common currency but in gold, which was at a premium; those who lived by lending money wanted as high a premium as possible to be put on their commodity by increasing its scarcity. The panics, depressions, and bankruptcies caused by their policies only added to their wealth;

such catastrophes offered opportunities to engross the wealth of others through business consolidations and foreclosures. Hence the interests actually relished and encouraged hard times. The Greenbackers had long since popularized this argument, insisting that an adequate legal-tender currency would break the monopoly of the "Shylocks." Their demand for $50 of circulating medium per capita, still in the air when the People's Party arose, was rapidly replaced by the less "radical" demand for free coinage of silver. But what both the Greenbackers and free-silverites held in common was the idea that the contraction of currency was a deliberate squeeze, the result of a long-range plot of the "Anglo-American Gold Trust." Wherever one turns in the Populist literature of the nineties one can find this conspiracy theory expressed. It is in the Populist newspapers, the proceedings of the silver conventions, the immense pamphlet literature broadcast by the American Bimetallic League, the Congressional debates over money; it is elaborated in such popular books as Mrs. S. E. V. Emery's *Seven Financial Conspiracies Which Have Enslaved the American People* or Gordon Clark's *Shylock: as Banker, Bondholder, Corruptionist, Conspirator.*

Mrs. Emery's book, first published in 1887, and dedicated to "the enslaved people of a dying republic," achieved great circulation, especially among the Kansas Populists. According to Mrs. Emery, the United States had been an economic Garden of Eden in the period before the Civil War. The fall of man had dated from the war itself, when "the money kings of Wall Street" determined that they could take advantage of the wartime necessities of their fellow men by manipulating the currency. "Controlling it, they could inflate or depress the business of the country at pleasure, they could send the warm life current through the channels of trade, dispensing peace, happiness, and prosperity, or they could check its flow, and completely paralyze the industries of the country." With this great power for good in their hands, the Wall Street men preferred to do evil. Lincoln's war policy of issuing greenbacks presented them with the dire threat of an adequate supply of currency. So the Shylocks gathered in convention and "perfected" a conspiracy to create a demand for their gold. The remainder of the book was a recital of a series of seven measures passed between 1862 and 1875 which were alleged to be a part of this continuing conspiracy, the total effect of which was to contract the currency of the country further and further until finally it squeezed the industry of the country like a hoop of steel.

Mrs. Emery's rhetoric left no doubt of the sustained purposefulness of this scheme—described as "villainous robbery," and as having been "secured through the most soulless strategy." She was most explicit about the so-called crime of 1873, the demonetization of silver, giving a fairly full statement of the standard greenback-silverite myth concerning that event. As they had it, an agent of the Bank of England, Ernest Seyd by name, had come to the United States in 1872 with $500,000 with which he had bought enough support in Congress to secure the passage of the demonetization measure. This measure was supposed to have greatly increased the value of American four percent bonds held by British capitalists by making it necessary to pay them in gold only. To it Mrs. Emery attributed the panic of 1873, its bankruptcies, and its train of human disasters: "Murder, insanity, suicide, divorce, drunkenness, and all forms of immorality and crime have increased from that day to this in the most appalling ratio."

"Coin" Harvey, the author of the most popular single document of the whole currency controversy, *Coin's Financial School,* also published a novel, *A Tale of Two Nations,* in which the conspiracy theory of history was incorporated into a melodramatic tale. In this story the powerful English banker Baron Rothe plans to bring about the demonetization of silver in the United States, in part for his own aggrandizement but also to prevent the power of the United States from outstripping that of England. He persuades an American Senator (probably John Sherman, the *bête noire* of the silverites) to cooperate in using British gold in a campaign against silver. To be sure that the work is successful, he also sends to the United States a relative and ally, one Rogasner, who stalks through the story like the villains in the plays of Dion Boucicault, muttering to himself such remarks as "I am here to destroy the United States—Cornwallis could not have done more. For the wrongs and insults, for the glory of my own country, I will bury the knife deep into the heart of this nation." Against the plausibly drawn background of the corruption of the Grant administration, Rogasner proceeds to buy up the American Congress and suborn American professors of economics to testify for gold. He also falls in love with a proud American beauty, but his designs on her are foiled because she loves a handsome young silver Congressman from Nebraska who bears a striking resemblance to William Jennings Bryan!

One feature of the Populist conspiracy theory that has been generally overlooked is its frequent link with a kind of rhetorical anti-Semitism. The slight current of anti-Semitism that existed in the United States before the 1890s had been associated with problems of money and credit.[2] During the closing years of the century it grew noticeably. While the jocose and rather heavy-handed anti-Semitism that can be found in Henry Adams's letters of the 1890s shows that this prejudice existed outside Populist literature, it was chiefly Populist writers who expressed that identification of the Jew with the usurer and the "international gold ring" which was the central theme of the American anti-Semitism of the age. The omnipresent symbol of Shylock can hardly be taken in itself as evidence of anti-Semitism, but the frequent references to the House of Rothschild make it clear that for many silverites the Jew was an organic part of the conspiracy theory of history. Coin Harvey's Baron Rothe was clearly meant to be Rothschild; his Rogasner (Ernest Seyd?) was a dark figure out of the coarsest anti-Semitic tradition. "You are very wise in your way," Rogasner is told at the climax of the tale, "the commercial way, inbred through generations. The politic, scheming, devious way, inbred through generations also." One of the cartoons in the effectively illustrated *Coin's Financial School* showed a map of the world dominated by the tentacles of an octopus at the site of the British Isles, labeled: "Rothschilds." In Populist demonology, anti-Semitism and Anglophobia went hand in hand.

The note of anti-Semitism was often sounded openly in the campaign for silver. A representative of the New Jersey Grange, for instance, did not hesitate to warn the members of the Second National Silver Convention of 1892 to watch out for political candidates who represented "Wall Street, and the Jews of Europe." Mary E. Lease described Grover Cleveland as "the agent of Jewish bankers and British gold." Donnelly represented the leader of the governing council of plutocrats in *Caesar's Column,* one Prince Cabano, as a powerful Jew, born Jacob Isaacs; one of the triumvirate who lead the Brotherhood of Destruction is also an exiled Russian Jew, who flees from the apocalyptic carnage with a hundred million dollars which he intends to use to "revive the ancient splendors of the Jewish race, in the midst

---

[2]Anti-Semitism as a kind of rhetorical flourish seems to have had a long underground history in the United States. During the panic of 1837, when many states defaulted on their obligations, many of which were held by foreigners, we find Governor McNutt of Mississippi defending the practice by baiting Baron Rothschild: "The blood of Judas and Shylock flows in his veins, and he unites the qualities of both his countrymen. . . ." Quoted by George W. Edwards: *The Evolution of Finance Capitalism* (New York, 1938), p. 149. Similarly we find Thaddeus Stevens assailing "the Rothschilds, Goldsmiths, and other large money dealers" during his early appeals for greenbacks.

of the ruins of the world." One of the more elaborate documents of the conspiracy school traced the power of the Rothschilds over America to a transaction between Hugh McCulloch, Secretary of the Treasury under Lincoln and Johnson, and Baron James Rothschild. "The most direful part of this business between Rothschild and the United States Treasury was not the loss of money, even by hundreds of millions. It was the resignation of the country itself INTO THE HANDS OF ENGLAND, as England had long been resigned into the hands of HER JEWS." [3]

Such rhetoric, which became common currency in the movement, later passed beyond Populism into the larger stream of political protest. By the time the campaign of 1896 arrived, an Associated Press reporter noticed as "one of the striking things" about the Populist convention at St. Louis "the extraordinary hatred of the Jewish race. It is not possible to go into any hotel in the city without hearing the most bitter denunciation of the Jews as a class and of the particular Jews who happen to have prospered in the world." This report may have been somewhat overdone, but the identification of the silver cause with anti-Semitism did become close enough for Bryan to have to pause in the midst of his campaign to explain to the Jewish Democrats of Chicago that in denouncing the policies of the Rothschilds he and his silver friends were "not attacking a race; we are attacking greed and avarice which know no race or religion."

It would be easy to misstate the character of Populist anti-Semitism or to exaggerate its intensity. For Populist anti-Semitism was entirely verbal. It was a mode of expression, a rhetorical style, not a tactic or a program. It did not lead to exclusion laws, much less to riots or pogroms. There were, after all, relatively few Jews in the United States in the late 1880s and early 1890s, most of them remote from the areas of Populist strength. It is one thing, however, to say that

[3] There was a somewhat self-conscious and apologetic note in populistic anti-Semitism. Remarking that "the aristocracy of the world is now almost altogether of Hebrew origin," one of Donnelly's characters explains that the terrible persecutions to which the Jews had been subjected for centuries heightened the selective process among them, leaving "only the strong of body, the cunning of brain, the long-headed, the persistent . . . and now the Christian world is paying, in tears and blood, for the sufferings inflicted by their bigoted and ignorant ancestors upon a noble race. When the time came for liberty and fair play the Jew was master in the contest with the Gentile, who hated and feared him." *Cæsar's Column,* p. 37. In another fanciful tale Donnelly made amends to the Jews by restoring Palestine to them and making it very prosperous. *The Golden Bottle* (New York and St. Paul, 1892), pp. 280–281.

this prejudice did not go beyond a certain symbolic usage, quite another to say that a people's choice of symbols is of no significance. Populist anti-Semitism does have its importance—chiefly as a symptom of a certain ominous credulity in the Populist mind. It is not too much to say that the Greenback-Populist tradition activated most of what we have of modern popular anti-Semitism in the United States. [4] From Thaddeus Stevens and Coin Harvey to Father Coughlin, and from Brooks and Henry Adams to Ezra Pound, there has been a curiously persistent linkage between anti-Semitism and money and credit obsessions. A full history of modern anti-Semitism in the United States would reveal, I believe, its substantial Populist lineage, but it may be sufficient to point out here that neither the informal connection between Bryan and the Klan in the twenties nor Thomas E. Watson's conduct in the Leo Frank case were altogether fortuitous. And Henry Ford's notorious anti-Semitism of the 1920s, along with his hatred of "Wall Street," were the foibles of a Michigan farm boy who had been liberally exposed to Populist notions.

The conspiratorial theory and the associated Anglophobic and Judophobic feelings were a part of a larger complex of fear and suspicion of the stranger that haunted, and still tragically haunts, the nativist American mind. This feeling, though hardly confined to Populists and Bryanites, was none the less exhibited by them in a particularly virulent form. Everyone remote and alien was distrusted and hated—even Americans, if they happened to be city people. The old agrarian conception of the city as the home of moral corruption reached a new

---

[4] I distinguish here between popular anti-Semitism, which is linked with political issues, and upper-class anti-Semitism, which is a variety of snobbery. It is characteristic of the indulgence which Populism has received on this count that Carey McWilliams in his *A Mask for Privilege: Anti-Semitism in America* (Boston, 1948) deals with early American anti-Semitism simply as an upper-class phenomenon. In his historical account of the rise of anti-Semitism he does not mention the Greenback-Populist tradition. Daniel Bell: "The Grass Roots of American Jew Hatred," *Jewish Frontier,* Vol. XI (June 1944), pp. 15–20, is one of the few writers who has perceived that there is any relation between latter-day anti-Semites and the earlier Populist tradition. . . . Arnold Rose has pointed out that much of American anti-Semitism is intimately linked to the agrarian myth and to resentment of the ascendancy of the city. The Jew is made a symbol of both capitalism and urbanism, which are themselves too abstract to be satisfactory objects of animosity. *Commentary,* Vol. VI (October 1948), pp. 374–378.

pitch. Chicago was bad; New York, which housed the Wall Street bankers, was farther away and worse; London was still farther away and still worse. This traditional distrust grew stronger as the cities grew larger, and as they were filled with immigrant aliens. As early as 1885 the Kansas preacher Josiah Strong had published *Our Country,* a book widely read in the West, in which the cities were discussed as a great problem of the future, much as though they were some kind of monstrous malignant growths on the body politic. Hamlin Garland recalled that when he first visited Chicago, in the late 1880s, having never seen a town larger than Rockford, Illinois, he naturally assumed that it swarmed with thieves. "If the city is miles across," he wondered, "how am I to get from the railway station to my hotel without being assaulted?" While such extreme fears could be quieted by some contact with the city, others were actually confirmed—especially when the farmers were confronted with city prices. Nativist prejudices were equally aroused by immigration, for which urban manufacturers, with their insatiable demand for labor, were blamed. "We have become the world's melting pot," wrote Thomas E. Watson. "The scum of creation has been dumped on us. Some of our principal cities are more foreign than American. The most dangerous and corrupting hordes of the Old World have invaded us. The vice and crime which they have planted in our midst are sickening and terrifying. What brought these Goths and Vandals to our shores? The manufacturers are mainly to blame. They wanted cheap labor: and they didn't care a curse how much harm to our future might be the consequence of their heartless policy."

Anglo-Saxons, whether Populist or patrician, found it difficult to accept other peoples on terms of equality or trust. Others were objects to be manipulated—benevolently, it was often said, but none the less firmly. Mary E. Lease, that authentic voice of inland Populism who became famous for advising farmers to "raise less corn and more hell," wrote a book in 1895 under the ingratiating title: *The Problem of Civilization Solved,* in which this ethnic condescension was rather ingenuously displayed. According to Mrs. Lease, Europe and America stood on the brink of one or two immense catastrophes—a universal reign of anarchistic terror or the establishment of a world-wide Russian despotism. The only hope of averting catastrophe was, as she put it, "the most stupendous migration of races the world has ever known, and thereby relieve the congested centers of the world's population of half their inhabitants and provide Free Homes for half of mankind." She proposed a vast reshuffling of peoples in which the tropics in both hemispheres be taken over by white planters with Negroes and Orientals as "tillers of the soil." "Through all the vicissitudes of time, the Caucasian has arisen to the moral and intellectual supremacy of the world, until now this favored race is fitted for the *Stewardship of the Earth and Emancipation from Manual Labor.*" This stewardship, far from being an imposition on the lesser breeds without the law, would be an act of mercy; it would take the starved and miserable ryots and coolies of the world and by giving them management and supervision provide them with the means of life, as well as rescue them from paganism. Such a change they would "hail with joy."

The proposal for colonization under government supervision and with governmental subsidies was supplemented by a grand plan for what Mrs. Lease candidly called the partitioning of the world, in which the Germanic and Latin peoples would be united into two racial confederations, and the British and Russian empires checked and neutralized by other powerful states. The role of the United States in this world was to be the head of the federated American republics. Canada should be annexed—so also Cuba, Haiti, Santo Domingo, and Hawaii. The Latin republics would be fertile fields for colonization by the surplus population of the United States—which no longer had a public domain to give its citizens—and the North Americans would import "vast swarms of Asiatics as laborers for the plantations." Mrs. Lease felt that the Latins, like the Asiatics, would certainly benefit from this and that they ought to like it. Moreover, they owed the United States a debt of gratitude: "We stand, and have stood for years, ready to extend our blood and treasure in defense of Latin American against European aggression. Can they not *reciprocate* by giving us the leadership on this continent? If not, we should take it! We should follow the example of European nations and annex all we can and establish protectorates wherever possible in America."

Mrs. Lease's book, the work of a naïve but imaginative mind driven to the pitch of its powers by an extraordinary capacity for suspicion, was hardly as representative or popular as *Coin's Financial School* or *Caesar's Column,* though its author was one of the indigenous products of Populist political culture. Mrs. Lease's peculiar ideas of *Weltpolitik,* her particular views on tropical colonization, were not common currency in Populist thinking. But other assumptions in her book could be found among the Populists with great frequency—the smug assumption of Anglo-Saxon superiority and benevolence, the sense of a need for some new area of expansion, the hatred of

England, the fear of Russia,[5] the anxiety over the urban masses as a potential source of anarchy.

The nationalist fervor of Mrs. Lease's book also represents one side of a curiously ambiguous aspect of Populism. On the surface there was a strong note of antimilitarism and anti-imperialism in the Populist movement and Bryan democracy. Populists were opposed to large standing armies and large naval establishments; most of them supported Bryan's resistance to the acquisition of the Philippines. They looked upon the military as a threat to democracy, upon imperialist acquisitions as gains only to financiers and "monarchists," not to the people. But what they chiefly objected to was institutional militarism rather than war itself, imperialism rather than jingoism. Under a patina of pacifist rhetoric they were profoundly nationalistic and bellicose. What the nativist mind most resolutely opposed was not so much war itself as cooperation with European governments for any ends at all. Those who have been puzzled in our own time by the anti-European attitudes of men like Senator Taft and General MacArthur, and by their alternating espousal of dangerously aggressive and near-pacifistic (or antimilitarist) policies, will find in the Populist mentality a suggestive precedent.

The Populists distinguished between wars for humanity and wars of conquest. The first of these they considered legitimate, but naturally they had difficulty in discriminating between the two, and they were quite ready to be ballyhooed into a righteous war, as the Cuban situation was to show. During the early nineteenth century popular sentiment in the United States, especially within the democratic camp, had been strong for the republican movements in Europe and Latin America. With the coming of the nineties and the great revulsion against the outside world, the emphasis was somewhat changed; where sympathy with oppressed and revolutionary peoples had been the dominant sentiment in the past, the dominant sentiment now seemed rather to be hatred of their governments. That there must always be such an opposition between peoples and governments the Populist mind did not like to question, and even the most democratic governments of Europe were persistently looked upon as though they were nothing but reactionary monarchies. . . .

It is no coincidence, then, that Populism and jingoism grew concurrently in the United States during the 1890s. The rising mood of intolerant nationalism was a nationwide thing, certainly not confined

---

[5] Since this was a commonplace in the nineteenth century, it would be too much to ascribe to Mrs. Lease any special prophetic stature.

to the regions of Populist strength; but among no stratum of the population was it stronger than among the Populists. Moreover it was on jingoist issues that the Populist and Bryanite sections of the country, with the aid of the yellow press and many political leaders, achieved that rapport with the masses of the cities which they never succeeded in getting on economic issues. Even conservative politicians sensed that, whatever other grounds of harmony were lacking between themselves and the populace of the hinterland, grounds for unity could be found in war.

The first, and for the Populists the preferred, enemy would have been England, the center of the gold power. *Coin's Financial School* closed with a better philippic against England: "If it is claimed we must adopt for our money the metal England selects, and can have no independent choice in the matter, let us make the test and find out if it is true. It is not American to give up without trying. If it is true, let us attach England to the United States and blot her name out from among the nations of the earth. A war with England would be the most popular ever waged on the face of the earth . . . the most just war ever waged by man." . . .

As we review these aspects of Populist emotion, an odd parallel obtrudes itself. Where else in American thought during this period do we find this militancy and nationalism, these apocalyptic forebodings and drafts of world-political strategies, this hatred of big businessmen, bankers, and trusts, these fears of immigrants and urban workmen, even this occasional toying with anti-Semitic rhetoric? We find them, curiously enough, most conspicuous among a group of men who are in all obvious respects the antithesis of the Populists. During the late 1880s and the 1890s there emerged in the eastern United States a small imperialist elite representing, in general, the same type that had once been Mugwumps, whose spokesmen were such solid and respectable gentlemen as Henry and Brooks Adams, Theodore Roosevelt, Henry Cabot Lodge, John Hay, and Albert J. Beveridge. While the silverites were raging openly and earnestly against the bankers and the Jews, Brooks and Henry Adams were expressing in their sardonic and morosely cynical private correspondence the same feelings, and acknowledging with bemused irony their kinship at this point with the mob. While Populist congressmen and newspapers called for war with England or Spain, Roosevelt and Lodge did the same, and while Mrs. Lease projected her grandiose schemes of world partition and tropical colonization, men like Roosevelt, Lodge, Beveridge, and Mahan projected more realistic plans for the conquest of markets and the annexation of territory. While Populist readers were pondering over Donnelly's apocalyptic fantasies, Brooks and Henry Adams were also bemoaning the approaching end of their type of civilization, and even the characteristically optimistic T. R. could share at moments in "Brooks Adams' gloomiest anticipations of our gold-ridden, capitalist-bestridden, usurer-mastered future." Not long after Mrs. Lease wrote that "we need a Napoleon in the industrial world who, by agitation and education, will lead the people to a realizing sense of their condition and the remedies," Roosevelt and Brooks Adams talked about the threat of the eight-hour movement and the danger that the country would be "enslaved" by the organizers of the trusts, and played with the idea that Roosevelt might eventually lead "some great outburst of the emotional classes which should at least temporarily crush the Economic Man."

Not only were the gentlemen of this imperialist elite better read and better fed than the Populists, but they despised them. This strange convergence of unlike social elements on similar ideas has its explanation, I believe, in this: both the imperialist elite and the Populists had been bypassed and humiliated by the advance of industrialism, and both were rebelling against the domination of the country by industrial and financial capitalists. The gentlemen wanted the power and status they felt due them, which had been taken away from their class and type by the *arriviste* manufacturers and railroaders and the all-too-potent banking houses. The Populists wanted a restoration of agrarian profits and popular government. Both elements found themselves impotent and deprived in an industrial culture and balked by a common enemy. On innumerable matters they disagreed, but both were strongly nationalistic, and amid the despairs and anxieties of the nineties both became ready for war if that would unseat or even embarrass the moneyed powers, or better still if it would topple the established political structure and open new opportunities for the leaders of disinherited farmers or for ambitious gentlemen. But if there seems to be in this situation any suggestion of a forerunner or analogue of modern authoritarian movements, it should by no means be exaggerated. The age was more innocent and fortunate than ours, and by comparison with the grimmer realities of the twentieth century many of the events of the nineties take on a comic-opera quality. What came in the end was only a small war and a quick victory; when the farmers and the gentlemen finally did coalesce in politics, they produced only the genial reforms of Progressivism; and the man on the white horse turned out to be just a graduate of the Harvard boxing squad, equipped with an immense bag of platitudes, and quite willing to play the democratic game.

8

The Tolerant Populists

Walter T. K. Nugent

Walter T. K. Nugent agrees with Richard Hofstadter that the Populists believed in the reality of an international banking conspiracy. Nugent argues, however, that the vast majority of Populists were not guilty of anti-Semitism or any other form of xenophobia.

The Populists, . . . lacked any consistent antipathy either to foreign countries or to immigrants, with the single exception of labor competition. But when they dealt with the deceptively innocent-looking problems of money and banking and land tenure, problems which lay at the very heart of their program, they laid themselves open to the double charge of Anglophobia and anti-Semitism; and it is on their expressions about these two specific problems that the whole case for Populist nativism must rest.

The money question, to Populist thinking, lay at the root of many evils. They blamed much on a lack of sufficient circulating medium:

Reprinted from The Tolerant Populists: Kansas Populism and Nativism *by Walter T. K. Nugent without footnotes by permission of The University of Chicago Press. Copyright 1963 by the University of Chicago. Pp. 102–121.*

low commodity prices; the oppressiveness of interest rates on loans contracted when more money could be had for a given amount of labor and produce; a lowered ability to buy equipment, improvements, or consumer goods; and the greater ease with which banking and finance could be controlled by small groups of specially interested men. As solutions, they continually advocated a return to the policy of the United States prior to 1873, either by the issuance of legal tender paper money, or by the remonetization of silver, freely coined and as legal as gold.

From 1865 to 1879 the United States had unquestionably followed a definite policy of contracting the currency, and in spite of the Bland-Allison Act of 1878 and the Sherman Silver Purchase Act of 1890, which allowed limited purchases of silver by the Treasury, this policy had not been effectively altered. This policy did not go down well with the western farmers, who laid many of their own most serious problems at the door of the tightly closed Treasury.

They also saw certain other obvious conditions. First, in spite of a stable or dwindling amount of currency, population and trade were constantly increasing. Second, more and more wealth of all kinds was concentrating in fewer and fewer hands. Third, powerful statesmen, including John Sherman, William McKinley, and Grover Cleveland, suggested laws and policies that speeded this concentration. Fourth, the primary beneficiary of concentration, as well as of the national banking system endorsed by the same statesmen, was the Wall Street financial community, which controlled the assets or stock of many smaller banks, important corporations and trusts, and mortgage loan agencies. And fifth, either through actual agency, as in the case of the Belmont firm, or simply because of the position of the United States as a debtor nation in the international balance of payments, Wall Street was also in part economically tributary to the larger and richer financial community on Lombard and Threadneedle streets, London, where the old Anglo-Jewish Rothschild family played an influential part. Under these circumstances, the western farmers with their crashing prices and crushing mortgages reacted with a remarkable lack of deviation from the facts.

Of course, this is a generalization, and Populism like any other American reform movement of large proportions had many voices and comprised a broad spectrum of groups and individuals. Even so, only a tiny, narrow band let their rhetoric get the better of them. Most of them were puzzled and angry but not irrational. . . . A farmer need not have been a hopeless neurotic to have taken a look at corporations, grain markets, finance capitalism, and the leaders of

Congress and mistaken a common nonagrarian outlook for positive cooperation. He agreed easily with the author of *The Riddle of the Sphinx* that "well-disciplined organizations of capital and handlers have forced the farmer to sell his products to them at prices fixed by themselves, and to buy his commodities of them at prices again fixed by themselves."

It is certainly true that if farmers had been more worldly-wise, if they had traveled to New York, Washington, Chicago, and London and seen at first hand what cities, industry, and finance were actually like, they would have realized that dogged competition, not class conspiracy, were more the hallmarks of urban, industrial life in the late nineteenth century. Yet no educational excursion would have rid them of the certain conviction that whatever may have been the regard of these groups for one another, they were united in a way of life, a common economic viewpoint, that left farmers and laborers out of account except as factors in production and, very often, as subjects for exploitation. Populism was shot through with naïveté and oversimplification. But at the same time, it had its roots and its being in a realistic conflict of economic interest.

In its salad days the party that had sprung from high mortgages, currency stringency, and high railroad freight rates settled upon reforming land, money, and transportation as its foremost aims, a trident for puncturing a bloated plutocracy. Even in 1890, the central prong, money reform, was a little longer than the others, and as time passed, it became by far the longest and sharpest of the three. The Populists were guilty of oversimplification and one-sidedness, and they have been accused of treating silver coinage as a panacea and of demonstrating a lack of principle by emphasizing the money question almost to the exclusion of the others, especially in the Bryan-McKinley campaign of 1896, but there are some plausible reasons for this concentration.

In a political campaign a single issue that subsumes other objectives is a valuable thing; . . . Both in Kansas and throughout the rest of the country, the money question seemed to have the broadest appeal among potential reform voters. Furthermore, currency expansion as a nearly exclusive issue was a long tradition with post-Civil War reformers. Most of all, it seemed solidly rooted in economic logic, which relieved fretful Populists of any worry that stressing it heavily would indicate a lack of principle. If money were more plentiful, buyers of farm commodities would have a greater supply of it relative to their demand for the available corn, wheat, and other crops, and commodity prices would rise. The farmer would receive more cash; he would be loosed from the vise of low crop returns and high prices on his purchases. He could buy more. He would have more cash to pay mortgages, and the debts that had seemed insignificant when he contracted them in prosperous times would become trifling again. In addition, with greater cash returns for crops, railroad rates would eat up a smaller percentage of the return. Laws passed in state legislatures to stay foreclosures or to set maximum freight rates would be helpful, but, essentially, they would operate only as stopgap or supplementary measures while the farmers awaited a more plentiful supply of money. As for those "well-disciplined organizations of capital," bankers agreed with farmers that a small amount of circulating medium was easier to control than a large amount; a greater money supply would even alleviate the worst effects of economic combinations and monopolies.

The money question, then, was not only an issue in itself, but as more and more Populists viewed it, it underlay political success, reform traditions, mortgage problems, freight rates, improvement of (or speculation in) land, and the reduction of monopoly power. They did not notice, they were not in a position to understand, that such knotty problems as trust formation, urban slums, inequitable wealth distribution, and unresponsiveness of governments were not ultimately soluble by money reform alone or even in large part. . . .

When they talked about the money question practically all Populists, including recent immigrants, had four things in common. First came actual, imminent, or proximate financial distress. Second, they professed a certain creed about America, which included a scorn for manipulators of wealth in contrast to producers of wealth, a strong dislike of any kind of "English oppression," which invoked patriotic "memories" of 1776 and 1812, a distrust of European decadence, and a humanitarian welcome for downtrodden Europeans who sought a breath of free and fresh American air. Third, they perceived a connection between United States Treasury contractionists, eastern financiers, and London-centered magnates of world finance. Fourth, they agreed that free coinage of silver, the issuance of legal tender paper money, and the abolition of the national banking system were the chief solutions to financial distress.

Many, perhaps most, Populists restricted their expressions on the money question to an exposition of the economic situation and an advocacy of free silver, legal tender paper money, and the end of the national banks in order to put an end to this rule by special interests. Many others, however, by a personalization of the combined facts, substituted for "money question" the term "money power."

After this, the next question was, of course, Who controls this power?

The answer, embedded in the facts, was Wall Street and Lombard Street, Cleveland and Sherman, Gould and Vanderbilt, the Belmonts and the Rothschilds. Perhaps the facts strictly construed proved only that these groups had common interests and agreed on financial theory and policies. With very slight extrapolation, however, this agreement became a collective self-interest—in a word, a conspiracy. Even here, the conspiracy involved in equal parts American bankers, English and Anglo-Jewish bankers, and members of the American government.

When it became specific, as it sometimes did, the conspiracy harked back to the Civil War, when by a "Hazzard Circular" of 1862 European capitalists were supposed to have warned American capitalists that together they had to keep the control of money in the hands of the international capitalist class when the war was over. As the story went, the London financiers sent a certain Ernest Seyd to Washington with one hundred thousand English pounds put up by themselves and (less important) some German bankers. This scheme, with the connivance of certain American financiers and political bigwigs, successfully brought about the demonetization of silver in 1873. The spreaders of the story were often at great pains to prove it by affidavits, witnesses, and the like. Silver Republicans along with Populists swallowed it. It has all the earmarks of fantasy, yet financial historians ignore it rather than explode it and place the cause of the demonetization of silver on the gold-silver ratio in 1873, the disappearance of silver coin from circulation, and inadvertence. If the story was true, the "conspiracy" was a fact. If it was false, it was nonetheless propagated with documentation and not gullibly or frantically. One Populist congressman, John Davis, called this particular story a tall tale that his fellow Populists should never swallow, but he not only knew of Seyd's existence but defended him as a bimetalist, a real friend of silver, who had been incautiously maligned.

Aside from the "Hazzard Circular"–Ernest Seyd story, different writers gave the money power or conspiracy argument different forms and textures. Mrs. Lease, as usual, violently erupted with it:

> The capitalistic press rejoiced in the power of Grover Cleveland, the American agent of Jewish bankers and British gold. . . . [The Populists are] the only political party in existence that says to robber England "Hands off our money; American finance for Americans!"

But more often it appeared something like this:

> The demonetization of silver was the result of a carefully laid conspiracy between capitalists of the loaning classes against the business and debtor classes. The United States government, as a debtor, and also as the chief silver country, allowed the European Rothschilds and their American allies, millionaire bankers, to overreach her in dealing with the money question.

Again, it is worth stressing that the "conspiracy," whatever its particulars, was international. Censure fell on bankers, whether American or English, Jewish or Gentile. This was the consensus of those Populists who dealt with the money question in terms of a "money power," and it indicates that even among these people, who were by no means the whole party or its ideologues, it was bankers, not Jews, bankers, not England, who were the conspirators. When the Populists talked of an "international money power," they meant just that: not a foreign power but a foreign and domestic power that cared nothing for national boundaries or ethnic origins. To a Populist it was indeed remarkable that there were dozens of millionaires in New York, but not remarkable that there were among them a handful of Jews.

There were exceptions who unambiguously proclaimed that American policy was dictated by England and that "monarchy . . . continues to suck the life's blood from the Nation while the Republic sleeps," but these statements were more than balanced by more frequent and equally unambiguous statements blaming everything on Wall Street. . . .

From their treatment of the "money power" this group of Populists derived their only two consistent antagonisms to foreign groups. The first antagonism was to Jews, or more properly, Jewish bankers. The second antagonism, evoked by land tenure questions as well as money, was to English bankers and landlords.

First, the Jews. A distinction is in order between two forms of anti-Semitism: social discrimination and ideological hatred. The connection between the two is more logical than historical, and in many cases, one exists in the absence of the other. The use of the word "anti-Semitism" involves an assumption that there is a connection between what may be unrelated anti-Jewish acts; but for present purposes it will be assumed that it is more than a catchword. As for the distinction between ideological hatred and social discrimination, it has been said that "Anglophobia, a political ideology, was as harmless to English immigrants as ideological anti-Semitism was to Jews," but both aspects are still worth looking at.

Social discrimination can be disposed of quickly: it was not a Populist trait. There were few Jews in Kansas, fewer still on farms, and as far as is known, they were well treated by Populists, Republicans, and Democrats alike. The relative absence of Jews in Kansas has been used to support the idea of Populist ill feeling, apparently on the ground that what one does not know, one is suspicious of. There is no denying that personal contact with minorities can often decrease suspicions and antagonistic attributions. But this "absence theory" fails to distinguish between personal and ideological antipathy; it fails to explain why Jews were so much more discriminated against in large cities and in the East, where they lived and were known in large numbers; it fails to explain why the Populists bore no resentment against other absent minorities; it fails to note that foreign groups or countries, whether represented in Kansas or not (as, for example, the English certainly were), were unfavorably regarded if they were significantly connected to gold standard finances and favorably regarded if they were pro-silver. Merchants with strongly Jewish names were mentioned favorably in the local press. Others, singly or in groups, were well-regarded in their communities. Jewish mayors administered, at various times, the Kansas towns of Rosedale, Wichita, and Dodge City, and probably others; Populists supported a Jew for postmaster of Salina, and the son of the Populist state chairman told me of his fond remembrance of the only Jew in his home town of Chetopa, one Sig Lehman, who was elected mayor "year after year."

Out of hundreds of Populist newspapers and pamphlets, there were only a few references to large noses, nearly all in boiler-plate cartoons of "Rothschild"; there were two or three sentences of dialect writing, such as Thomas Bailey Aldrich or Finley Peter Dunne were using for other minorities; there were no references at all to ritual murder or other vicious libels that were getting some mention, if not acceptance, in the large city press of the time. . . .

Ideological anti-Semitism is a more complex problem. Populist discussions of the money question were by no means studded with possibly anti-Jewish references, but two words—"Rothschild" and "Shylock"—recur frequently and demand attention. Other anti-Jewish references are conspicuous by their great rarity, and even when they do occur they lack a tone of irrational opprobriousness. Leaving Shylock and Rothschild aside for the moment, a search of several thousand Populist newspapers, pamphlets, and books yielded only nine antagonist references, all of which can be mitigated in small or large part by reasonable analysis. For example, a series of fictitious letters in the *Advocate* in 1894 between "K. Gold Isaacs," a Wall Street banker, and his nephew, "W. M. Naut, Boomtown, Kansas," contained, other than the name, not a single implication of anti-Semitism unless mentions of Lombard Street are to be construed as such. The choice of name meant nothing more than the use of a stereotype of a harmless kind in order to achieve economic ends, if "Isaacs's" advice to play up the appointment of Edward White, a Roman Catholic, to the United States Supreme Court because "bloodshed over difference of creed would be much more agreeable than conflicts between the rich and poor" means anything.

Another example is Ignatius Donnelly's *Caesar's Column,* which probably sold well enough in Kansas and which has been given as clinching proof of "Populist anti-Semitism." Unlike Bellamy's *Looking Backward,* in which the problems of industrialism in the 1880s came to a happy solution, *Caesar's Column* was antiutopian. Its world of the future drew out the worst aspects of industrial society to a "logical" conclusion, in which a submerged mass of slaves existed in a world in the grip of an oligarchy of malefactors who possessed all wealth worth having. A secret revolutionary group rose gradually, however, and with the help of the oligarchy's jet air force, destroyed the oligarchy in a bloody purge and set up a popular dictatorship in its place. The good elements fled both. There are three important "anti-Semitic" aspects: the most powerful malefactor was Jacob Isaacs, alias "Prince Cabano"; the oligarchy was nearly all Jewish; the Jewish nation was reborn in the chaos of the revolutionary upheaval.

As for Jacob Isaacs, Donnelly portrayed him as an outcast, "driven from his synagogue"; and furthermore, the second in command of the opposing revolutionary forces was a Russian Jew, like his colleagues driven to violent rebellion by a traumatic personal incident produced by a vicious economic system beyond his control. This has been interpreted to mean that Donnelly thought Jews to be radicals on both sides of the fence, "working toward hidden Jewish ends," but it is just as likely, since the revolutionary forces are portrayed as Jewish-inspired but justice-seeking, that the evil Jew, Isaacs, is cancelled out by the good, if not always well-advised, Jew of the revolution. If the oligarchy was nearly all Jewish and was extremely powerful, this was because, Donnelly explained carefully, any weak Jews had long since been purged by Christian persecution, and not unnaturally they had become "as merciless to the Christian as the Christian had been to them." If the Jews were powerful, it was because Christians had started a fight they were too weak to finish. The idea that the Jewish nation was reborn out of the revolution's chaos may indicate a fear of Zionism, but it more likely showed Donnelly's admiration for the ancient chosen people, whom he praised in another novel of fantasy, *The Golden Bottle.*

Donnelly, the "K. Gold Isaacs" series, and references in other writings may be "ambiguous" in their attitude toward the Jew, but that is the worst that can legitimately be said, and it is probably too much. Even if they should receive the harshest interpretation, they would still remain nothing more than scattered references. . . .

In the more important Populist financial treatises such references are missing. N. B. Ashby, for example, mentioned Shylocks once in connection with control of the money market and Rothschilds once as part of "the interests which profit by a shrunken volume of money," in neither case making any explicitly Jewish reference. In his opening sketch of agriculture in world history, he described the biblical Jews as a group with a high respect for, and skill at, agriculture. W. S. Morgan used the word "Shylock" about a dozen and a half times but never made it specifically Jewish, and in his concluding list of the major aims of reform did not, of course, include elimination or confinement in ghettos of the Jews as one of them. Furthermore, his references to Shylock were balanced by many references to Vanderbilts, Goulds, Huntington, and monopolists in general. N. A. Dunning's 742-page *Farmers' Alliance History* hardly used the word "Shylock." W. A. Peffer, in *The Farmer's Side,* came down hard on Wall Street but avoided Shylock, Rothschild, London, and the Jews. These books were the lengthiest and most involved expositions of Populist financial doctrine. . . .

It should be needless to say that discriminatory laws, exclusion, mob action, and overt agitation were not a part of Populism.

The use of "Shylock," although frequent, fell far short of anti-Semitism. Even a critic of Populism has said that "the American stereotype [of Shylock] involved no hostility, no negative judgment"; and another analyst pointed out that it was never vicious until combined with the new stereotype of the "quintessential parvenu" in areas, particularly the East, where discriminatory patterns were taking shape. The mass of evidence supports this. Very infrequently is there an identification of Shylock and Rothschild, and in any case Shylock was not a symbol or collective title for Jews but rather for Wall Street or English moneylenders.

The Rothschild reference, less common than Shylock but a favorite subject of cartoons, needs two comments. The first is that it indicates a specific person who was in fact one of the world's leading bankers. Like Gould, Morgan, and Vanderbilt, who are mentioned at least as often, Rothschild was a flesh-and-blood person, and if he symbolized anything, it was the power of selfish finance not the power of world Jewry. The second is that Rothschild's Englishness is more significant than his Jewishness. . . . Rothschild is recognized as a Jew, but the significant facts are that he is an English banker Jew and that his interests are representative of other bankers, whether in London or New York, whether Jew or Gentile. . . .

A much better case can be made for Populist Anglophobia. . . .

Some Populist criticism of England was more than financial, however. They heatedly recalled Sir Lionel Sackville-West's alleged interference in domestic politics in 1888. They chauvinistically raised "American language . . . literature . . . education . . . inventions . . . advancement in the arts and sciences" above Britain's. They reviled many Americans for agreeing with Andrew Carnegie that England should "accept the headship of the race" in a unification of England and America. Too many Americans, they thought, "do nothing but ape the English aristocracy." England was supposed to have subsidized Hinton Rowan Helper's 1857 book, *The Impending Crisis in the South,* in order to bring on the self-destructive American Civil War. Britain was said to have tried in two wars to take over the United States and now concentrated her efforts on financial control. And one said, "Queen Victoria has a pet dog named Cleveland."

All the same, these were minority expressions. Others believed that the English labor system bore down on the English people harder than American pre-Civil War slavery bore upon the Negroes and admitted that British merchants were generally honest. The distinction between oppressors and oppressed was clearly made. English financial hegemony was unquestionably real. . . .

One possible source of their anglophobia lay in the curious and recurrent Populist references to Ireland, not, usually, in relation to the money question but to the problem of land tenure. Beginning with third-party and Alliance platforms in the late eighties and running through the nineties, agrarians frequently praised Parnell, Irish attempts to throw off the yoke of landlordism and rack-renting, and in general such putative Irish virtues as frugality, industriousness, bravery in battle, and fortitude in economic distress. Could it be that the anti-English feelings of many Populists came in part from Irish-American nationalism? Mrs. Lease was not the only Populist with personal knowledge of Irish political exile. Furthermore, Irish-Americans in Kansas seem to have forsaken their usual Democratic affinities and voted Populist when three-ticket campaigns gave them the opportunity.

Whatever contribution Irish-American nationalism may have made to Populism, Irish experience with English landlords had much to do with the frequent Populist injunctions against alien ownership of land, probably for the most part by providing a topical issue by which to reawaken ideas of Jeffersonian physiocracy and the natural goodness of the homestead principle.

Populist platform planks and other statements against alien land ownership comprise the only overt official references, except those against contract labor, to foreign countries or the foreign-born. Were they intended to be anti-immigrant? The platforms could leave that impression, except that they very often include a clause to the effect that land should be held "for actual settlers only" and often use the Irish situation to warn Americans. A typical and important formulation was the Kansas state Alliance plank of 1890:

> We demand the passage of laws prohibiting alien ownership of land, and that Congress take early steps to devise some plan to obtain all land now owned by aliens and foreign syndicates, and that all land now held by railroads and other corporations in excess of such as are actually used and needed by them be reclaimed by the government and held for actual settlers only.

If one takes for granted, as the farmers did, that land should not be held for speculation or for renting when smallholders are readily available, then the alien land problem was certainly real. . . .

But aside from the fact that not only Populists but Republicans and Prohibitionists supported alien land legislation, the content of Populist statements on the question makes it virtually certain that they had nothing against the individual foreign settler and in fact welcomed him. The enemy, as with the money question, was the man who profited by other men's labor. The Homestead Act of 1862 was not only the great charter of the American rural freeholder, in the Populists' opinion, but made land available to any immigrant who had declared his intention to become a citizen. . . .

The question of nativism in Kansas Populism, as just discussed, can perhaps be summed up as follows.

1. Antagonistic references to foreigners occurred on two issues only: money and land tenure.
2. Antagonistic references were limited to England and Jews, specifically to English landlords and bankers and to Anglo-Jewish bankers.
3. Such references emanated from a small minority, a wing that

generally favored prohibition and women's suffrage, opposed fusion, and perhaps drew more of its strength from former Republicans than from former Democrats.

4. Even within this group, the unfavorable references were remarkably infrequent and the expressions of a tiny fringe.
5. Nearly all antagonistic references were based on factual situations; for example, it was true that English bankers, including Rothschild, were powerful, self-interested, and unsympathetic to the farmer-debtors.
6. Such Populist antagonism as there was was rooted in democratic ideals nourished by the American Revolution, the War of 1812, and pre-Civil War nineteenth-century experience, not on later racist theories.
7. Populists who dealt in these terms found Wall Street and Lombard Street, Gentile financiers and Jewish financiers, equally opprobrious, with if anything the greater stress on the American and Gentile financiers than on the English and Jewish ones.
8. Antagonism was seldom directed to Englishness, practically never to Jewishness; rather to the financial power and aims of certain classes of Englishmen, Jews, and Americans.
9. Republicans, especially silver Republicans, made similar references.
10. Populists often supported their arguments with laudatory references to successful instances of reform practices in foreign countries.
11. Populist antagonism did not exist on a personal, individual basis and almost never on a racial basis, as did the antagonism of contemporary eastern restrictionists; it can be considered an infrequent emotional or rhetorical overflow which resulted from membership drives, political campaigns, and bleak agricultural depression.

9

Communism and the Great Steel Strike of 1919

Robert K. Murray

The rise of labor unions in the late nineteenth century was one of several major changes destined to alter traditional institutional arrangements in American society. For decades many Americans associated labor unions with foreign political radicalism. For example, the bombing at Chicago's Haymarket Square in 1886 aroused widespread fear that labor movements were infected by anarchism. These fears grew with the emergence of the IWW and the Socialist Party, reaching a climax after the Bolshevik Revolution in Russia. Robert K. Murray, who has written extensively on the Red Scare of 1919–1920, explains how fear of communism crippled the unions in the steel strike of 1919. An important question raised by his article is the degree to which fear of conspiracy was used deliberately by management and its supporters to obscure the fact that labor had legitimate grievances.

From Robert K. Murray, "Communism and the Great Steel Strike of 1919," The Mississippi Valley Historical Review, *XXXVIII (December 1951), 445–466. Reprinted with most of the footnotes omitted by permission of the author and the publishers.*

The year 1919 dawned full of hope and promise. The nation had just emerged from the greatest of all wars and peace again reigned. To millions of Americans standing on the threshold of a new year, this meant the possibility of a return to an existence wherein war stories, battles, and casualty lists would be absent from the front pages of their newspapers and it would only be necessary to glance briefly at the headlines before plunging on into the sports section.

Such a condition, however, was not easily or quickly attained. In the months following the armistice, inflation, demobilization, reconversion, labor unrest, and the struggle to establish a lasting peace filled the void left by silent guns and mute cannon. Moreover, all the hate, prejudice, and intolerance fostered by wartime anti-Hun emotionalism spilled over into this period and further clouded the postwar scene. The confusion, uncertainty, and fear that naturally surrounded such events precluded from the beginning a rapid return to the idyllic state of "normalcy," and the year 1919 is remembered for its turbulence and chaos rather than for its hope and promise.

Undoubtedly, the most spectacular phenomenon of this tempestuous year was the almost hysterical and paranoiac fear which the American public harbored for bolshevism. From the beginning of the Bolshevik Revolution in 1917, Americans had regarded the movement as an unmitigated evil, and the later bolshevik duplicity with respect to the Brest-Litovsk Treaty apparently confirmed earlier suspicions. Subsequent Allied and American intervention in Russia merely served to sharpen public animosity toward the doctrine, while superpatriotic organizations, such as the American Defense Society and the National Security League, as well as a majority of the nation's press, succeeded in inflaming public sentiment all the more. Amid sensational press reporting, several frenzied and frankly biased bolshevik investigations, and much misinformation, it was inevitable that the average American should become firmly convinced that bolshevism was inimical to his security and represented the very essence of lawlessness, brutality, and crime.

As a result, the bolshevik quickly and easily replaced the Hun as the factor most responsible for many of the nation's ills. No strike, no act of violence, no deviation from the norm failed to bring charges that the probable cause was domestic bolshevik activity. Inevitably, ever greater exaggerations were made by the press and various conservative pressure groups concerning the number of bolshevists who were active on the American scene. Although some native radicals openly espoused the bolshevik philosophy and worked for internal revolution, the number was actually never very large (the various domestic communist factions had about 75,000 members in 1919) and there was no real reason to believe that the nation was in serious danger. However, as the postwar months of 1919 slipped by, the Seattle general strike, the May Day riots and bombs, and the Boston police strike gave almost any kind of exaggeration a semblance of validity, and the alleged number of domestic communists rapidly increased from an estimated 500,000 to 5,000,000!

This schizophrenic fear of radicalism underlay, at least partially, much of the mob violence and general intolerance that characterized the year 1919, and was almost totally responsible for such vicious outbursts as the May Day riots and the infamous Centralia murders.[1] In a more subtle, but equally deadly, fashion, this public fear also underwrote the vigorous suppression of liberalism and plunged nonconformists into the full glare of public censure. Clergymen, government officials, schoolteachers, college professors, Negroes, and others were automatically condemned as "bolshevists" if they did not cleave to the accepted superpatriotic line.

Particularly was this true with respect to labor leaders and the activities of organized labor. The tremendous increase in the number of strikes and strikers in 1919 greatly alarmed the general public, and, influenced by the propaganda of employers and antiunion groups (who had lost little love for Wilsonian liberalism and desperately wanted to break the power of organized labor), it began to fear that radicalism was capturing American labor. Although nothing could have been farther from the truth, such events as the Seattle general strike of February and the Boston police strike of September, together with the May Day riots and bombings, appeared to many citizens as final proof that American labor was indeed becoming "bolshevized." [2]

Only with this background in mind can one understand properly the alleged connection between communism and the greatest of the turbulent labor struggles of 1919—the Great Steel Strike. The ground-

---

[1] May Day rioting occurred in numerous American cities, among the most important being New York, Cleveland, and Boston. . . . The Centralia murders occurred on November 11, 1919, in Centralia, Washington, where four American Legionnaires were shot by members of the local IWW and one Wobbly was subsequently lynched by the enraged populace.

[2] The Seattle general strike involved 60,000 workers in all lines of activity who walked off the job and permitted the city government to rest for a time in the hands of a labor strike committee. . . .The Boston police strike resulted from the fact that the police commissioner refused to permit the local policemen's union to affiliate with the AFL.

work for this conflict had been laid in August 1918, when a conference of twenty-four trade unions met in Chicago and established a National Committee for Organizing Iron and Steel Workers with Samuel Gompers as its honorary chairman, John Fitzpatrick as acting chairman, and William Z. Foster as secretary-treasurer. Throughout the ensuing months of 1918 and 1919 this committee achieved remarkable success, particularly within the ranks of the unorganized immigrant steel workers. It organized steel men in Johnstown, Youngstown, Chicago, Cleveland, Wheeling, Buffalo, and also, to some extent, in Pittsburgh, the stronghold of the United States Steel Corporation. Naturally, the steel organizers' activities met bitter resistance from the steel interests who retaliated against the budding unions by discharging known union men and prohibiting local union meetings. Nevertheless, Foster, who was the director of the campaign, continued on the basis that the "industry could be organized in spite of all the Steel Trust could do," and it was asserted that by the summer of 1919 he had a steel union in every important mill town.

William Z. Foster was not a typical AFL organizer. While most of the Federation's leaders were basically conservative and unalterably opposed to radicalism of all types, Foster exhibited a background and held economic philosophies which ran counter to the general pattern. He had been a Bryan follower; then he became a Socialist. Later he joined the Industrial Workers of the World and in 1910 studied French syndicalism in Paris. While there he became convinced that dual unionism was a mistake and that radicals should stay in the old trade unions. Failing, however, in his subsequent attempt to transform the IWW into a propaganda league to "bore from within," Foster abandoned syndicalism in 1916 for "pure and simple" trade unionism. During the war he evidenced a real conversion by giving patriotic services in Liberty Bond drives and by participating as a four-minute speaker. However, in spite of these appearances he retained a sufficient amount of his earlier radicalism to desire the overthrow of the conservative labor machine "by the mass organization of the unorganized." To the National Association of Manufacturers he was always known simply as "Red" Foster.

Foster's crusade to "organize the unorganized" could not possibly have found a better milieu than that of the steel industry. Many of the steel workers were uneducated immigrants of a dozen different nationalities who were completely at the mercy of the Steel Trust. Living conditions for such workmen were often wretched, many of their homes being "mere unpainted shacks without running water or plumbing." Almost half the men worked twelve hours a day, seven days a week, while the average work week for the whole industry was slightly under sixty-nine hours. An unskilled steel laborer's average annual income was only $1466, while the estimated minimum subsistence level for a family of five in 1919 was at least $1575.

As a result of these deplorable conditions, steel workers were extremely interested in bettering their economic position and joined the new steel union movement to force remedial action. The AFL, in turn, backed the steel workers in their demands, and the *American Federationist* sounded the keynote of all organized labor's attitude toward the steel companies by declaring that "Steel autocracy must capitulate" and that "Steel in America must be democratized." Hence, on June 20, 1919, the AFL, acting in the interests of the steel workers, asked Judge Elbert H. Gary, chairman of the United States Steel's board of directors, for a conference to discuss conditions in the steel industry and the betterment of the workers' position. When no reply was forthcoming, the steel union leaders circulated a strike ballot among the local steel unions, all of which by August 20 registered a desire for a strike, the date to be set by the National Committee for Organizing Iron and Steel Workers. With this warning to the steel companies that they were serious in their demands, Fitzpatrick and Foster on August 26 requested of Judge Gary an arbitration conference to settle all differences. His reply of the following day declared that because of the open shop policy of United States Steel, "The officers of the corporation respectfully decline to discuss with you, as representatives of a labor union, any matters relating to employees." Fitzpatrick and Foster immediately asked Judge Gary to reconsider, but he again refused.

In view of these events it was obvious that a tremendous industrial struggle was in the making. Labor had been rebuffed in securing what it felt were legitimate demands, while Judge Gary was firm in his desire to hold the line against the growing power of steel unionism. President Woodrow Wilson, acting in the interest of industrial peace, immediately appealed to both sides to stay the conflict and on August 31, in a Labor Day message to the nation, declared that he was going to call an industrial conference in the near future "to discuss fundamental means of bettering the whole relationship of capital and labor." The President fervently hoped that a steel struggle might thereby be averted.

But neither Gary nor the steel union leaders showed any willingness to avert the impending strife and, despite the plea of the President, refused to change their original positions. Therefore, on September 10, under tremendous pressure from the local steel unions, the National Committee for Organizing Iron and Steel Workers voted for the strike to begin on September 22. Two hundred thousand copies of the strike call were immediately issued in seven different languages: "STRIKE SEPTEMBER 22, 1919. The Workers in the iron and steel mills and blast furnaces . . . are requested not to go to work on September 22, and to refuse to resume their employment until such time as the demands of the organizations have been conceded by the steel corporations." The basic demands for which the strike was called were "The right of collective bargaining; reinstatement of all men discharged for union activities with pay for time lost; the eight-hour day; one day's rest in seven; the abolition of the twenty-four hour shift; an American living wage; double pay for overtime; the check-off and seniority; and the abolition of company unions."

Given to the public at a time when the sensational Boston police strike had not yet been settled, this steel strike announcement caused national consternation. The business world, in particular, was shaken as steel stocks wavered on the exchanges. Again President Wilson frantically urged conciliation and appealed directly to Samuel Gompers to use his influence to postpone the strike at least until after the proposed industrial conference should convene on October 6. The conservative Gompers, who reluctantly continued to serve as honorary chairman of the organizing committee, suggested to Fitzpatrick and Foster that they abide by the President's request, but they immediately replied "that any vague, indefinite postponement would mean absolute demoralization and utter ruin" for the steel union movement. They also informed President Wilson of this fact, further buttressing their decision with a recital of instances of oppression and of denial of workers' rights by the steel companies.

It has since been asserted that Gompers, although favoring postponement, refused to force the hand of the steel union leaders because he feared radicals might promote the strike anyway. There is certainly an element of truth in this contention, for the steel organizers' radicalism was well known and a favorite topic of the day.[3] For some time newspapers had been parading the "bolshevism" of the steel labor leaders by quoting Fitzpatrick as saying, "We are going to socialize the basic industries of the United States," and also by publicizing excerpts from Foster's earlier syndicalist writings. Newspapers such as the New York *Times* continually cautioned Gompers against this " 'Red' element" within the AFL and early declared that the proposed steel strike was not a strike for wages and hours but a "strike for power, for the control of the industry." Meanwhile, the Washington *Post* warned,

[3] Writing in 1925 Gompers declared that he knew from the beginning the strike would fail because of the radicalism involved. He asserted that Foster wanted to reconstruct the AFL "upon the Soviet revolutionary basis."

"The public is not in a long-suffering mood just at present," and suggested that the AFL keep its leadership firmly in line.

At first glance it would appear that the general public and the press had already lined up against the steel workers, and yet closer examination reveals that Judge Gary was not faring too well at their hands either. Indeed, his arbitrary stand on the open shop principle and his absolute refusal to confer with the union chiefs had aroused considerable animosity. The Springfield *Republican,* for example, thought Gary was acting like an "extreme reactionary," and the Chicago *Tribune* predicted that his actions would drive even the conservative unionist into the arms of the Reds. The liberal press, as represented by the *Survey,* the *New Republic,* and the *Nation,* agreed with these papers and declared that Gary was utterly in the wrong in his drive to "smash unionism." It was inevitable, of course, that the *Wall Street Journal* should assert that these charges were wholly false and that Judge Gary was actually "fighting the battle of the American Constitution."

Amid these conflicting opinions as to the real purport of the antagonists, the steel strike began on September 22. Although the steel companies minimized the extent of the walkout, and conservative labor leaders such as Gompers withheld wholehearted support, an estimated 275,000 steel workmen left their jobs on that day. Shortly thereafter their ranks were swelled by other thousands of steel workers, and, by the end of the first week, the strikers numbered in excess of 365,000. According to Foster, the strike was about 90 percent effective, although he did admit that in the Pittsburgh area only about three-fourths of the plants were shut down.

The magnitude of the strike was a shocking revelation to the nation. Up to the very moment of the walkout, the public, along with the President, had hoped that the struggle might somehow be averted and that conservative AFL leaders might hold the steel zealots in line. Now, however, it appeared to many observers that radicalism had gained the upper hand. The Boston *Evening Transcript* and the *Ohio State Journal* expressed the similar fear that the strike was a revolutionary attempt to change the character of the government, while the New York *Tribune* flatly declared that the struggle was "another experiment in the way of Bolshevizing American industry." Other newspapers which did not believe that the steel strike was actually a "revolution" agreed that it was indeed a "serious mistake" and that organized labor in the long run would be the chief sufferer from the consequences.

On the other hand, the radical press hailed the steel strike in glowing terms and completely identified itself with the struggle. The *Socialist*

News declared that the strike threw "HALF MILLION WORKERS IN OPEN CLASS WAR," while the New York *Call* (Socialist) insisted that labor was entering what might be "the last battle with the industrial overlords of America." The *New Solidarity* (IWW) maintained that "possibilities of revolution are in what may develop during the strike," and the *Communist* (CP) immediately urged all laborers to support the steel workers for a final battle to "crush the capitalists." Meanwhile, the *One Big Union* (IWW) exclaimed: "we are cooperating with Foster at every step in the fight. Many of our members [Wobblies] are in the Steel Workers' Union; some of them sit in the councils of that body. . . . Let Foster build his one big union; may it grow, may it increase, may it win its battle with the Steel Trust."

In such manner the illusion was created from the beginning that the steel strike was an attempt at revolution. And yet there is every reason to believe that, in spite of the exaggerated assertions of both radicals and conservatives, many citizens at first were basically sympathetic to the strikers' demands for better working conditions and opposed to the arbitrary actions of the Steel Trust. The steel companies were certainly aware of this fact and their most pressing problem therefore was to promote a more favorable public opinion toward their own position. Perceiving that their greatest ally was the latent public fear of the strike's radicalism, the steel interests realized that much of the current animosity to Judge Gary's actions would disappear and the strike would fail if the public could be convinced that "bolshevism" was the *only* strike issue. Steel officials and other antiunion conservatives therefore began a concerted drive to mold public opinion along this line.

The ruses used were many. The fiction was spread through the press that steel workers received up to $70 per day, and certain newspapers even carried reports "that the more luxurious New York hotels expected an influx of striking steel-workers who would use the occasion to take a vacation and spend their 'high wages.' " The inference, of course, was that the strike could not possibly be for higher wages. It was also constantly maintained that the strike would not prove a success because native American workmen were refusing to leave their jobs and that their action was causing many foreign strikers to return to work. The native element, it was said, was opposed to the radicalism of the foreign workers and considered the strike "disloyal" and "un-American." A whole host of false reports were made upon this assumption, for at a time when Foster claimed the strike was 90 percent effective, newspaper headlines read as follows: "CONDITIONS ALMOST NORMAL IN ALL STEEL PLANTS," "WORKERS

FLOCK BACK TO JOBS," "STRIKE CRUMBLING." Pittsburgh papers, such as the *Dispatch, Leader, Chronicle-Telegraph, Post,* and *Press,* in particular, kept up a constant barrage of such propaganda.

Then, too, between September 27 and October 8 no less than thirty full-page advertisements appeared in the various Pittsburgh papers, condemning the strike and asking the steel workers to return to their jobs. These appeals were printed in as many as nine different languages and, in addition to exhorting workmen to "GO BACK TO WORK" and to "STAND BY AMERICA," maintained that the native workers who clearly understood the radicalism involved were already back. Through such advertisements the idea was also circulated "that the U. S. in the name U. S. Steel Corporation signified that the Corporation was an official part of the federal government, and that a strike against it was a rebellion against the United States"! As the strike progressed, similar advertisements also appeared in other newspapers such as the Baltimore *Sun,* Cincinnati *Enquirer,* and Los Angeles *Times* asking labor to "SHOW UP THE RED AGITATOR FOR WHAT HE IS" and warning workers to "BEWARE THE AGITATOR WHO MAKES LABOR A CATSPAW FOR BOLSHEVISM."

Important as this propaganda was, however, it was William Z. Foster who actually bore the brunt of the steel companies' attack. Steel officials circulated widely copies of his *Syndicalism,* a pamphlet written in 1911 while he was still a member of the IWW, in which he declared:

> In his choice of weapons to fight his capitalist enemies, the Syndicalist is no more careful to select those that are "fair," "just," or "civilized" than is a householder attacked in the night by a burglar. He knows he is engaged in a life and death struggle . . . and considers his tactics only from the standpoint of their effectiveness. With him the end justifies the means.

While these views had been publicized prior to the strike, it was mainly after the strike began that they gained their widest publicity. Under the tutelage of antiunion conservatives, the press of the country, with few exceptions, centered on Foster's radical past and made of him a thoroughly revolutionary leader. Although Foster constantly denied such charges and declared that no radicalism of any kind was involved in the steel strike, the majority of the press remained firm in its conviction that he was "an avowed syndicalist," "an uncompromising enemy of the existing political order," and "a revolutionist." He engineered the steel strike, agreed the press "not for the purpose of improving labor conditions, but for the purpose of revolutionizing industry."[4] Meanwhile, even the House and Senate gave Foster's background a cautious look. Senator Henry L. Myers characterized Foster as "a notorious syndicalist, revolutionist, and enemy of organized government." Senator Charles S. Thomas labeled him a radical who wanted economic chaos in the United States. Representative John G. Cooper of Ohio branded him as a man unfit for "the name of an American citizen and the protection of that flag."

Had no violence occurred during the strike, it might have been more difficult for the general public to accept wholeheartedly these charges of "revolution" which were so cleverly built up by conservative antiunion forces and strengthened by press assertions and the statements of public men. However, as riot after riot ensued between embattled strikers, nonstrikers, and law enforcement officers, charges of "bolshevism" gained increasing credence. Antiunion elements and steel officials used such events to influence further the public mind, and the public became increasingly convinced of the radical nature of the strike without realizing that strike disturbances were often the result of police belligerency or of insidious action on the part of steel representatives.

The day before the strike began, headlines in the Washington *Post* declared "STEEL MILLS READY TO FIGHT STRIKERS—POLICE PLANS RUSHED." Three days later headlines read: "RIOTING SPREADS IN STRIKE," "GUARDS RAID PENNSYLVANIA MILL PICKETS," "MANY SHOT—2 DEAD." Such headlines tersely explain what happened throughout the strike. From the very beginning the steel companies openly prepared for war and surrounded their plants with guards armed with rifles and riot guns. Also, because of their control over local politics (particularly in western Pennsylvania), the steel corporations strengthened and assumed charge of the law enforcement agencies in many local communities where citizens were sworn in by the droves as special deputies and were armed to prevent picketing and violence. It was estimated, for example, that along the Monongahela from Pittsburgh to Clairton (a distance of twenty miles), 25,000 men were under arms at the onset of the strike and that in some areas there was a deputy sheriff for almost every striker!

---

[4] Foster, in his *Great Steel Strike,* 154–155, declared such charges were wholly fictious and were invented by the steel companies to kill the strike. However, seventeen years later, writing as America's No. 1 Communist, he declared in his *From Bryan to Stalin* (1937), 133, that he was really a "borer from within" and hoped success in the steel strike would supplant the AFL with a militant majority.

Such a condition opened the way to violence. Police Officials and local deputies were often overzealous in displaying their authority. In certain areas union meetings were summarily broken up, picket lines were dispersed, and orderly participants were clubbed. In some small mill towns the local mounted police rode over pedestrians on the sidewalks, injuring peaceful groups of men and women. When strikers attempted to defend themselves from such brutal action, they were treated ruthlessly. For example, at Farrell, Pennsylvania, in a skirmish between strikers and police (arising from the latter's oppressive curtailment of free speech), four strikers were killed and eleven badly wounded. The result of such police activity was that in many areas, particularly in western Pennsylvania, civil liberty became a dead letter.

Besides this use of special deputies and police, the steel companies' employment of labor spies and strikebreakers also served to inflame hatred and incite violence. Probably of all the weapons used by the steel interests to quell the strike, these two were the most reprehensible. The steel companies purposely aroused racial hatred and prejudice by instructing their agents "to stir up as much bad feeling as you possibly can," and by using Negro strikebreakers against white pickets. As a result of such activities, riots broke out in some mill towns between nationalities and between races. In Donora, Pennsylvania, a riot between Negro strikebreakers and foreign strikers cost two of the strikers their lives. Similarly, in Braddock twenty persons were injured and one killed in a riot involving two excited foreign mobs.

Unfortunately, these ruthless methods used by the steel companies were not emphasized to any extent in the press. Instead, reports of riot disturbances were written in such a manner as to make it appear that steel officials were on the defensive against those who were carrying the attack against existing law and order. The public, therefore, received a biased picture of the strike situation since newspapers dwelt mostly on the evidences of radicalism involved and related all other factors to them. In reply to the New York *Call's* question, "Why Must There Be Cossacks?" the *Wall Street Journal* said it was simply because "the leaders of the steel strike are apostles of violence with the destruction of any form of law as a first principle."

Actually, the vast majority of the riot disturbances contained little or no trace of radicalism. However, one such disturbance definitely did possess some evidence of radical activity; hence, it was all the more publicized in the press and capitalized on by the steel companies. Occurring at Gary, Indiana, on October 4, this incident deepened the growing fear of labor radicalism, hurt the steel strikers' cause, and added credence to all the various claims of the Steel Trust.

From the outset of the strike, reports from Gary emphasized the radicalism of the strike leaders in that city. They were quoted as making such extreme statements as "The strike won't stop until the steel workers become the lawmakers at Washington, D. C." As a result, even the federal government became alarmed and sent federal agents into the area to prevent radical elements from capitalizing on the strike. Nevertheless, the situation at Gary became increasingly tense, and the steel companies finally decided to break the influence of the strike leaders in that city. Negro strikebreakers were brought into the area in large numbers and on October 4 violent rioting inevitably ensued. Governor James P. Goodrich of Indiana immediately ordered eleven companies of the state militia into East Chicago and Gary, and these soldiers plus 500 special police and 300 deputies set about to restore order, filling the city's hospitals with wounded and its jails with arrests.

This restoration of order was short-lived, however, for on the following day rioting flared anew when 500 strikers stormed the Tyler Street gates of the United States Steel Corporation's plant, while another group attempted to force its way into the Buchanan Street entrance. Again militiamen were hurried to the scene, but this time they were unable to quell the disturbance before a number of persons were killed and many injured. In desperation the Indiana Governor now appealed for federal troops, and a pouring rain on the afternoon and evening of October 5 tended to cool heated tempers until the arrival the following day of regular army soldiers under General Leonard Wood.

Immediately after his arrival, the General placed Gary under martial law, forbade assembly in the city's streets or parks, and made the carrying of firearms a major offense. He then asked Army Intelligence to begin a thorough investigation of radical influence among the workmen in the city. The sifting process purportedly uncovered those who were attempting to make the steel strike a revolution. According to Army Intelligence, radical pamphlets were found which had been circulated freely among the strikers, and which reportedly advised such actions as "Capture the power of the state [and] establish the dictatorship of the workers." Furthermore, evidence of a bomb plot designed to blow up the homes of prominent Gary citizens was discovered, and it was rumored that participants in the infamous May–June bombings might be involved. As a result of these discoveries, a whirlwind raid on known nests of Gary radicals was suddenly conducted by the army on October 15, netting scores in arrests and much bolshevist literature.

Although Gary strike leaders immediately denied all connection with this radical element, and General Wood's investigation showed that most of the Gary radicals were neither regular steel workers nor organizers, the damage to the steel strikers' cause had been done. Newspapers throughout the nation seized upon the army raid and the various Gary riots as further proof of the radicalism of all steel workers. The Portland *Oregonian* declared that these incidents at Gary proved that the steel struggle was "an attempted revolution, not a strike," while the Atlanta *Constitution* advanced the belief that the Gary workers represented a "Red Guard" in American industry. The Boston *Evening Transcript* concluded, "[The Gary incident] shows the extraordinary hold which 'Red' principles have upon the foreign born population in the steel districts."

Meanwhile, the manner in which bona fide radicals reacted to the situation in Gary did little to allay the mounting public fear that the steel strike was a revolutionary movement. Some radicals readily admitted their complicity in the Gary riots and openly urged strikers to kill police and soldiers. One of their pamphlets demanded that laborers everywhere arm themselves and take reprisals "for every worker killed." Mother Jones, ancient labor agitator, shouted to a radical meeting in Gary that in spite of all opposition "We're going to take over the steel mills and run them for Uncle Sam," while the *Communist* (CP) shrieked, "RESIST THE TERROR!" and added, "Armed force must not prevail! . . . Workers, act! Out of your mass strikes will come . . . a state of the workers, proletarian dictatorship, which will crush the capitalist as the capitalist state now crushes the workers."

Unfortunately for the cause of industrial peace, the Gary riots with their resultant army investigation and raid were the immediate background against which the President's National Industrial Conference operated. Convening in the Pan-American Union Building in Washington, D. C., on October 6 (the very day that General Wood declared martial law in Gary), this body was composed of the representatives of capital, labor, and the public, and began work to allay the current industrial unrest. Although the Pittsburgh *Post* hailed it as "the only method that can produce a better understanding" and other newspapers fervently hoped it would succeed, the conference really had little chance for success. The steel industry was paralyzed, charges of "revolution" were flying, and public animosity toward organized labor was growing. Capital was in the driver's seat and could afford to be obstinate. Labor was on the defensive and somewhat belligerent. As usual, the public sat uncomfortably in-between.[5]

For several weeks the conference paid lip service to industrial co-operation. However, when Samuel Gompers offered a resolution on October 21 declaring for "the right of wage earners . . . to bargain collectively . . . in respect to wages, hours of labor, and relations and conditions of employment," the conference fell to pieces. Here, after all, was the central issue of the industrial unrest, *not* radicalism. Capital was determined *not* to allow its position to be compromised by the collective bargaining power of labor, and organized labor was equally determined to force capital to concede. The representatives of the public, meanwhile, held the balance of power, and their action illustrated that the constant charges of radicalism and the propaganda of antiunion elements were bearing rich fruit. By a coalition vote of capital and the public, Gompers' resolution was voted down. Immediately thereafter, on October 22, the AFL's chief declared, "I have sung my swan song in this conference; . . . and with a feeling of regret that I am not able with a clear conscience to remain longer, I go."

The next day's headlines of the Chicago *Tribune* briefly told the story: "LABOR QUITS, CAPITAL FLITS, PUBLIC SITS!" Although some papers, such as the Washington *Evening Star,* thought the employer group was just as guilty as labor in the breakup of the conference, general sentiment placed the blame squarely on Gompers' shoulders. The Baltimore *Sun* declared that "Labor's action was not justified," while the *Rocky Mountain News* said its withdrawal made of the conference "An industrial Sarajevo." Gompers' action, concluded the *Wall Street Journal,* was merely further proof that organized labor was succumbing to "the IWW's and Russian Bolshevists."

From the time of the Gary riots and labor's withdrawal from the Industrial Conference, the steel strike was utterly doomed. Although the struggle dragged on for two more months, public sentiment had become so adverse to the strikers that they could not hope to win. During this two-month period, conservative pressure groups and government officials continued to emphasize the strikers' supposed radical-

---

[5] It is interesting to notice that of the twenty-two men who represented the public, eighteen had corporation affiliations, among them John D. Rockefeller and Judge Elbert H. Gary! That these two, in particular, should have represented the public, said the Columbus *Citizen,* September 23, 1919, p. 6, was "absolutely absurd."

ism, not only because of their own real fear, but also because of the calculated effect which such propaganda would have on the public mind. The National Security League and the *Open Shop Review* persistently reiterated the charge that the steel struggle was purely "an effort of anarchists . . . to destroy the government," while conservative government officials such as Senator Miles Poindexter openly avowed that "there is a real danger that the Government will fall." The press also continued to present the public with an entirely false picture of the strength of labor radicalism by filling their columns with phrases like "a bolshevist campaign," "the bolshevism in it," and "not an ordinary labor dispute." Conservative labor officials, who had been cool to the strike from the beginning, also fanned the flames of public fear by stating that some of the strike leaders were indeed "noted IWW's and Anarchists . . . and outspoken Bolshevists from the tops of their heads to the soles of their feet." The radical press promoted this hysterical fear of bolshevism by declaring that of course there were radicals in the steel strike who "do not need the newspapers to tell them that they are Bolsheviki."

Since it became increasingly obvious to all concerned that these widespread charges of bolshevism were strangling the strike, two investigations of the real purport of the conflict were watched with particular interest. One was made by the Senate Committee on Education and Labor, the full results of which were made public before the strike officially closed. The other was handled by a special commission of inquiry of the Interchurch World Movement, and, although its final report did not appear until the fall of 1920, its summary findings were also given to the public while the strike was yet in progress.

While admitting that the steel companies were guilty of industrial despotism in their arbitrary refusal to bargain collectively with the steel union leaders, the Senate report placed special emphasis on organized labor's shortcomings. Besides assailing union leaders for refusing to postpone the strike upon the President's request, it declared the AFL had committed a colossal blunder in permitting Foster to conduct the struggle and that the evidence showed he had not renounced his earlier syndicalist views. The Senate report boldly concluded that behind the strike was massed "a considerable element of IWW's anarchists, revolutionists, and Russian Soviets" who were using the conflict "as a means of elevating themselves to power."

The findings of the Commission of Inquiry reversed the emphasis by minimizing the extent of radical influence among both strikers and strike leaders, and, although admitting that a few workers wanted "big changes," it declared that these had no voice in the strike. It then attacked vigorously the role played by the steel companies and bitterly denounced the use of "strikebreakers," "undercover men," and "labor spies." It further charged that the grievances of the workers were just and that the steel interests used their control over the press and police agencies to abrogate free speech and restrict an airing of the true causes of the struggle. This struggle, it continued, was conducted in an orthodox fashion according to the rules of the AFL, and Foster, regardless of his earlier bent for syndicalism, had harmonized his actions perfectly with those of the AFL in the steel fight. The Church report concluded that under the influence of the steel companies, the general press and other interested elements had built up false "Red" charges to make the public lose sight of the real issues.

The report of the Commission of Inquiry was much closer to the truth than that of the Senate committee. But, regardless of the many possible points of difference, one fact could receive universal agreement —the words "revolution" and "bolshevism" had killed all chance of the strikers' success. This fact was no less known to the investigators and the public than to the strike leaders themselves, and, on January 8, 1920, at a time when less than 100,000 men were still out and when steel production was about 70 percent normal, the National Committee for Organizing Iron and Steel Workers voted to end the struggle. The men had gained not "a single concession," twenty lives had been sacrificed (of which eighteen had been strikers), and approximately $112,000,000 in wages lost. The tremendous cost to the steel companies cannot be calculated, but they obviously considered the expense well worthwhile to crush the embryonic steel union movement. After the strike defeat Foster resigned from the AFL and rapidly gravitated toward the Communist party, while conservative union leaders vainly attempted to repair the damage done by ruthlessly purging all suspected radicals from the organized labor movement. On the other hand, the United States Steel Corporation, with its vast resources and its control over subsidiaries, independent companies, banks, and mines, emerged from the struggle as the recognized champion of the American conservative tradition as well as the primary industrial bulwark against unionism. Backed by a favorable public opinion which was based to a large extent on an exaggerated fear of communism, this corporation proved that not even 350,000 strikers could prevail against it.

The effect of the Great Steel Strike upon the already turbulent postwar scene is of course readily obvious. Public hatred for bolshevism increased immeasurably as the fear grew that American labor unions were succumbing to that doctrine. Constant antiunion propaganda, press sensationalism, official sentiment, and a few actual instances of radical activity, more than the basic issues of the strike itself, had succeeded in establishing this belief. Hagridden by the specter of labor radicalism, the public held organized labor in such complete suspicion by the close of the steel conflict that despite all labor's attempts to prove that subsequent strikes, such as the 1919 coal strike, were justifiable, it was unable to make its voice heard. As soon as the word "Red" was injected into any industrial dispute, the immediate issues were lost completely. Wages and hours were regarded by the public as little more than a ruse while union recognition carried with it the connotation of "sovietism." The open shop principle rapidly became the "American way," since all labor-management conflicts suddenly were no longer mere squabbles between employers and employees, but in every case were thought to represent a crucial fight in which the government and American democratic traditions were at stake.[6]

Such antiunion animosity, based in the main upon a false fear of radicalism, fell heavily upon the future fortunes of organized labor. Subsequent to its bitter defeat in the steel strike (and in the famous coal strike which followed), labor lapsed into the doldrums. Its strength and militancy rapidly declined as the open shop campaign gained momentum and as fewer and fewer workers expressed a willingness to brave the storm of public criticism which was almost certain to greet any new labor dispute. In short, much of the decline which organized labor experienced during the twenties stemmed originally from the alleged connection between communism and the steel strike of 1919.

More specifically, the effect of the steel strike upon the future of steel unionism was particularly disastrous. The strike's utter collapse and the successful stand of Judge Gary on the open shop principle brought an end to the organizing campaign in the steel industry for the time being. The National Committee for Organizing Iron and Steel Workers was crippled by the immediate withdrawal of various unions, such as the Amalgamated Association of Iron and Steel Workers, which "refused to be further 'subject to outside interference.'" Of the

---

[6] The 1919 coal strike began on November 1 and, despite bitter opposition by the public, officialdom, and the nation's press, 394,000 miners left the mines. Meanwhile, on October 30, a temporary injunction was secured by the government forbidding the leaders to participate in the strike. On November 8 this injunction was made permanent and the union leaders were summarily ordered to rescind the strike call. This they did on November 11. However, amid widespread charges of "bolshevism," "radicalism," and "revolution," the leaderless miners remained on strike until December 10.

workers organized during the 1918–1919 whirlwind campaign, estimated at 250,000, only a handful remained in the unions by late 1920.

Subsequent American labor history clearly demonstrates that the catastrophic defeat for steel unionism in 1919 was not quickly remedied, for it would not be until 1937 that organized labor under the leadership of the newly created CIO could muster sufficient strength to contest again the authority of Big Steel, wipe out the humiliation of 1919, and force the industry to meet labor's basic demands. Perhaps in the final analysis, this delayed success on the part of labor in storming the bastions of Big Steel illustrates more graphically than anything else the lasting and important effect of "communism" upon the Great Steel Strike of 1919.

10

The American Red Scare of 1919–1920

Stanley Coben

The great steel strike of 1919 was one of a number of forces and events that combined to produce the "Red Scare." Stanley Coben argues that the Scare must be understood as a reaction to a series of severe social and economic dislocations, upheavals that convinced many observers that American culture was threatened by disintegration. Coben also suggests that some politicians, notably Attorney-General A. Mitchell Palmer and General Leonard Wood, tried to utilize fear of subversion to advance their own political careers.

At a victory loan pageant in the District of Columbia on May 6, 1919, a man refused to rise for the playing of "The Star-Spangled Banner." As soon as the national anthem was completed an enraged sailor fired three shots into the unpatriotic spectator's back. When the man fell, the *Washington Post* reported, "the crowd burst into cheering and handclapping." In February of the same year, a jury in Hammond,

---

From "A Study in Nativism: The American Red Scare of 1919–1920" by Stanley Coben. Reprinted with permission from the Political Science Quarterly, *79 (March 1964), 52–75. Most of the footnotes have been omitted by permission of the author and the publisher.*

Indiana, took two minutes to acquit the assassin of an alien who yelled, "To Hell with the United States." Early in 1920, a clothing store salesman in Waterbury, Connecticut, was sentenced to six months in jail for having remarked to a customer that Lenin was "the brainiest," or "one of the brainiest" of the world's political leaders. Dramatic episodes like these, or the better known Centralia Massacre, Palmer Raids, or May Day riots, were not everyday occurrences, even at the height of the Red Scare. But the fanatical one hundred percent Americanism reflected by the Washington crowd, the Hammond jury, and the Waterbury judge pervaded a large part of our society between early 1919 and mid-1920.

Recently, social scientists have produced illuminating evidence about the causes of eruptions like that of 1919–1920. They have attempted to identify experimentally the individuals most responsive to nativistic appeals, to explain their susceptibility, and to propose general theories of nativistic and related movements. These studies suggest a fuller, more coherent picture of nativistic upheavals and their causes than we now possess, and they provide the framework for this attempt to reinterpret the Red Scare.

Psychological experiments indicate that a great many Americans—at least several million—are always ready to participate in a "red scare." These people permanently hold attitudes which characterized the nativists of 1919–1920: hostility toward certain minority groups, especially radicals and recent immigrants, fanatical patriotism, and a belief that internal enemies seriously threaten national security.

In one of the most comprehensive of these experiments, psychologists Nancy C. Morse and Floyd H. Allport tested seven hypotheses about the causes of prejudice and found that one, national involvement or patriotism, proved to be "by far the most important factor" associated with prejudice. Other widely held theories about prejudice—status rivalry, frustration-aggression, and scapegoat hypotheses, for example—were found to be of only secondary importance. Summarizing the results of this and a number of other psychological experiments, Gordon W. Allport, a pioneer in the scientific study of prejudice, concluded that in a large proportion of cases the prejudiced person is attempting to defend himself against severe inner turmoil by enforcing order in his external life. Any disturbance in the social status quo threatens the precarious psychic equilibrium of this type of individual, who, according to Allport, seeks "an island of institutional safety and security. The nation is the island he selects. . . . It has the definiteness he needs." . . .

Substantial evidence, then, suggests that millions of Americans are both extraordinarily fearful of social change and prejudiced against those minority groups which they perceive as "threatening intruders." Societal disruption, especially if it can easily be connected with the "intruders," not only will intensify the hostility of highly prejudiced individuals, but also will provoke many others, whose antagonism in more stable times had been mild or incipient, into the extreme group.

A number of anthropologists have come to conclusions about the roots of nativism which complement these psychological studies. Since the late nineteenth century, anthropologists have been studying the religious and nativistic cults of American Indian tribes and of Melanesian and Papuan groups in the South Pacific. Recently, several anthropologists have attempted to synthesize their findings and have shown striking parallels in the cultural conditions out of which these movements arose. In every case, severe societal disruption preceded the outbreak of widespread nativistic cult behavior. According to Anthony F. C. Wallace, who has gone farthest toward constructing a general theory of cult formation, when the disruption has proceeded so far that many members of a society find it difficult or impossible to fulfill their physical and psychological needs, or to relieve severe anxiety through the ordinary culturally approved methods, the society will be susceptible to what Wallace has termed a "revitalization movement." This is a convulsive attempt to change or revivify important cultural beliefs and values, and frequently to eliminate alien influences. Such movements promise and often provide participants with better means of dealing with their changed circumstances, thus reducing their very high level of internal stress.

American Indian tribes, for example, experienced a series of such convulsions as the tide of white settlers rolled west. The Indians were pushed onto reservations and provided with Indian agents, missionaries, and physicians, who took over many of the functions hitherto assumed by chiefs and medicine men. Indian craftsmen (and craftswomen) were replaced by dealers in the white man's implements. Most hunters and warriors also lost their vocations and consequently their self-respect. What an anthropologist wrote of one tribe was true of many others: "From cultural maturity as Pawnees they were reduced to cultural infancy as civilized men."

One of the last major religious upheavals among the Indians was the Ghost Dance cult which spread from Nevada through Oregon and northern California in the 1870s, and a similar movement among the Rocky Mountain and western plains Indians about 1890. Although cult beliefs varied somewhat from tribe to tribe, converts generally were persuaded that if they followed certain prescribed rituals, including the dance, they would soon return to their old ways of living. Even their dead relatives would be restored to life. Most Indians were too conscious of their military weakness to challenge their white masters directly. Ghost Dancers among the Dakota Sioux, however, influenced by the militant proselyter Sitting Bull, became convinced that true believers could not be harmed by the white man's bullets and that Sioux warriors would drive the intruders from Indian lands. Their dreams were rudely smashed at the massacre of Wounded Knee Creek in December 1890.

The Boxer movement in China, 1898 to 1900, resembled in many respects the Indian Ghost Dance cults; however, the Boxers, more numerous and perhaps less demoralized than the Indians, aimed more directly at removing foreign influences from their land. The movement erupted first in Shantung province where foreigners, especially Japanese, British, and Germans, were most aggressive. A flood of the Yellow River had recently deprived about a million people in the province of food and shelter. Banditry was rampant, organized government ineffective. The Boxer movement, based on the belief that these tragic conditions were due almost entirely to the "foreign devils" and their agents, determined to drive the enemy out of China. Boxers went into action carrying charms and chanting incantations supposed to make them invulnerable to the foreigners' bullets. The first object of the Boxers' nativistic fury were Chinese who had converted to Christianity, the intruders' religion. The patriots then attacked railroad and telegraph lines, leading symbols of foreign influence. Finally, the Boxers turned against the foreigners themselves, slaughtering many. Not until after the Boxers carried on a two-month siege of the foreign community in Peking did American, European, and Japanese armies crush the movement.

Other revitalization attempts proved more successful than the Boxers or Ghost Dancers. The Gaiwiio movement, for example, helped the Iroquois Indians of western New York State to retain their identity as a culture while adjusting successfully to an encroaching white civilization during the first decade of the nineteenth century. The movement implanted a new moral code among the Indians, enjoining sobriety and family stability and encouraging acceptance of Western technology, while revivifying cohesive Indian traditions.

Dominant as well as conquered peoples, Ralph Linton has pointed out, undergo nativistic movements. Dominant groups, he observed, are sometimes threatened "not only by foreign invasion or domestic revolt but also by the invidious process of assimilation which might, in the long run, destroy their distinctive powers and privileges." Under such circumstances, Linton concluded, "the frustrations which motivate nativistic movements in inferior or dominated groups" are "replaced by anxieties which produce very much the same [nativistic] result" in dominant groups.

Communist "brainwashers" have consciously attempted to achieve results comparable to those obtained by prophets of movements like the Ghost Dance cult and the Boxers. They create intolerable stress within individuals, not through rapid societal change, but by intentional physical debilitation and continual accusations, cross-examinations, and use of other anxiety-provoking techniques. Then they offer their prisoners an escape from the induced psychological torment: conversion to the new gospel.

The similarity in the mental processes involved in "brainwashing" and in the formation of nativistic movements becomes even clearer upon examination of the Chinese Communist attempt to establish their doctrines in mainland China. Again, the Communists intentionally have created conditions like those out of which nativistic cults have arisen more spontaneously in other societies. In addition to the stress which ordinarily would accompany rapid industrialization of an economically backward society, the Chinese leaders have provoked additional anxiety through the systematic use of group confessions and denunciations and have intentionally disrupted family life. Hostility toward the American enemy has been purposely aroused and used to unify the masses, as well as to justify the repression of millions of alleged internal enemies. The whole population has been continually urged to repent their sins and to adopt wholeheartedly the Communist gospel, which had a strong nativistic component. As a psychologist has remarked, to a large extent the Chinese Communists provide both the disease and the cure.

The ferocious outbreak of nativism in the United States after World War I was not consciously planned or provoked by any individual or group, although some Americans took advantage of the movement once it started. Rather, the Red Scare, like the Gaiwiio and the Boxer movements described above, was brought on largely by a number of severe social and economic dislocations which threatened the national equilibrium. The full extent and the shocking effects of these disturbances of 1919 have not yet been adequately described. Runaway prices, a brief but sharp stock market crash and business depression, revolutions throughout Europe, widespread fear of domestic revolt, bomb explosions, and an outpouring of radical literature were distressing enough. These sudden difficulties, moreover, served to exaggerate the disruptive effects already produced by the social and intellectual ravages of the World War and the preceding reform era, and by the arrival, before the war, of millions of new immigrants. This added stress intensified the hostility of Americans strongly antagonistic to minority groups, and brought new converts to blatant nativism from among those who ordinarily were not overtly hostile toward radicals or recent immigrants.

Citizens who joined the crusade for one hundred percent Americanism sought, primarily, a unifying force which would halt the apparent disintegration of their culture. The movement, they felt, would eliminate those foreign influences which the one hundred percenters believed were the major cause of their anxiety.

Many of the postwar sources of stress were also present during World War I, and the Red Scare, as John Higham has observed, was partly an exaggeration of wartime passions. In 1917–1918 German-Americans served as the object of almost all our nativistic fervor; they were the threatening intruders who refused to become good citizens. "They used America," a patriotic author declared in 1918 of two million German-Americans, "they never loved her. They clung to their old language, their old customs, and cared nothing for ours. . . . As a class they were clannish beyond all other races coming here." Fear of subversion by German agents was almost as extravagant in 1917–1918 as anxiety about "reds" in the postwar period. Attorney General Thomas Watt Gregory reported to a friend in May 1918 that "we not infrequently receive as many as fifteen hundred letters in a single day suggesting disloyalty and the making of investigations."

Opposition to the war by radical groups helped smooth the transition among American nativists from hatred of everything German to fear of radical revolution. The two groups of enemies were associated also for other reasons. High government officials declared after the war that German leaders planned and subsidized the Bolshevik Revolution. When bombs blasted homes and public buildings in nine cities in June 1919, the director of the Justice Department's Bureau of Investigation asserted that the bombers were "connected with Russian bolshevism, aided by Hun money." In November 1919, a year after the armistice, a popular magazine warned of "the Russo-German movement that is now trying to dominate America.". . .

Even the wartime hostility toward German-Americans, however, is more understandable when seen in the light of recent anthropological and psychological studies. World War I disturbed Americans not only because of the real threat posed by enemy armies and a foreign ideology. For many citizens it had the further effect of shattering an already weakened intellectual tradition. When the European governments decided to fight, they provided shocking evidence that man was not, as most educated members of Western society had believed, a rational creature progressing steadily, if slowly, toward control of his environment. When the great powers declared war in 1914, many Americans as well as many Europeans were stunned. . . .

Americans were jolted by new blows to their equilibrium after entering the war. Four million men were drafted away from familiar surroundings and some of them experienced the terrible carnage of trench warfare. Great numbers of women left home to work in war industries or to replace men in other jobs. Negroes flocked to northern industrial areas by the hundreds of thousands, and their first mass migration from the South created violent racial antagonism in northern cities.

During the war, also, Americans sanctioned a degree of government control over the economy which deviated sharply from traditional economic individualism. Again, fears aroused before the war were aggravated, for the reform legislation of the Progressive era had tended to increase government intervention, and many citizens were further perturbed by demands that the federal government enforce even higher standards of economic and social morality. By 1919, therefore, some prewar progressives as well as conservatives feared the gradual disappearance of highly valued individual opportunity and responsibility. Their fears were fed by strong postwar calls for continued large-scale government controls—extension of federal operation of railroads and of the Food Administration for example.

The prime threat to these long-held individualistic values, however, and the most powerful immediate stimulus to the revitalistic response, came from Russia. There the Bolshevik conquerors proclaimed their intention of exporting Marxist ideology. If millions of Americans were disturbed in 1919 by the specter of communism, the underlying reason was not fear of foreign invasion—Russia, after all, was still a backward nation recently badly defeated by German armies. The real threat was the potential spread of communist ideas. These, the one hundred percenters realized with horror, possessed a genuine appeal for reformers and for the economically underprivileged, and if accepted they would complete the transformation of America.

A clear picture of the Bolshevik tyranny was not yet available; therefore, as after the French Revolution, those who feared the newly successful ideology turned to fight the revolutionary ideals. So the *Saturday Evening Post* declared editorially in November 1919 that

"History will see our present state of mind as one with that preceding the burning of witches, the children's crusade, the great tulip craze, and other examples of softening of the world brain." The *Post* referred not to the Red Scare or the impending Palmer Raids, but to the spread of communist ideology. Its editorial concluded: "The need of the country is not more idealism, but more pragmatism; not communism, but common sense." One of the most powerful patriotic groups, the National Security League, called upon members early in 1919 to "teach 'Americanism.' This means the fighting of Bolshevism . . . by the creation of well-defined National Ideals." Members "must preach Americanism and instil the idealism of America's Wars, and that American spirit of service which believes in giving as well as getting." New York attorney, author, and educator Henry Waters Taft warned a Carnegie Hall audience late in 1919 that Americans must battle "a propaganda which is tending to undermine our most cherished social and political institutions and is having the effect of producing widespread unrest among the poor and the ignorant, especially those of foreign birth."

When the war ended Americans also confronted the disturbing possibility, pointed up in 1919 by the struggle over the League of Nations, that Europe's struggles would continue to be their own. These factors combined to make World War I a traumatic experience for millions of citizens. As Senator James Reed of Missouri observed in August 1919, "This country is still suffering from shell shock. Hardly anyone is in a normal state of mind. . . . A great storm has swept over the intellectual world and its ravages and disturbances still exist."

The wartime "shell shock" left many Americans extraordinarily susceptible to psychological stress caused by postwar social and economic turbulence. Most important for the course of the Red Scare, many of these disturbances had their greatest effect on individuals already antagonistic toward minorities. First of all, there was some real evidence of danger to the nation in 1919, and the nation provided the chief emotional support for many Americans who responded easily to charges of an alien radical menace. Violence flared throughout Europe after the war and revolt lifted radicals to power in several Eastern and Central European nations. Combined with the earlier Bolshevik triumph in Russia these revolutions made Americans look more anxiously at radicals here. Domestic radicals encouraged these fears; they became unduly optimsitic about their own chances of success and boasted openly of their coming triumph. Scores of new foreign language anarchist and communist journals, most of them written by and for Southern and Eastern European immigrants, commenced publication, and the established radical press became more exuberant. These periodicals never tired of assuring readers in 1919 that "the United States seems to be on the verge of a revolutionary crisis." American newspapers and magazines reprinted selections from radical speeches, pamphlets, and periodicals so their readers could see what dangerous ideas were abroad in the land. Several mysterious bomb explosions and bombing attempts, reported in bold front page headlines in newspapers across the country, frightened the public in 1919. To many citizens these seemed part of an organized campaign of terror carried on by alien radicals intending to bring down the federal government. The great strikes of 1919 and early 1920 aroused similar fears.

Actually American radical organizations in 1919 were disorganized and poverty-stricken. The Communists were inept, almost without contact with American workers and not yet dominated or subsidized by Moscow. The IWW was shorn of its effective leaders, distrusted by labor, and generally declining in influence and power. Violent anarchists were isolated in a handful of tiny, unconnected local organizations. One or two of these anarchist groups probably carried out the "bomb conspiracy" of 1919; but the extent of the "conspiracy" can be judged from the fact that the bombs killed a total of two men during the year, a night watchman and one of the bomb throwers, and seriously wounded one person, a maid in the home of a Georgia senator.

Nevertheless, prophesies of national disaster abounded in 1919, even among high government officials. Secretary of State Robert Lansing confided to his diary that we were in real peril of social revolution. Attorney General A. Mitchell Palmer advised the House Appropriations Committee that "on a certain day, which we have been advised of," radicals would attempt "to rise up and destroy the Government at one fell swoop." Senator Charles Thomas of Colorado warned that "the country is on the verge of a volcanic upheaval." And Senator Miles Poindexter of Washington declared, "There is real danger that the government will fall." . . .

The slight evidence of danger from radical organizations aroused such wild fear only because Americans had already encountered other threats to cultural stability. However, the dislocations caused by the war and the menace of communism alone would not have produced such a vehement nativistic response. Other postwar challenges to the social and economic order made the crucial difference.

Of considerable importance was the skyrocketing cost of living.

Retail prices more than doubled between 1915 and 1920, and the price rise began gathering momentum in the spring of 1919. . . .

Then the wave of postwar strikes—there were 3,600 of them in 1919 involving over 4,000,000 workers—reached a climax in the fall of 1919. A national steel strike began in September and nationwide coal and rail walkouts were scheduled for November 1. Unions gained in membership and power during the war, and in 1919 labor leaders were under strong pressure to help workers catch up to or go ahead of mounting living costs. Nevertheless, influential government officials attributed the walkouts to radical activities. Early in 1919, Secretary of Labor William B. Wilson declared in a public speech that recent major strikes in Seattle, Butte, Montana, and Lawrence, Massachusetts, had been instituted by the Bolsheviks and the IWW for the sole purpose of bringing about a nationwide revolution in the United States. During the steel strike of early fall, 1919, a Senate investigating committee reported that "behind this strike there is massed a considerable element of IWW's, anarchists, revolutionists, and Russian soviets." . . . In April 1920 the head of the Justice Department's General Intelligence Division, J. Edgar Hoover, declared in a public hearing that at least fifty percent of the influence behind the recent series of strikes was traceable directly to communist agents.

Furthermore, the nation suffered a sharp economic depression in late 1918 and early 1919, caused largely by sudden cancellations of war orders. Returning servicemen found it difficult to obtain jobs during this period, which coincided with the beginning of the Red Scare. The former soldiers had been uprooted from their homes and told that they were engaged in a patriotic crusade. Now they came back to find "reds" criticizing their country and threatening the government with violence, Negroes holding good jobs in the big cities, prices terribly high, and workers who had not served in the armed forces striking for higher wages. A delegate won prolonged applause from the 1919 American Legion Convention when he denounced radical aliens, exclaiming, "Now that the war is over and they are in lucrative positions while our boys haven't a job, we've got to send those scamps to hell." The major part of the mobs which invaded meeting halls of immigrant organizations and broke up radical parades, especially during the first half of 1919, was comprised of men in uniform.

A variety of other circumstances combined to add even more force to the postwar nativistic movement. Long before the new immigrants were seen as potential revolutionsts they became the objects of widespread hostility. The peak of immigration from Southern and Eastern Europe occurred in the fifteen years before the war; during that period almost ten million immigrants from those areas entered the country. Before the anxious eyes of members of all classes of Americans, the newcomers crowded the cities and began to disturb the economic and social order. Even without other postwar disturbances a nativistic movement of some strength could have been predicted when the wartime solidarity against the German enemy began to wear off in 1919.

In addition, not only were the European revolutions most successful in Eastern and to a lesser extent in Southern Europe, but aliens from these areas predominated in American radical organizations. At least ninety percent of the members of the two American Communist parties formed in 1919 were born in Eastern Europe. The anarchist groups whose literature and bombs captured the imagination of the American public in 1919 were composed almost entirely of Italian, Spanish, and Slavic aliens. Justice Department announcements and statements by politicians and the press stressed the predominance of recent immigrants in radical organizations. Smoldering prejudice against new immigrants and identification of these immigrants with European as well as American radical movements, combined with other sources of postwar stress to create one of the most frenzied and one of the most widespread nativistic movements in the nation's history.

The result, akin to the movements incited by the Chinese Boxers or the Indian Ghost Dancers, was called Americanism or one hundred percent Americanism.[1] Its objective was to end the apparent erosion of American values and the disintegration of American culture. By reaffirming those beliefs, customs, symbols, and traditions felt to be the foundation of our way of life, by enforcing conformity among the population, and by purging the nation of dangerous foreigners, the one hundred percenters expected to heal societal divisions and to tighten defenses against cultural change.

Panegyrics celebrating our history and institutions were delivered regularly in almost every American school, church, and public hall in 1919 and 1920. Many of these fervent addresses went far beyond the usual patriotic declarations. Audiences were usually urged to join a crusade to protect our hallowed institutions. Typical of the more moderate statements was Columbia University President Nicholas

---

[1] The word "Americanism" was used by the nativists of the 1840s and 1850s. During World War I, the stronger phrase "100 percent Americanism" was invented to suit the belligerent drive for universal conformity.

Murray Butler's insistence in April 1919 that "America will be saved, not by those who have only contempt and despite for her founders and her history, but by those who look with respect and reverence upon the great series of happenings extending from the voyage of the Mayflower." . . .

The American flag became a sacred symbol. Legionaires demanded that citizens "Run the Reds out from the land whose flag they sully." Men suspected of radical leanings were forced to kiss the stars and stripes. . . .

Recent immigrants, especially, were called upon to show evidence of real conversion. Great pressure was brought to bear upon the foreign-born to learn English and to forget their native tongues. As Senator William S. Kenyon of Iowa declared in October 1919, "The time has come to make this a one-language nation." An editorial in the *American Legion Weekly* took a further step and insisted that the one language must be called "American. Why even in Mexico they do not stand for calling the language the Spanish language."

Immigrants were also expected to adopt our customs and to snuff out remnants of Old World cultures. Genteel prewar and wartime movements to speed up assimilation took on a "frightened and feverish aspect." Welcoming members of an Americanization conference called by his department, Secretary of the Interior Franklin K. Lane exclaimed in May 1919, "You have been gathered together as crusaders in a great cause. . . . There is no other question of such importance before the American people as the solidifying and strengthening of true American sentiment." A Harvard University official told the conference that "The Americanization movement . . . gives men a new and holy religion. . . . It challenges each one of us to a renewed consecration and devotion to the welfare of the nation." The National Security League boasted, in 1919, of establishing one thousand study groups to teach teachers how to inculcate "Americanism" in their foreign-born students. A critic of the prevailing mood protested against "one of our best advertised American mottoes, 'One country, one language, one flag,' " which, he complained, had become the basis for a fervent nationwide program.

As the postwar movement for one hundred percent Americanism gathered momentum, the deportation of alien nonconformists became increasingly its most compelling objective. Asked to suggest a remedy for the nationwide upsurge in radical activity, the Mayor of Gary, Indiana, replied, "Deportation is the answer, deportation of these leaders who talk treason in America and deportation of those who agree with them and work with them." "We must remake

America," a popular author averred, "We must purify the source of America's population and keep it pure. . . . We must insist that there shall be an American loyalty, brooking no amendment or qualification." . . .

Politicians quickly sensed the possibilities of the popular frenzy for Americanism. Mayor Ole Hanson of Seattle, Governor Calvin Coolidge of Massachusetts, and General Leonard Wood became the early heroes of the movement. The man in the best political position to take advantage of the popular feeling, however, was Attorney General A. Mitchell Palmer. In 1919, especially after the President's physical collapse, only Palmer had the authority, staff, and money necessary to arrest and deport huge numbers of radical aliens. The virulent phase of the movement for one hundred percent Americanism came early in 1920, when Palmer's agents rounded up for deportation over six thousand aliens and prepared to arrest thousands more suspected of membership in radical organizations. Most of these aliens were taken without warrants, many were detained for unjustifiably long periods of time, and some suffered incredible hardships. Almost all, however, were eventually released.

After Palmer decided that he could ride the postwar fears into the presidency, he set out calculatingly to become the symbol of one hundred percent Americanism. The Palmer raids, his antilabor activities, and his frequent pious professions of patriotism during the campaign were all part of this effort. Palmer was introduced by a political associate to the Democratic party's annual Jackson Day dinner in January 1920 as "an American whose Americanism cannot be misunderstood." In a speech delivered in Georgia shortly before the primary election (in which Palmer won control of the state's delegation to the Democratic National Convention), the Attorney General asserted: "I am myself an American and I love to preach my doctrine before undiluted one hundred percent Americans, because my platform is, in a word, undiluted Americanism and undying loyalty to the republic." . . .

Unfortunately for political candidates like Palmer and Wood, most of the social and economic disturbances which had activated the movement they sought to lead gradually disappeared during the first half of 1920. The European revolutions were put down; by 1920 communism seemed to have been isolated in Russia. Bombings ceased abruptly after June 1919, and fear of new outrages gradually abated. Prices of food and clothing began to recede during the spring. Labor strife almost vanished from our major industries after a brief railroad walkout in April. Prosperity returned after mid-1919 and by early 1920 business activity and employment levels exceeded their wartime peaks. At the same time, it became clear that the Senate would not pass Wilson's peace treaty and that America was free to turn its back on the responsibilities of world leadership. The problems associated with the new immigrants remained; so did the disillusionment with Europe and with many old intellectual ideals. Nativism did not disappear from the American scene; but the frenzied attempt to revitalize the culture did peter out in 1920. The handful of unintimidated men, especially Assistant Secretary of Labor Louis F. Post, who had used the safeguards provided by American law to protect many victims of the Red Scare, found increasing public support. On the other hand, politicians like Palmer, Wood, and Hanson were left high and dry, proclaiming the need for one hundred percent Americanism to an audience which no longer urgently cared.

It is ironic that in 1920 the Russian leaders of the Comintern finally took charge of the American Communist movement, provided funds and leadership, and ordered the Communist factions to unite and participate actively in labor organizations and strikes. These facts were reported in the American press. Thus a potentially serious foreign threat to national security appeared just as the Red Scare evaporated, providing a final illustration of the fact that the frenzied one hundred percenters of 1919–1920 were affected less by the "red menace" than by a series of social and economic dislocations.

Although the Red Scare died out in 1920, its effects lingered. Hostility toward immigrants, mobilized in 1919–1920, remained strong enough to force congressional passage of restrictive immigration laws. Some of the die-hard one hundred percenters found a temporary home in the Ku Klux Klan until that organization withered away during the mid-twenties. As its most lasting accomplishments, the movement for one hundred percent Americanism fostered a spirit of conformity in the country, a satisfaction with the status quo, and the equation of reform ideologies with foreign enemies. Revitalization movements have helped many societies adapt successfully to new conditions. The movement associated with the American Red Scare, however, had no such effect. True, it unified the culture against the threats faced in 1919–1920; but the basic problems—a damaged value system, an unrestrained business cycle, a hostile Russia, and communism—were left for future generations of Americans to deal with in their own fashion.

11

The Klan's Fight for Americanism

Hiram Wesley Evans

The hysteria and repression associated with the Red Scare began to subside in 1920. Nevertheless, "100 percent Americanism" remained a significant factor throughout the 1920s, finding dramatic expression in the activities of the Ku Klux Klan. In 1926, Hiram Wesley Evans, a Klan leader, wrote a remarkably candid and revealing article justifying the Klan's struggle for "Native, White, Protestant Supremacy." It is interesting to compare Evans' revelations about the thinking of people prone to believe in conspiracy theories with the analyses of scholars. Particularly important is Evans' emphasis on immigration as a source of "racial and spiritual treason," a fear reflected in the restrictive immigration laws passed in the early twenties.

The Ku Klux Klan on last Thanksgiving Day passed its tenth anniversary. In one decade it has made a place and won a record for achievement which are almost, if not quite, unique in the history of great popular movements. It has not merely grown from a handful to a membership of millions, from poverty to riches, from ob-

Reprinted from The North American Review, *CCXXIII, 8 (March 1926), 33–63, by permission of the University of Northern Iowa.*

scurity to great influence, from fumbling impotence to the leadership in the greatest cause now before the American people. . . .

The greatest achievement so far has been to formulate, focus, and gain recognition for an idea—the idea of preserving and developing America first and chiefly for the benefit of the children of the pioneers who made America, and only and definitely along the lines of the purpose and spirit of those pioneers. The Klan cannot claim to have created this idea: it has long been a vague stirring in the souls of the plain people. But the Klan can fairly claim to have given it purpose, method, direction, and a vehicle. When the Klan first appeared the nation was in the confusion of sudden awakening from the lovely dream of the melting pot, disorganized and helpless before the invasion of aliens and alien ideas. After ten years of the Klan it is in arms for defense.This is our great achievement.

The second is more selfish; we have won the leadership in the movement for Americanism. Except for a few lonesome voices, almost drowned by the clamor of the alien and the alien-minded "Liberal", the Klan alone faces the invader. This is not to say that the Klan has gathered into its membership all who are ready to fight for America. The Klan is the champion, but it is not merely an organization. It is an idea, a faith, a purpose, an organized crusade. No recruit to the cause has ever been really lost. Though men and women drop from the ranks they remain with us in purpose, and can be depended on fully in any crisis. Also, there are many millions who have never joined, but who think and feel and—when called on—fight with us. This is our real strength, and no one who ignores it can hope to understand America today.

Other achievements of these ten years have been the education of the millions of our own membership in citizenship, the suppression of much lawlessness and increase of good government wherever we have become strong, the restriction of immigration, and the defeat of the Catholic attempt to seize the Democratic party. All these we have helped, and all are important.

The outstanding proof of both our influence and our service, however, has been in creating, outside our ranks as well as in them, not merely the growing national concentration on the problems of Americanism, but also a growing sentiment against radicalism, cosmopolitanism, and alienism of all kinds. We have produced instead a sane and progressive conservatism along national lines. We have enlisted our racial instincts for the work of preserving and developing our American traditions and customs. This was most strikingly shown in the elections last fall, when the conservative reaction amazed all politicians—especially the LaFollette rout in the Northwest. This reaction added enormously to the plurality of the President, the size of which was the great surprise of the election.

I wish it might fairly be claimed that the Klan from the beginning had this vision of its mission. Instead the beginnings were groping and futile, as well as feeble; they involved errors which long prevented any important achievement. The chief idea of the founders seems to have been merely to start a new fraternal society, based on rather vague sentiments of brotherhood among white Americans, and of loyalty to the nation and to Protestantism. There was also a sentimental reverence for the Klan of the 'sixties which led to revival of the old name and some of the ritual. There was finally the basic idea of white supremacy, but this was also at the time a mere sentiment, except as it applied to some Negro unrest. . . .

To us who know the Klan today, its influence, purpose and future, the fact that it can have grown from such beginnings is nothing less than a miracle, possible only through one of those mysterious interventions in human affairs which are called Providence. The fact is, as we see now, that beneath the stupid or dangerous oratory of those early leaders lay certain fundamental truths, quite unseen by them, and then hardly bigger than the vital germ in a grain of corn, but which matured automatically.

The hate and invisible government ideas, however, were what gave the Klan its first great growth, enlisted some 100,000 members, provided wealth for a few leaders, and brought down upon the organization the condemnation of most of the country, leaving it a reputation from which it has not yet recovered. But even before outside indignation had appeared there began an inside reaction, caused by abuses and excesses and by the first stirrings of the purposes which now dominate. Thus began the reform of the Klan by itself, which gained steadily until it won full control in 1922. It laid the basis for the astounding growth of the last three years, and for the present immense influence.

This reform did more than merely rectify the old abuses; it developed into full life the hidden but vital germs, and released one of the most irresistible forces in human affairs, the fundamental instinct of race pride and loyalty—what Lothrop Stoddard calls "the imperious urge of superior heredity." Closely associated with it are two other instincts vital to success among the northern races: patriotism, stimulated to unusual activity by the hyphenism revealed in the World War; and spiritual independence, a revival of the individualism which sprang up just as the Nordic races began to assert themselves in their great blossoming of the last four centuries, and which found its chief expression in Protestantism. These ideas gave direction and guidance to the reforms demanded by the rank and file three years ago. They have been further developed, made more definite and more purposeful, and they are the soul of the Klan today.

The direct reforms brought about were several. First was the stopping of any exercise of "invisible government." This was reinforced by a change in the oath, by which all Klansmen are sworn to uphold legally constituted officers in enforcing the law at all times. One result of this is to be seen in the decrease of lawlessness in Klan territory. We can justly claim credit for the remarkable improvement as regards lynching in the last two years. . . .

Most important of all has been the formulation of the true Klan purposes into definite principles. This has been a gradual process. We in the lead found ourselves with a following inspired in many ways beyond our understanding, with beliefs and purposes which they themselves only vaguely understood and could not express, but for the fulfillment of which they depended on us. We found ourselves, too, at the head of an army with unguessable influence to produce results for which responsibility would rest on us—the leaders—but which we had not foreseen and for which we were not prepared. As the solemn responsibility to give right leadership to these millions, and to make right use of this influence, was brought home to us, we were compelled to analyze, put into definite words, and give purpose to these half-conscious impulses.

The Klan, therefore, has now come to speak for the great mass of Americans of the old pioneer stock. We believe that it does fairly and faithfully represent them, and our proof lies in their support. To understand the Klan, then, it is necessary to understand the character and present mind of the mass of old-stock Americans. The mass, it must be remembered, as distinguished from the intellectually mongrelized "Liberals."

These are, in the first place, a blend of various peoples of the so-called Nordic race, the race which, with all its faults, has given the world almost the whole of modern civilization. The Klan does not try to represent any people but these. . . .

Nordic Americans for the last generation have found themselves increasingly uncomfortable, and finally deeply distressed. There appeared first confusion in thought and opinion, a groping and hesitancy about national affairs and private life alike, in sharp contrast to the clear, straightforward purposes of our earlier years. There was futility in religion, too, which was in many ways even more distressing. Presently we began to find that we were dealing with strange ideas; policies that always sounded well [*sic*], but somehow always made us still more uncomfortable.

Finally came the moral breakdown that has been going on for two decades. One by one all our traditional moral standards went by the boards, or were so disregarded that they ceased to be binding. The sacredness of our Sabbath, of our homes, of chastity, and finally even of our right to teach our own children in our own schools fundamental facts and truths were torn away from us. Those who maintained the old standards did so only in the face of constant ridicule.

Along with this went economic distress. The assurance for the future of our children dwindled. We found our great cities and the control of much of our industry and commerce taken over by strangers, who stacked the cards of success and prosperity against us. Shortly they came to dominate our government. The bloc system by which this was done is now familiar to all. Every kind of inhabitant except the Americans gathered in groups which operated as units in politics, under orders of corrupt, self-seeking and un-American leaders, who both by purchase and threat enforced their demands on politicians. Thus it came about that the interests of Americans were always the last to be considered by either national or city governments, and that the native Americans were constantly discriminated against, in business, in legislation, and in administrative government.

So the Nordic American today is a stranger in large parts of the land his fathers gave him. Moreover, he is a most unwelcome stranger, one much spit upon, and one to whom even the right to have his own opinions and to work for his own interests is now denied with jeers and revilings. "We must Americanize the Americans," a distinguished immigrant said recently. Can anything more clearly show the state to which the real American has fallen in this country which was once his own?

Our falling birth rate, the result of all this, is proof of our distress. We no longer feel that we can be fair to children we bring into the world, unless we can make sure from the start that they shall have capital or education or both, so that they need never compete with those who now fill the lower rungs of the ladder of success. We dare no longer risk letting our youth "make its own way" in the conditions under which we live. So even our unborn children are being crowded out of their birthright!

All this has been true for years, but it was the World War that gave us our first hint of the real cause of our troubles, and began to crystallize our ideas. The war revealed that millions whom we had allowed to share our heritage and prosperity, and whom we had assumed had become part of us, were in fact not wholly so. They had other loyalties: each was willing—anxious!—to sacrifice the interests of the country that had given him shelter to the interests of the one he was supposed to have cast off; each in fact did use the freedom and political power we had given him against ourselves whenever he could see any profit for his older loyalty.

This, of course, was chiefly in international affairs, and the excitement caused by the discovery of disloyalty subsided rapidly after the war ended. But it was not forgotten by the Nordic Americans. They had been awakened and alarmed; they began to suspect that the hyphenism which had been shown was only a part of what existed; their quiet was not that of renewed sleep, but of strong men waiting very watchfully. And presently they began to form decisions about all those aliens who were Americans for profit only.

They decided that even the crossing of salt water did not dim a a single spot on a leopard; that an alien usually remains an alien no matter what is done to him, what veneer of education he gets, what oaths he takes, nor what public attitudes he adopts. They decided that the melting pot was a ghastly failure, and remembered that the very name was coined by a member of one of the races—the Jews—which most determinedly refuses to melt. They decided that in every way, as well as in politics, the alien in the vast majority of cases is unalterably fixed in his instincts, character, thought, and interests by centuries of racial selection and development, that he thinks first for his own people, works only with and for them, cares entirely for their interests, considers himself always one of them, and never an American. They decided that in character, instincts, thought, and purposes—in his whole soul—an alien remains fixedly alien to America and all it means.

They saw, too, that the alien was tearing down the American standard of living, especially in the lower walks. It became clear that while the American can outwork the alien, the alien can so far under-live the American as to force him out of all competitive labor. So they came to realize that the Nordic can easily survive and rule and increase if he holds for himself the advantages won by strength and daring of his ancestors in times of stress and peril, but that if he surrenders those advantages to the peoples who could not share the stress, he will soon be driven below the level at which he can exist by their low standards, low living, and fast breeding. And they saw that the low standard aliens of Eastern and Southern Europe were doing just that thing to us.

They learned, though more slowly, that alien ideas are just as dangerous to us as the aliens themselves, no matter how plausible such ideas may sound. With most of the plain people this conclusion is based simply on the fact that the alien ideas do not work well for them. Others went deeper and came to understand that the differences in racial background, in breeding, instinct, character, and emotional point of view are more important than logic. So ideas which may be perfectly healthy for an alien may also be poisonous for Americans.

Finally they learned the great secret of the propagandists: that success in corrupting public opinion depends on putting out the subversive ideas without revealing their source. They came to suspect that "prejudice" against foreign ideas is really a protective device of nature against mental food that may be indigestible. They saw, finally, that the alien leaders in America act on this theory, and that there is a steady flood of alien ideas being spread over the country, always carefully disguised as American.

As they learned all this the Nordic Americans have been gradually arousing themselves to defend their homes and their own kind of civilization. They have not known just how to go about it; the idealist philanthropy and good-natured generosity which led to the philosophy of the melting pot have died hard. Resistance to the peaceful invasion of the immigrant is no such simple matter as snatching up weapons and defending frontiers, nor has it much spectacular emotionalism to draw men to the colors.

The old-stock Americans are learning, however. They have begun to arm themselves for this new type of warfare. Most important, they have broken away from the fetters of the false ideals and philanthropy which put aliens ahead of their own children and their own race.

To do this they have had to reject completely—and perhaps for the moment the rejection is a bit too complete—the whole body of "liberal" ideas which they had followed with such simple, unquestioning faith. The first and immediate cause of the break with liberalism was that it had provided no defense against the alien invasion, but instead had excused it—even defended it against Americanism. Liberalism is today charged in the mind of most Americans with nothing less than national, racial, and spiritual treason.

But this is only the last of many causes of distrust. The plain people now see that liberalism has come completely under the dominance of weaklings and parasites whose alien "idealism" reaches its logical peak in the Bolshevist platform of "produce as little as you can, beg or steal from those who do produce, and kill the producer for thinking he is better than you." Not that all liberalism goes so far, but it all seems to be on that road. The average liberal idea is apparently that those who can produce should carry the unfit, and let the unfit rule them.

This aberration would have been impossible, of course, if American liberalism had kept its feet on the ground. Instead it became wholly academic, lost all touch with the plain people, disowned its instincts and common sense, and lived in a world of pure, high, groundless logic.

Worse yet, this became a world without moral standards. Our forefathers had standards—the liberals today say they were narrow—and they had consciences and knew that liberalism must be kept within fixed bounds. They knew that tolerance of things that touch the foundations of the home, of decency, of patriotism, or of race loyalty is not lovely but deadly. Modern American liberalism has no such bounds. If it has a conscience it hides it shamefacedly; if it has any standards it conceals them well. If it has any convictions—but why be absurd? Its boast is that it has none except conviction in its own decadent religion of liberalism toward everything; toward the right of every man to make a fool or degenerate of himself and to try to corrupt others; in the right of any one to pull the foundations from under the house or poison the wells; in the right of children to play with matches in a powdermill!

The old stock Americans believe in liberalism, but not in this thing. It has undermined their Constitution and their national customs and institutions, it has corrupted the morals of their children, it has vitiated their thought, it has degenerated and perverted their education, it has tried to destroy their God. They want no more of it. They are trying to get back to decency and common sense. . . .

But the plain people realize also that merely stopping the alien flood does not restore Americanism, nor even secure us against final utter defeat. America must also defend herself against the enemy within, or we shall be corrupted and conquered by those to whom we have already given shelter. . . .

An equal danger is from disunity, so strikingly shown during the war and from a mongrelization of thought and purpose. It is not merely foreign policy that is involved; it is all our thought at home, our morals, education, social conduct—everything. We are already confused and disunited in every way; the alien groups themselves, and the skilful alien propaganda, are both tearing steadily at all that makes for unity in nationhood, or for the soul of Americanism. If the word "integrity" can still be used in its original meaning of singleness of purpose or thought, then we as a nation have lost all integrity. Yet our old American motto includes the words ". . . divided we fall!"

One more point about the present attitude of the old stock American: he has revived and increased his long-standing distrust of the Roman Catholic Church. It is for this that the native Americans, and the Klan as their leader, are most often denounced as intolerant and prejudiced. This is not because we oppose the Catholic more than we do the alien, but because our enemies recognize that patriotism and race loyalty cannot safely be denounced, while our own tradition of religious freedom gives them an opening here, if they can sufficiently confuse the issue.

The fact is, of course, that our quarrel with the Catholics is not religious but political. The Nordic race is, as is well-known, almost entirely Protestant, and there remains in its mental heritage an anti-Catholic attitude based on lack of sympathy with the Catholic psychology, on the historic opposition of the Roman Church to the Nordics' struggle for freedom and achievement, and on the memories of persecutions. But this strictly religious prejudice is not now active in America, and so far as I can learn, never has been. I do not know of a single manifestation in recent times of hostility to any Catholic because of his religion, nor to the Catholic Church because of its beliefs. Certainly the American has always granted to the Catholic not only full religious liberty, without interference or abuse either public or private, but also every civil, social, and political equality. Neither the present day Protestant nor the Klan wishes to change this in any degree. . . .

The real indictment against the Roman Church is that it is, fundamentally and irredeemably, in its leadership, in politics, in thought, and largely in membership, actually and actively alien, un-American and usually anti-American. The old stock Americans, with the exception of the few such of Catholic faith—who are in a class by themselves, standing tragically torn between their faith and their racial and national patriotism—see in the Roman Church today the chief leader of alienism, and the most dangerous alien power with a foothold inside our boundaries. It is this and nothing else that has revived hostility to Catholicism. By no stretch of the imagination can it fairly be called religious prejudice, though, now that the hostility has become active, it does derive some strength from the religious schism.

We Americans see many evidences of Catholic alienism. We believe that its official position and its dogma, its theocratic autocracy and its claim to full authority in temporal as well as spiritual matters, all make it impossible for it as a church, or for its members if they obey it, to cooperate in a free democracy in which Church and State have been separated. It is true that in this country the Roman Church speaks very softly on these points, so that many Catholics do not know them. It is also true that the Roman priests preach Americanism, subject to their own conception of Americanism, of course. But the Roman Church itself makes a point of the divine and unalterable character of its dogma, it has never seen fit to abandon officially any of these un-American attitudes, and it still teaches them in other countries. Until it does renounce them, we cannot believe anything except that they all remain in force, ready to be called into action whenever feasible, and temporarily hushed up only for expediency.

The hierarchical government of the Roman Church is equally at odds with Americanism. The Pope and the whole hierarchy have been for centuries almost wholly Italian. It is nonsense to suppose that a man, by entering a church, loses his race or national loyalties. The Roman Church today, therefore, is just what its name says—Roman; and it is impossible for its hierarchy or the policies they dictate to be in real sympathy with Americanism. Worse, the Italians have proven to be one of the least assimilable of people. The autocratic nature of the Catholic Church organization, and its suppression of free conscience or free decision, need not be discussed; they are unquestioned. Thus it is fundamental to the Roman Church to demand a supreme loyalty, overshadowing national or race loyalty, to a power that is inevitably alien, and which at the best must inevitably inculcate ideals un-American if not actively anti-American.

We find, too, that even in America, the majority of the leaders and of the priests of the Roman Church are either foreign-born, or of foreign parentage and training. They, like other aliens, are unable to teach Americanism if they wish, because both race and education prevent their understanding what it is. The service they give it, even if sincere, can at best produce only confusion of thought. Who would ask an American, for instance, to try to teach Italians their own language, history, and patriotism, even without the complication of religion?

Another difficulty is that the Catholic Church here constantly represents, speaks for, and cares for the interests of a large body of alien peoples. Most immigration of recent years, so unassimilable and fundamentally un-American, has been Catholic. The Catholics of American stock have been submerged and almost lost; the aliens and their interests dictate all policies of the Roman Church which are not dictated from Rome itself.

Also, the Roman Church seems to take pains to prevent the assimilation of these people. Its parochial schools, its foreign-born priests, the obstacles it places in the way of marriage with Protestants unless the children are bound in advance to Romanism, its persistent use of the foreign languages in church and school, its habit of grouping aliens together and thus creating insoluble alien masses—all these things strongly impede Americanization. Of course they also strengthen and solidify the Catholic Church, and make its work easier, and so are very natural, but the fact remains that they are hostile to Americanism.

Finally, there is the undeniable fact that the Roman Church takes an active part in American politics. It has not been content to accept in good faith the separation of Church and State, and constantly tries through political means to win advantages for itself and its people—in other words, to be a political power in America, as well as a spiritual power. Denials of Catholic activity in politics are too absurd to need discussion. The "Catholic vote" is as well recognized a factor as the "dry vote." All politicians take it for granted.

The facts are that almost everywhere, especially in the great industrial centers where the Catholics are strongest, they vote almost as a unit, under control of leaders of their own faith, always in support of the interests of the Catholic Church and of Catholic candidates without regard to other interests, and always also in support of alienism whenever there is an issue raised. They vote, in short, not as American citizens, but as aliens and Catholics! They form the biggest, strongest, most cohesive of all the alien blocs. On many occasions they form alliances with other alien blocs against American interests, as with the Jews in New York today, and with others in the case of the great opposition to immigration restriction. Incidentally they have been responsible for some of the worst abuses in American politics, and today are the chief support of such machines as that of Brennan in Chicago, Curley in Boston, and Tammany in New York.

All this might occur without direct sanction from the Roman Church, though that would not make it less a "Catholic" menace. But the evidence is that the Church acts directly and often controls these activities. The appearance of Roman clergy in "inside" political councils, the occasional necessity of "seeing" a prelate to accomplish political results, and above all the fact that during the fight in the

Democratic National Convention of 1924 the hotel lobbies and the corridors of Madison Square Garden were suddenly black with priests, all seem to prove that the Catholic Church acts in politics *as a church,* and that it must bear responsibility for these evils. . . .

This is the general state of mind of the Nordic Americans of the pioneer stock today. Many of them do not understand the reasons for their beliefs so fully as I have stated them, but the state of mind is there beyond doubt, and the reasons are true at all vital points. It is inevitable that these people are now in revolt. This is the movement to which the Klan, more through Providence than its own wisdom, has begun to give leadership.

The Ku Klux Klan, in short, is an organization which gives expression, direction, and purpose to the most vital instincts, hopes, and resentments of the old stock Americans, provides them with leadership, and is enlisting and preparing them for militant, constructive action toward fulfilling their racial and national destiny. Madison Grant summed up in a single sentence the grievances, purpose and type of membership of the Klan: "Our farmers and artisans . . . of American blood, to recognize and meet this danger." The Klan literally is once more the embattled American farmer and artisan, coordinated into a disciplined and growing army, and launched upon a definite crusade for Americanism!

This Providential history of the Klan, and the Providential place it has come to hold, give it certain definite characteristics. The disadvantages that go with them, as well as the advantages, may as well be admitted at once.

We are a movement of the plain people, very weak in the matter of culture, intellectual support, and trained leadership. We are demanding, and we expect to win, a return of power into the hands of the everyday, not highly cultured, not overly intellectualized, but entirely unspoiled and not de-Americanized, average citizen of the old stock. Our members and leaders are all of this class—the opposition of the intellectuals and liberals who held the leadership, betrayed Americanism, and from whom we expect to wrest control, is almost automatic.

This is undoubtedly a weakness. It lays us open to the charge of being "hicks" and "rubes" and "drivers of second-hand Fords." We admit it. Far worse, it makes it hard for us to state our case and advocate our crusade in the most effective way, for most of us lack skill in language. Worst of all, the need of trained leaders constantly hampers our progress and leads to serious blunders and internal troubles. If the Klan ever should fail it would be from this cause. All this we on the inside know far better than our critics, and regret more. Our leadership is improving, but for many years the Klan will be seeking better leaders, and the leaders praying for greater wisdom.

Serious as this is, and strange though our attitude may seem to the intellectuals, it does not worry us greatly. Every popular movement has suffered from just this handicap, yet the popular movements have been the mainsprings of progress, and have usually had to win against the "best people" of their time. Moreover, we can depend on getting this intellectual backing shortly. It is notable that when the plain people begin to win with one of their movements, such as the Klan, the very intellectuals who have scoffed and fought most bitterly presently begin to dig up sound—at least well-sounding—logic in support of the success. . . .

We are sure of the fundamental rightness of our cause, as it concerns both ourselves and the progress of the world. We believe that there can be no question of the right of the children of the men who made America to own and control America. We believe that when we allowed others to share our heritage, it was by our own generosity and by no right of theirs. We believe that therefore we have every right to protect ourselves when we find that they are betraying our trust and endangering us. We believe, in short, that we have the right to make America *American* and for Americans.

We believe also that only through this kind of a nation, and through development along these lines, can we best serve America, the whole world today, and the greater world yet unborn. We believe the hand of God was in the creation of the American stock and nation. We believe, too, in the right and duty of every man to fight for himself, his own children, his own nation and race. We believe in the parable of the talents, and mean to keep and use those entrusted to us—the race, spirit, and nationhood of America!

Finally, we believe in the vitality and driving power of our race: a faith based on the record of the Nordics throughout all history, and especially in America. J. P. Morgan had a motto which said, in effect, "Never bet against the future of America." We believe it is equally unsafe to bet against the future of any stock of the Nordic race, especially so finely blended and highly bred a stock as that of the sons of the pioneers. Handicaps, weaknesses, enemies and all, we will win!

Our critics have accused us of being merely a "protest movement," of being frightened; they say we fear alien competition, are in a panic because we cannot hold our own against the foreigners. That is partly true. We are a protest movement—protesting against being robbed. We are afraid of competition with peoples who would destroy our standard of living. We are suffering in many ways, we have been betrayed by our trusted leaders, we are half beaten already. But we are not frightened nor in a panic. We have merely awakened to the fact that we must fight for our own. We are going to fight—and win! . . .

Thus the Klan goes back to the American racial instincts, and to the common sense which is their first product, as the basis of its beliefs and methods. The fundamentals of our thought are convictions, not mere opinions. We are pleased that modern research is finding scientific backing for these convictions. We do not need them ourselves; we know that we are right in the same sense that a good Christian knows that he has been saved and that Christ lives—a thing which the intellectual can never understand. These convictions are no more to be argued about than is our love for our children; we are merely willing to state them for the enlightenment and conversion of others.

There are three of these great racial instincts, vital elements in both the historic and the present attempts to build an America which shall fulfill the aspirations and justify the heroism of the men who made the nation. These are the instincts of loyalty to the white race, to the traditions of America, and to the spirit of Protestantism, which has been an essential part of Americanism ever since the days of Roanoke and Plymouth Rock. They are condensed into the Klan slogan: "Native, white, Protestant supremacy."

First in the Klansman's mind is patriotism—America for Americans. He believes religiously that a betrayal of Americanism or the American race is treason to the most sacred of trusts, a trust from his fathers and a trust from God. He believes, too, that Americanism can only be achieved if the pioneer stock is kept pure. There is more than race pride in this. Mongrelization has been proven bad. It is only between closely related stocks of the same race that interbreeding has improved men; the kind of interbreeding that went on in the early days of America between English, Dutch, German, Hugenot, Irish, and Scotch.

Racial integrity is a very definite thing to the Klansman. It means even more than good citizenship, for a man may be in all ways a good citizen and yet a poor American, unless he has racial understanding of Americanism, and instinctive loyalty to it. It is in no way a reflection on any man to say that he is un-American; it is merely a statement that he is not one of us. It is often not even wise to try to make an American of the best of aliens. What he is may be spoiled without his becoming American. The races and stocks of men are as distinct as breeds of animals, and every boy knows that if one tries to train a bulldog to herd sheep, he has in the end neither a good bulldog nor a good collie.

Americanism, to the Klansman, is a thing of the spirit, a purpose and a point of view, that can only come through instinctive racial understanding. . . . The Klansman believes in the greatest possible diversity and individualism within the limits of the American spirit. But he believes also that few aliens can understand that spirit, that fewer try to, and that there must be resistance, intolerance even, toward anything that threatens it, or the fundamental national unity based upon it.

The second word in the Klansman's trilogy is "white". The white race must be supreme, not only in America but in the world. This is equally undebatable, except on the ground that the races might live together, each with full regard for the rights and interests of others, and that those rights and interests would never conflict. Such an idea, of course, is absurd; the colored races today, such as Japan, are clamoring not for equality but for their supremacy. The whole history of the world, on its broader lines, has been one of race conflicts, wars, subjugation, or extinction. This is not pretty, and certainly disagrees with the maudlin theories of cosmopolitanism, but it is truth. The world has been so made that each race must fight for its life, must conquer, accept slavery, or die. The Klansman believes that the whites will not become slaves, and he does not intend to die before his time.

Moreover, the future of progress and civilization depends on the continued supremacy of the white race. The forward movement of the world for centuries has come entirely from it. Other races each had its chance and either failed or stuck fast, while white civilization shows no sign of having reached its limit. Until the whites falter, or some colored civilization has a miracle of awakening, there is not a single colored stock that can claim even equality with the white; much less supremacy.

The third of the Klan principles is that Protestantism must be supreme; that Rome shall not rule America. The Klansman believes this not merely because he is a Protestant, nor even because the colonies that are now our nation were settled for the purpose of wresting America from the control of Rome and establishing a land of free conscience. He believes it also because Protestantism is an essential part of Americanism; without it America could never have been created and without it she cannot go forward. Roman rule would kill it. . . .

So long as politicians cater to alien racial and religious groups, it is the merest self-defense to have also a Protestant and an American "vote" and to make it respected. The hatred and prejudice are, as has been evident to every candid person, displayed by our enemies and not by us.

As to the charge that the Klan brought race and religion into politics, that simply is not true. That was done by the very people who are now accusing us, because we are cutting into the profits they had been making in politics out of *their* races and *their* religions. Race and religion have for years been used by the aliens as political platforms. The Klan is in no way responsible for this condition. We merely recognized it when others dared not, and we fight it in the open. Our belief is that any man who runs for office or asks political favors, or advocates policies or carries on any other political activity, either as a member of any racial or religious group, or in the interests of or under orders from such a group or of any non-American interest whatever, should be opposed for that very reason. The Klan's ambition is to get race and religion out of politics, and that cannot be done so long as there is any profit in exploiting them. It therefore fights every attempt to use them.

This vicious kind of politics has mostly been more or less secret. We of the Klan wish we could claim credit for bringing the scandal into the open, but we cannot even do that. The open issue was raised for the first time on a national scale at the Democratic National Convention of 1924. This was the doing of the Catholic politicians, who seized upon Catholicism as a cement for holding the anti-McAdoo forces together. The bitter cleavage that followed was inevitable, and it was they—the Catholic leaders—who so nearly wrecked the party and were quite ready to wreck it completely if that would have helped their local Catholic machines.

One of the Klan's chief interests is in education. We believe that it is the duty of government to insure to every child opportunity to develop its natural abilities to their utmost. We wish to go to the very limit in the improvement of the public schools; so far that there will be no excuse except snobbery for the private schools.

Further, the Klan wishes to restore the Bible to the school, not only because it is part of the world's great heritage in literature and philosophy and has profoundly influenced all white civilization, but because it is the basis on which all Christian religions are built, and to which they must look for their authority. The Klan believes in the right of each child to pass for itself on the ultimate authority behind the creed he is asked to adopt; it believes in preserving to all children their right to religious volition, to full freedom of choice. This is impossible if they are barred from the Bible. We oppose any means by which any priesthood keeps its hold on power by suppressing, hiding, or garbling the fundamental Christian revelation.

This is one of the reasons for the Klan's objection to parochial schools of any church. They very readily become mere agencies of propaganda. Another reason is that in many the teaching is in the hands of aliens, who cannot possibly understand Americanism or train Americans to citizenship. In many, even, the textbooks have been so perverted that Americanism is falsified, distorted, and betrayed. The Klan would like to see all such schools closed. If they cannot be abolished, the Klan aims to bring them under control of the State, so as to eliminate these evils, insure religious volition, and enforce the teaching of true Americanism. . . .

We of the Klan admit that we are intolerant and narrow in a certain sense. We do not think our intolerance is so serious as that of our enemies. It is not an intolerance that tries to prevent free speech or free assembly. The Klan has never broken up a meeting, nor tried to drive a speaker to cover, nor started a riot, nor attacked a procession or parade, nor murdered men for belonging to the Knights of Columbus or the B'nai B'rith.

And we deny that either bigotry or prejudice enters into our intolerance or our narrowness. We are intolerant of everything that strikes at the foundations of our race, our country or our freedom of worship. We are narrowly opposed to the use of anything alien—race, loyalty to any foreign power or to any religion whatever—as a means to win political power. We are prejudiced against any attempt to use the privileges and opportunities which aliens hold only through our generosity as levers to force us to change our civilization, to wrest from us control of our own country, to exploit us for the benefit of any foreign power—religious or secular—and especially to use America as a tool or cat's-paw for the advantage of any side in the hatreds and quarrels of the Old World. This is our intolerance; based on the sound instincts which have saved us many times from the follies of the intellectuals. We admit it. More and worse, we are proud of it.

But this is all of our intolerance. We do not wish harm to any man, even to those we fight. We have no desire to abuse, enslave, exploit, or deny any legal, political, or social right to any man of any religion, race, or color. We grant them full freedom—except freedom to destroy our own freedom and ourselves. In many ways we honor and respect them. Every race has many fine and admirable traits, each has made notable achievements. There is much for us to learn from each of them. But we do insist that we may learn what we choose, and what will best fit the peculiar genius of our own race, rather than have them choose our lessons for us, and then ram them down our throats.

The attitude of the Klan toward outsiders is derived logically from these beliefs. From all Americans except the racial and spiritual expatriates we expect eventual support. Of the expatriates nothing can be hoped. They are men without a country and proud of it.

The Negro, the Klan considers a special duty and problem of the white American. He is among us through no wish of his; we owe it to him and to ourselves to give him full protection and opportunity. But his limitations are evident; we will not permit him to gain sufficient power to control our civilization. Neither will we delude him with promises of social equality which we know can never be realized. The Klan looks forward to the day when the Negro problem will have been solved on some much saner basis than miscegenation, and when every State will enforce laws making any sex relations between a white and a colored person a crime.

For the alien in general we have sympathy, opportunity, justice, but no permanent welcome unless he becomes truly American. It is our duty to see that he has every chance for this, and we shall be glad to accept him if he does. We hold no rancor against him; his race, instincts, training, mentality, and whole outlook of life are usually widely different from ours. We cannot blame him if he adheres to them and attempts to convert us to them, even by force. But we must see that he can never succeed.

The Jew is a more complex problem. His abilities are great, he contributes much to any country where he lives. This is particularly true of the Western Jew, those of the stocks we have known so long. Their separation from us is more religious than racial. When freed from persecution these Jews have shown a tendency to disintegrate and amalgamate. We may hope that shortly, in the free atmosphere of America, Jews of this class will cease to be a problem. Quite different are the Eastern Jews of recent immigration, the Jews known as the Askhenasim. It is interesting to note that anthropologists now tell us that these are not true Jews, but only Judaized Mongols—Chazars. These, unlike the true Hebrew, show a divergence from the American type so great that there seems little hope of their assimilation.

The most menacing and most difficult problem facing America today is this of the permanently unassimilable alien. The only solution so far offered is that of Dr. Eliot, president emeritus of Harvard. After admitting that the melting pot has failed—thus supporting the primary position of the Klan—he adds that there is no hope of creating here a single, homogeneous race-stock of the kind necessary for national unity. He then suggests that, instead, there shall be a congeries of diverse peoples, living together in sweet harmony, and all working for the good of all and of the nation! This solution is on a par with the optimism which foisted the melting pot on us. Diverse races never have lived together in such harmony; race antipathies are too deep and strong. If such a state were possible, the nation would be too disunited for progress. One race always ruled, one always must, and there will be struggle and reprisals till the mastery is established—and bitterness afterwards. And, speaking for us Americans, we have come to realize that if all this could possibly be done, still within a few years we should be supplanted by the "mere force of breeding" of the low standard peoples. We intend to see that the American stock remains supreme. . . .

One more charge against the Klan is worth noting: that we are trying to cure prejudice by using new and stronger prejudice, to end disunity by setting up new barriers, to speed Americanization by discriminations and issues which are un-American. This is a plausible charge, if the facts alleged were true, for it is certain that prejudice is no cure for prejudice, nor can we hope to promote Americanism by violating its principles.

But the Klan does not stimulate prejudice, nor has it raised race or religious issues, nor violated the spirit of Americanism in any way. We simply recognize facts, and meet the situation they reveal, as it must be met. Nonresistance to the alien invasion, and ostrich-like optimism have already brought us to the verge of ruin. The time has come for positive action. The Klan is open to the same charge of creating discord that lies against any people who, under outside attack, finally begin resistance when injuries have become intolerable—it is blamable to that extent, but no more. There can be no hope of curing our evils so long as it is possible for leaders of alien groups to profit by them, and by preventing assimilation. Our first duty is to see to it that no man may grow rich or powerful by breeding and exploiting disloyalty.

The future of the Klan we believe in, though it is still in the hands of God and of our own abilities and consecration as individuals and as a race. Previous movements of the kind have been short-lived, killed by internal jealousies and personal ambitions, and partly, too, by partial accomplishment of their purposes. If the Klan falls away from its mission, or fails in it, perhaps even if it succeeds—certainly whenever the time comes that it is not doing needed work—it will become a mere derelict, without purpose or force. If it fulfills its mission, its future power and service are beyond calculation so long as America has any part of her destiny unfulfilled. Meantime we of the Klan will continue, as best we know and as best we can, the crusade for Americanism to which we have been providentially called.

12

Fascism and Father Coughlin

James P. Shenton

The Depression of the 1930s produced the most massive social and economic disruption in American history. Father Charles E. Coughlin kept millions of radio listeners spellbound with his charges that the Great Depression was the result of "an insidious conspiracy of international bankers and world communism." An early supporter of Franklin D. Roosevelt, Coughlin eventually attacked the President and described the New Deal as a bureaucratic monster that had one foot mired in the "red mud of Soviet Communism," and the other in the "stinking cesspool of pagan plutocracy." His furious attacks on Jews led many observers to see him as an American fascist. James P. Shenton doubts that the radio priest was fascist, and he suggests that Coughlin failed to create an effective political coalition because the disaffected minority groups to whom he appealed hated each other even more than they feared capitalism, communism, or Jews.

James P. Shenton, "Fascism and Father Coughlin," Wisconsin Magazine of History, *XLIV (Autumn 1960), 6–11. Reprinted without footnotes by permission of the author and the publishers.*

Americans have notoriously refused to define political terms exactly. Often a single term has been used to cover such a multitude of sins and virtues that the historian or political scientist is left with the impression that he has entered into a wonderland of nonsense. An excellent example of this propensity is the scope with which the word "fascism" was used in depression America. A person unfamiliar with the New Deal era might, after reading the popular magazines and journals of the day, be justified in assuming that fascism was the dominant political mood of America during the 1930s. The frequency with which repeated charges of fascist infiltration were made leaves the question of how valid were the accusations. An exploration of the career of Father Charles E. Coughlin provides both the opportunity to indicate the scope of the usage and the applicability of the description to the "radio priest."

A Texas congressman writing a preface to a postwar congressional report on Fascism unwittingly revealed the extent of American confusion concerning its precise meaning when he wrote, "Opinions vary as to whether this movement is economic, social, political, or philosophical." One need not blame his confusion since fascism had been used to describe the Daughters of the American Revolution, Boss Frank Hague, the New Deal—and particularly its NIRA experiment—Huey Long, Franklin D. Roosevelt, the Roman Catholic hierarchy, local chambers of commerce, the American Legion, Tammany, and the Reverend Charles E. Coughlin, among others.

The indictment of American institutions and individuals came in a plentitude of pejoratives. Fascism appeared to one contemporary critic as the legitimate "teammate for our other authority . . . efficiency"; to another as "radical"; while another deprecated it as "reactionary." Others thought fascism threatened "collectivism," which promised to eliminate the "last vestiges of chaotic democracy and confused liberalism," while still others thought it insured a resurgence of an "individualism freed from want."

Fascism, frequently, received an unsupported identification with either Big Business or with the middle class—usually a segment of that class. When Henry Ford, for example, accepted a decoration from Adolph Hitler, he signified for some the corruption of all businessmen. The treatment given migrating Okies, described as "workers of old American stock," in the California vineyards evoked an image of their being "harried and dragooned . . . by uniformed blackshirts." From such examples came the deduction that "fascism is the reorganization of society by undemocratic means to maintain the capitalist system."

Huey Long, often called a fascist, commented caustically that "if ever fascism came to America it would come in the guise of anti-fascism." The squire of Hyde Park, ever the optimist, dismissed the threat of both fascism and communism "to the continuation of our form of government" unless "old-time Tory Republicanism" aided these alien systems in frustrating his reform program. Opponents of Roosevelt reciprocated with charges that "the New Deal, like Fascism, recognizes not one class, but the equilibrium of classes." This slipshod usage achieved a cavalier result with the argument, "The New Dealers, strangely enough, have been employing Fascist means to gain liberal ends; while their Old Guard opponents are strongly in favor of liberal and constitutional means to gain Fascist ends."

The comprehensive meaning given fascism by Americans left thoughtful contemporaries complaining that "In our common scale of speech the word fascism has reached the stage where it is applied to almost any kind of thing or person one does not like." Some felt that the multitude of social inequities and injustices covered by the word led to the question of whether "we have not had fascism in America for generations."

The question brought from some an affirmative response. "Our fascism probably entails," one observer noted, "a merger of the Hamiltonian tradition with the Jacksonian, producing a social revolution in the name of monopoly." This seemingly contradictory development would come about when the "Jacksonian 'little' people" willingly imposed upon themselves the direction of "Hamiltonian hierarchs" who, they believed, would relieve them of their burdens. Others, foreshadowing a recent historical revisionism, described fascism as an extreme statement of populism, a political attitude which supposedly presented a hostile face to both capitalism and socialism. Any alliance between fascism and capitalism was assumed to be temporary, terminating in the subservience of capitalism.

Populism so used received a comprehensive definition; it included among others John Dewey and the League for Independent Political Action, midwestern agriculture, the railroad brotherhoods, the American Federation of Labor, and southern rural democracy. Only the latter seemed to promise a plausible base for fascism. The assassination of Huey Long, however, had deprived this faction of its natural leader. The chauvinistic and moralizing tone of southern demagoguery led to timid predictions that Father Coughlin might assume leadership of a southern fascism. But even a brief contemplation of southern bias persuaded proponents of this idea of its implausibility; they concluded that

Big Business rather than populism would sponsor "capitalist fascism."

As the foregoing indicates, few Americans understood what fascism meant. The most cogent definition appeared in the *Encyclopaedia of the Social Sciences* which stated that only "when viewed as a peculiarly Italian phenomenon" did fascism reveal distinctive features. Its repudiation of "Rousseau's dogma of natural rights as well as the infallibility of majority rule," expressed both a rejection of parliamentary government, and an emphasis upon the organic unity of the state expressed through the supremacy of a governing elite. It achieved political expression through a single party, organized on the hierarchic principle, and possessed of exclusive power.

If one accepts this definition, it is reasonable to assume that men labeled as fascist ought to have shown an affinity to the program set forth by Italian fascists. An application of this test to Father Coughlin and his program of Social Justice proves suggestive. However, only the loosest use of the term makes it applicable to Coughlin.

An extensive reading of Coughlin's speeches and editorials reveals that he used a rhetoric which had a thoroughly familiar ring to American audiences. He argued against "entangling alliances," denounced the evils of the "money trust," railed against "an international money plutocracy," which Coughlin described as eager to nail the simple American to "a cross of gold." He called for "a re-awakened America —an America that stands 100 percent for Americanism—an America that will have no patience either with Nazism or Communism; an America that still stands by the traditions of our forefathers—traditions of liberty, traditions of Godliness, traditions upon which we must establish a sane Christian nationalism." The language rang with Populist and Progressive imagery.

"Our ancestors departed from Europe," Coughlin thundered, "to establish here a new nation free from the plots and intrigues which fester practically in every capital from the North Sea to the Red Sea." To escape the contaminating influence of Europe, he opposed entrance into the League of Nations, arguing that it would involve Americans in "entanglements for destruction." British imperialists used the League as a disguise which Coughlin felt made its protests against Italian aggression hypocritical. To protest the tragedy of Ethiopia while tolerating the subjugation of the remainder of Africa moved him to vivid deununciations of perfidious Albion.

To keep America free and innocent is the repeated theme of Coughlin's discourses on foreign affairs. At home he pleaded for the restoration of an equalitarian justice. Both internal and external threats to the republic are described as being of alien origin. An insidious conspiracy of international bankers and world communism, he repeatedly charged, sought to destroy the nation. "The intelligence . . . and intestinal fortitude of [an] Andrew Jackson," he declared, "alone can meet both threats."

Coughlin predicted that only sweeping reforms would prevent the Republic from lapsing into oblivion. Capitalism had lost its chance to achieve a just distribution of its fruits. "Communism," he admitted, "has a just complaint." Only through a return to the teachings of Christ could the nation achieve salvation. In his sixteen principles of social justice he presented a program which called for "freedom of conscience and of education," "a just, living, annual wage," "public ownership of public necessities," "nationalization of the Federal Reserve System," government control of all property necessary for the public welfare, a guaranteed fair profit for the farmer, and a graduated tax system. None could be designated as novel, all had the virtue of support by some segment of public opinion. Several of them implied, however, the erection of a considerable government apparatus to administer the program. Coughlin overlooked this implication and demanded the maintenance of a government of Jeffersonian proportions which would attempt a program of Hamiltonian dimensions. In his opposition to Big Government he insisted that its end result would be either Fascism or Nazism. As his disenchantment towards the New Deal increased, he charged that it floundered toward such a result.

He indicted the New Deal as an administrative monster whose feet were mired, "one in the red mud of Soviet communism, and the other, in the stinking cesspool of pagan plutocracy." To complete the confusion, he described it as "staggering towards Fascism." When Coughlin expressed sympathy with the Italian experiment, he invariably pointed to its desire to achieve a self-sufficient nationalism. It appealed to his own fierce hostility to anything which threatened American isolation. His political theme reiterated that alien faiths and values threatened with destruction "the temple of America."

Fundamentally, the appeal of the radio priest rested upon his exploitation of a nation groggy with depression, preoccupied with its plight, and often willing to look abroad for its villains. His plea for inflationary policies struck a responsive chord among a people who agreed that they needed money. The hard core of his supporters, after his break with Roosevelt, often denounced the New Deal for the inadequacy of its relief efforts. His identification with the enormously popular President originally added to his immense radio audiences. His support of Roosevelt enabled his listener to see him as a prop of the established order. Though his support occasionally embarrassed the administration, it preferred to allow him the distinction of indirect identification. However, when Coughlin chose to break with the President, he exposed the limits of his own appeal.

Once Coughlin had forced his audience to choose between himself and Roosevelt, the response was prompt and blunt. "I am sorry to say," wrote more than one irate listener, "I couldn't under any consideration continue to support you if you feel it your duty to criticize [Roosevelt]." The extent of his popular repudiation compelled Coughlin to attempt to retrieve his loss of prestige. "It is not my purpose to destroy," he explained, "but to perfect the New Deal." But his efforts came to naught.

As he continued to lose public support, the Roman Catholic hierarchy, overwhelmingly supporters of Roosevelt and less than enthusiastic about Coughlin and his overt political agitation, expressed private dismay at the increasing public identification of Coughlin with the Church. In Boston, Cardinal O'Connell, who viewed Coughlin with withering contempt, denied him access to his episcopal jurisdiction and instructed his clergy not to listen to his radio sermons. Cardinal Hayes closed the Archdiocese of New York to Coughlin and invited members of the teaching clergy to refute him at every opportunity. Bishop Bernard J. Sheil, speaking for Cardinal Mundelein of Chicago, expressed the hierarchical attitude succinctly: "As an American citizen, Father Coughlin has the right to express his personal views on current events, but he is not authorized to speak for the Catholic Church, nor does he represent the doctrine or sentiments of the Church."

As Coughlin became more explicitly anti-Semitic, *Commonweal*, the liberal Catholic journal, warned: "We can't forget that modern anti-Semitism, condemned in a noble way as racism, must also be recognized from a most practical, everyday point of view, as one side of a coin on whose reverse is inscribed: 'No Popery!' " Not only at home, but also at the Vatican, the fear grew that the wholesale indictment which Coughlin levelled against the international banker, the international Jew, and international communism, left Roman Catholicism with its supranational character painfully exposed.

Pius XI evidently took severe exception to Coughlin's calling Roosevelt a liar. Despite a public apology by the radio priest, supporters of Roosevelt among the American prelates persuaded the Vatican to forestall similar incidents during the 1936 campaign by having the then Cardinal Pacelli visit the United States during October 1936. It was widely accepted in Catholic circles that Coughlin would be publicly repudiated by Pacelli if he were to make injudicious attacks. The day that the Vatican Secretary of State landed in New York, all the Union

Party candidates in New York State withdrew from the election. Within a week, "crowds at Coughlin rallies began falling off." Influential lay Catholics joined in the attack. Even Joseph Kennedy, a longtime friend of Coughlin, made the point of emphatically supporting Roosevelt. The Catholic minority had no intention of isolating itself from the mainstream of American political life by following Coughlin into his backwater.

After his repudiation at the polls, Coughlin found growing hostility in newspapers and magazines, and numerous radio stations were unwilling to carry his sermons. Rumors soon circulated that he might seek to exploit the inheritance of Huey Long; and his developing association with Gerald L. K. Smith and the German-American Bund seemed to lend these rumors credibility. But there existed an insurmountable obstacle to such an alliance: Coughlin still wore the Roman collar. In his home state, Michigan, the Black Legion—a vicious variant of the Ku Klux Klan sharing many of Coughlin's antipathies—flourished, but its anti-Catholicism precluded cooperation. The Molotov-Ribbentrop Pact of 1939 broke off his association with the German-American Bund. Coughlin, bound by his religion and a decade of vehement anticommunism, denounced the Pact "as the union of anti-God and Antichrist." Catholic supporters bridled at his association with the fundamentalist Smith. Father Edward Curran, a key organizer of the Christian Front, Coughlin's attempt to create a single movement of right-wing dissidence, exposed the difficulty of such an effort when he denounced FDR for nominating to the Supreme Court Hugo Black, a "former KKK man." Between the fundamentalist and the Catholic there existed an unbridgeable gap.

From 1939 onward, Coughlin thrashed about for an issue. Confronted with a world involved in a growing war, he returned to an argument which had always proved congenial: America must retreat into a self-sufficient isolation. Only then could she hope to maintain—or was it recapture—her original purity. He charged bitterly that both communism and fascism were "abominable" outgrowths of capitalism. As it became evident that the United States was moving away from neutrality, Coughlin moved dangerously close to treason. He seemed willing to allow the destruction of a nation which had repudiated its isolationist faith and himself, and left him with only a belligerent claque. In Detroit, his superior, Archbishop Mooney, who had always suspected that Coughlin's contempt for the principle of hierarchical authority threatened a Church schism, imposed an increasingly restrictive discipline. The most noteworthy lay member of the Detroit Archdiocese, Justice Frank Murphy, concluded: "Father

Coughlin is trying to work himself into jail, as [he] is giving aid and comfort to the enemy." Shortly after Pearl Harbor, Coughlin finally found himself compelled to accept disciplinary silence, one which remains unbroken.

Coughlin, who had drawn heavily upon traditional agrarian democracy, had finally been frustrated by the pluralistic democracy. The authority of the Roman Catholic Church had repudiated him rather than lose contact with traditional political authority. Time and again ethnic minorities revealed their unwillingness to forget past loyalties; southern Democrats refused to relinquish their anti-Papist sentiments; dissident Catholics proved unable to forget the excesses of the KKK. Though each shared, with varying intensity, hostility to capitalism, to the complexities of industrial-urban life, to the Jew, to Communism, Coughlin proved unable to forge an effective coalition of minorities. For though there existed ample discontent, the groups to whom he appealed also shared an even greater antipathy to one another.

Most certainly, for Coughlin to have effectively met the definition of fascism he would have had to create an organic state. There is little evidence that he tried, and even if he had, there simply did not exist the human materials from which to create such a state. But lest we conclude that there is no lesson to be learned from the career of Coughlin, it is well to remind ourselves of David Riesman's belief that the absence of "agreement on fundamental values is essential for democratic functioning." It may deprive us of ideological symmetry, but it does keep the enemy within the gate at bay—or did in the 1930s.

13

The Attack on Japanese Americans during World War II

Jacobus ten Broek, Edward N. Barnhart, and Floyd W. Matson

Prejudice and fear of subversion produced one of the most glaring episodes of repression in American history. During the early months of World War II approximately 100,000 Japanese American citizens were evacuated from the West Coast and herded into "relocation centers." Jacobus ten Broek, Edward N. Barnhart, and Floyd W. Matson observe that although the Japanese attack on Pearl Harbor was the immediate cause of repression, the deeper causes date from the beginnings of Oriental immigration to the United States at the end of the nineteenth century. The development of a racial stereotype depicting both the Japanese and Chinese as sly, inscrutable, and potentially dangerous resulted in a policy of excluding Oriental immigrants and laid the basis for the assault on the rights of Japanese Americans.

From Jacobus ten Broek, Edward N. Barnhart, and Floyd W. Matson, Prejudice, War and the Constitution *(Berkeley 1954), "Conclusion; The Faces of the Stereotype," pp. 91–96. Originally published by the University of California Press; reprinted by permission of the Regents of the University of California.*

Viewed in the perspective of a decade, with all the advantages of hindsight and subsequent disclosure, the Japanese American episode of World War II looms as a great and evil blotch upon our national history. The whole vast, harsh, and discriminatory program of uprooting and imprisonment—initiated by the generals, advised, ordered, and supervised by the civilian heads of the War Department, authorized by the President, implemented by Congress, approved by the Supreme Court, and supported by the people—is without parallel in our past and full of ominous forebodings for our future.

The entire Japanese American program violated and degraded the basic individualism which sustains a democracy. It impaired the trial tradition of the common law. It disparaged the principle that guilt is individual. It sapped the vitality of the precept of equality. It made racism a constitutional principle. It tolerated preventive incarceration for assumed disloyal beliefs and attitudes—unaccompanied by acts—attributing them without proof, probable cause, or reasonable suspicion to an entire group on a basis of race. Recklessly and unnecessarily, it loosened judicial control of the military and produced dangerous imbalance in our government.

The episode embodied one of the most "sweeping and complete deprivations of constitutional rights in the history of this nation." It destroyed basic and precious rights of personal security: the right—without arbitrary or constitutionally irrelevant interference—to move about freely, to live and work where one chooses, to establish and maintain a home; the right not to be deprived of constitutional safeguards except upon an individual basis and after charges, notice, hearing, fair trial, and all of the procedural requirements of due process. It destroyed, as well, basic and precious rights of democratic participation: the right of peaceable assembly to discuss the general welfare and problems of government; the rights of free speech and a free press; the right freely to hear, read, and learn; the rights of petition and remonstrance; the rights of franchise and election, of seeking and holding office; and, not least of all, the right and responsibility to defend one's native land, if need be with one's life.

The Japanese American episode culminated in a constitutional sanctification of these deprivations by the highest court in the land—a court dedicated to justice, defense of the Constitution, determination of the powers and limitations of government, and protection of the rights of men.

In the historical view, the wisdom of a decision is tested principally by subsequent events. Contemporary plausibility is only a minor criterion. Judged by the historical test, military necessity arising out of the war emergency does not provide justification of the program of removal and imprisonment. It is true that Japanese arms, in the winter of 1941–42, advanced rapidly in southeast Asia and the southwest Pacific. Damaging blows were dealt the American navy. A foothold was gained on Attu and Kiska in the Aleutians, Dutch Harbor in Alaska was bombed. But it is also true that Japanese strength had been fully committed in the far Pacific. The mainland Pacific coastline of the United States was adequately protected even before December was out. The Battle of Midway on June 6, 1942, brought Japanese naval expansion in the Pacific to an end. Thereafter, the enemy forces on Attu and Kiska withered from lack of support.

There was no invasion of the coastal mainland. There were not even commando raids or air strikes upon it. One submarine lobbed a few shells harmlessly near an oil installation not far from Santa Barbara (February 23, 1942). Another sent a midget airplane with an incendiary bomb over an Oregon forest (September 9, 1942); the bomb ignited nothing. A third submarine fired on coast defenses at Astoria, Oregon (June 21, 1942). In December 1941 there were only three successful enemy submarine attacks on ships leaving West Coast ports. In January 1942 there were none; in February none; in March none; in April none; in May none. No Japanese surface ship ever operated in the eastern part of the Pacific between Hawaii and the mainland.

Thus, in the calm retrospect of history, it is evident that military necessity warranting the program simply did not exist. After Midway, there was no justification at all for either mass detention or mass exclusion. Even before Midway, there was no justification for mass detention or for the mass exclusion of American citizens of Japanese ancestry. There was no justification at any time for treating Japanese aliens differently from other enemy aliens.

The absence of any acts of espionage and sabotage by Japanese Americans between Pearl Harbor and evacuation—while numerous persons of other extractions were being convicted of such acts—sufficiently testifies (1) to the active or passive loyalty of the major part of the Japanese American population, and (2) to the adequacy of existing methods of control and prevention. Even were this not so, alternative methods of control were available, less drastic than evacuation and detention combined or than either of them separately, more consonant with the Constitution and wholly adequate to meet the actual danger.

All this can now be seen clearly. But even if we abandon the vantage point of history and judge the military only by what they then knew, the same conclusion must be reached. For the fact is that much of what was learned by the public only years later was, at the time, known to our military leaders. It was their judgment then that Japanese strength had been fully committed elsewhere; that, after December, the Pacific Coast was adequately protected. They knew the Japanese strength on land, sea, and in the air. They knew where it was deployed and what its capabilities were. The Navy especially believed that invasion was virtually out of the question by the spring of 1942. The significance of Midway was correctly appraised at the time. Yet it was after that battle that the inland Japanese Americans were evacuated and all Japanese Americans removed from assembly centers to relocation centers.

The weakness of the case for military necessity was spotlighted rather than concealed by General DeWitt's *Final Report,* which is a flimsy tissue of misstatements, preposterous absurdities, patently fallacious reasoning, unacknowledged quotations, and uses facts and arguments developed after the event in an obvious attempt to show that, at the time the decision for evacuation was made, it was based on facts and sound reasoning. Most remarkable of all are these two assertions, contained in a single paragraph: "The very fact that no sabotage has taken place to date is a disturbing and confirming indication that such action will be taken"; and "The Japanese race is an enemy race and while many second and third generation Japanese born on United States soil, possessed of United States citizenship, have become 'Americanized,' the racial strains are undiluted."

The responsibility for this flagrant breach of the nation's constitutional and moral ideals may be readily assigned.

It rests first and primarily with the people: the people of the nation in general; the people of the West Coast in particular. Popular feelings and attitudes were complex, but the two major forces which contributed to their development may be identified. First, of course, was the war itself.

Germany had conquered the European continent with amazing speed and show of invincibility. She had annexed Austria, humbled England and France at Munich, overrun Czechoslovakia. She had conquered Poland in twenty-six days. She had seized Denmark and Norway; had crushed the Netherlands in four days, Belgium in seventeen, France in ten. She had taken Roumania, Bulgaria, Yugoslavia, Greece, and Crete. She had invaded Russia on a 2,000-mile front and had pushed 500 miles into that country. She had held Kharkov and Rostov, beseiged

Leningrad, and approached the gates of Moscow. Thus, in December 1941, Hitler held Europe from Norway to Sicily and from the Pyrenees practically to Moscow. In the Mediterranean only Malta and Gibraltar were in British hands. The Germans were in French North Africa. Rommel was threatening Suez, which could only be reinforced by way of the Cape of Good Hope. From bases along the Atlantic Coast line, German U-boats, aircraft, and surface raiders ranged the North Sea, the Channel, and the Bay of Biscay. Shipping to Britain was under constant attack, with losses mounting to 500,000 tons a month early in 1941. Countermeasures reduced that staggering total to the still staggering figure of 180,000 tons a month in late 1941, but the British situation was still precarious. German arms, ships, and submarines terrorized shipping within 100 miles of the eastern coast of the United States.

Then came Pearl Harbor. The United States itself was suddenly in the war—a total global war, for the German declaration against us followed immediately—a war in which prior commitments and the overall strength of the enemy oriented our principal effort first toward the Atlantic. In the light of later events, it is difficult now to believe that at the time public reaction to Pearl Harbor included the wildest kind of overconfidence in our ability to deal with Japan and underestimation of her military potential. Military experts, lay commentators, and sidewalk reporters differed only as to whether it would take one, two, or three months to wipe out the Japanese navy and bring complete and overwhelming victory. But within one month the Japanese had occupied Thailand, Guam, Wake Island, Hong Kong, and Manila; they had made landings in Malaya; they had sunk the *Prince of Wales* and the *Repulse*. In the second month Japanese conquests mounted. They invaded Burma from Thailand; they pushed British forces back in Malaya toward Singapore. From landings in Borneo and the Celebes they worked down Macassar Straits despite bombings from Flying Fortresses and attacks by American destroyers. Spreading out from Truk they landed at Rabaul, New Britain, and New Ireland on January 23 and pushed into the Solomons on January 29, having seized the Admiralty Islands earlier. The sea lanes from Australia to India were now hazardous. There was a real threat that communications between Australia and the United States might be cut and shipping forced far to the east. By the end of the third month the Japanese had won a major victory in the battle of the Java Sea, established control over the Dutch East Indies, completely occupied Rangoon and Burma, and placed Bataan and Corregidor under siege. They had taken Singapore and its British army of 100,000 men. Communications between the Middle East and Australia had been rendered subject to attack. Port Darwin on the northern coast of Australia had been bombed from the air.

The reaction of the American people to these catastrophic events was not merely one of disbelief and incredulity; it was one of rising anger, fear, apprehension, and frustration. In this atmosphere few were heard to protest the removal from the western coastal area of those who had ancestral connections with Japan.

The second major force operating in the formation of popular attitudes, especially on the West Coast, was a long history of anti-Oriental and specifically anti-Japanese agitation. The Japanese attack on Pearl Harbor activated, but it did not begin, the Japanese American episode. The basis for the episode is to be found in the history of the Pacific frontier, when the first Japanese immigrants arrived to share the popular prejudice against the Chinese and eventually to inherit it. This part of the story concerns the creation, development, and widespread diffusion of an Oriental stereotype depicting first the Chinese and subsequently the Japanese as sly, tricky, inscrutable; as untrustworthy neighbors and unscrupulous competitors; and, most important of all, as spies and secret agents of the homeland government. Rising Japanese military and national strength, coupled with an aggressive policy of expansion following the Russo-Japanese War, gave seeming substance to the secret-agent element of the stereotype. The attack on Pearl Harbor provided, in the minds of the public, its complete substantiation. That Japanese immigrants and their descendants should now aid and support the ancestral government was all that was needed to bring about a total realization of the stereotype of the "yellow peril."

The primary responsibility of the people for the action taken against the Japanese Americans cannot be shifted to the shoulders of pressure groups and politicians. The activity of such organizations and individuals before the basic decision of mid-February 1942 (and indeed after) has been greatly exaggerated both as to extent and influence. The pressure groups of all varieties, the politicians in Congress, the state legislatures, and the executive departments, did not so much lead as follow the people. Many of them, in fact, pulled in the opposite direction; still more took no public stand at all. Some who moved against the Japanese Americans were prompted by the hope of economic gain; others acted contrary to their own self-interest. In the scattered and spasmodic, not to say desultory, actions of these varied groups along the coast in the early months of war there is little sign of systematic organization or crafty connivance; all that can be said is that if a mountainous plot existed its labors brought forth a mouse. But although the voices raised in discordant chorus against the Japanese Americans had no common organization, they did have a common heritage and a common fear. For politicians, farmers, businessmen, and exalted rulers are also people, private citizens, and members of the general public, who share the prevailing attitudes, beliefs, and habits of their communities. Not only do they respond to and exploit the prejudices of their fellows, they also possess them. In early 1942, their expression of anti-Orientalism was basically neither premonitory nor self-serving. It was an illustration and reflection of public sentiment.

Responsibility for the episode rests, secondarily, with the military, particularly with General DeWitt and the Western Defense Command. To portray General DeWitt as the sole or even the chief villain in this tragic drama, as has so often been done, is as much an injustice as to absolve him altogether. But his role, though subordinate, was important. The governmental activity which resulted in the establishment of the Japanese American program was initiated by General DeWitt. He made the proposal to his superiors and requested authority to execute it. For having done so he must stand convicted by history of committing a military blunder—the perpetration of an outrage on citizen civilians which was not required by the emergency. The plea of military necessity cannot be sustained. Statements from General DeWitt's *Final Report* make it plain that the proposal to evacuate and imprison the Japanese Americans was not the product of a military estimate of the military situation. That the program of exclusion and incarceration resulted from a proper and commendable concern about the security of the West Coast does not mean that the decision to inaugurate it was not based on palpable race prejudice in the Western Defense Command. That General DeWitt honestly believed that race and racial strains had a decisive bearing upon the danger of espionage and sabotage from Japanese Americans does not mean that his belief was a military factor in a military judgment.

Even greater responsibility rests upon President Franklin D. Roosevelt and his civilian aides in the War Department, Secretary Henry L. Stimson and Assistant Secretary John J. McCloy, and upon the Congress of the United States. General DeWitt did not order evacuation and incarceration independently and without prior authorization from his superiors. We do not have here the imaginary problem, posed by Justice Jackson in his *Korematsu* dissent, of an "irresponsible" and "unscrupulous" commander refusing to submit to higher civil authority. What we have, on the contrary, is a commander who proceeded meticulously through duly constituted channels. He presented his plan and request for authority to the War Department, thence to the President, and eventually to Congress. In response, the President, as the President alone could, issued Executive Order 9066, fully empowering the Secretary of War to put the proposed plan into operation. Thereafter, and pursuant to this delegation of authority, Secretary Henry L. Stimson, the civilian head of the War Department, and John J. McCloy, his civilian assistant, first modified the plan by exempting German and Italian American citizens and aliens, then ordered it put into effect, and, finally, continuously supervised its execution. Meanwhile, the Congress of the United States duly enacted Public Law 503, encompassing and providing civilian sanctions for Executive Order 9066 and the sub-delegations under it.

Thus, for these days which in their own way will live in infamy, President Roosevelt bears a large share of the responsibility. He bears it not only in the inert and formal sense that he was the chief executive of the nation and hence accountable for the acts of his subordinates whether he knew of them or not, but also in the immediate and active sense that he deliberately and knowingly authorized the program through the issuance of Executive Order 9066, thereafter supplemented it by other executive orders, and personally directed that its termination be delayed until after the presidential election of 1944. The action of Congress was also taken after due consideration. The President and the Congress of the United States were in fact, as well as in every proper constitutional and democratic sense, the agencies of ultimate decision. That their decision conformed to popular clamor and a request from the military does not and cannot relieve them of ultimate responsibility.

McCloy's apologetic statement that "the military men made the decision—it was a military decision" may indicate the attitude of the Washington officials involved in the decison. It does not and it cannot, however, explain the failure of McCloy and of Secretary Stimson to perform the function implicit in the historic purpose behind the requirement that the War Department must have civilian heads.

Responsibility rests, finally, with the courts, and especially with the Supreme Court of the United States. In many ways the failure of the Supreme Court was the greatest failure of all. For the military is preoccupied with war, not with the Constitution and men's rights. The President and Congress, too, are "war-waging" branches of government. The primary action and affirmative decision was theirs; but they moved on the brink of the event when the general course and outcome of the war were altogether uncertain. In 1945 General Marshall pointed out that in "the black days of 1942 when the Japanese conquered all of Malaysia, occupied Burma, and threatened India while the German armies approached the Volga and the Suez . . . Germany and Japan came so close to complete domination of the world that we do not yet realize how thin the thread of Allied survival had been stretched."

Among the branches of government, the Supreme Court occupies a unique position. It is not so much an active as a reflective body. Its decisions are made on the nether side of the event. Its job is not primary but secondary. It is the historian of events as much as it is their maker. It exerts only such constructive leadership as derives from the power to negate the policy of others. Its self-arrogated and perhaps inherent function is to strike the governmental balance between motion and stability, between new action and old doctrines, between the powers of the nation and men's rights.

If the court had struck down the program, the Japanese American episode would have lived in history as nothing worse than a military blunder. But the court approved the program as constitutional, a step with implications and consequences accurately described by Justice Jackson in his dissenting opinion on the *Korematsu* case:

> Much is said of the danger to liberty from the Army program for deporting and detaining these citizens of Japanese extraction. But a judicial construction of the due process clause that will sustain this order is a far more subtle blow to liberty than the promulgation of the order itself. A military order, however unconstitutional, is not apt to last longer than the military emergency. Even during that period a succeeding commander may revoke it all. But once a judicial opinion rationalizes such an order to show that it conforms to the Constitution, or rather rationalizes the Constitution to show that the Constitution sanctions such an order, the Court for all time has validated the principle of racial discrimination in criminal procedure and of transplanting American citizens. The principle then lies about like a loaded weapon ready for the hand of any authority that can bring forward a plausible claim of an urgent need. Every repetition imbeds that principle more deeply in our law and thinking and expands it to new purposes. All who observe the work of courts are familiar with what Judge Cardozo described as "the tendency of a principle to expand itself to the limit of its logic." A military commander may overstep the bounds of constitutionality, and it is an incident. But if we review and approve, that passing incident becomes the doctrine of the Constitution. There it has a generative power of its own, and all that it creates will be in its own image.

Grant that the function of the court, in reviewing war-power decisions made by the military, the President, and Congress, is not to determine whether those decisions were reasonable in the light of all the circumstances down to the date of judicial review—a very questionable concession. Grant further that the function of the court is not to substitute its judgment for that of the military, the President, and Congress on a basis of what it would have regarded as reasonable in the situation obtaining at the time of the military action—though the substantial-basis test to some degree requires just that. Grant, finally, that even with respect to military orders not strictly military in characer that affect civilians within the country, the court, reviewing the military as it would a civilian agency making the same decision, must allow a fair amount of latitude to the military both in deciding whether and to what extent a danger exists and in choosing the means to cope with it. Grant all this, and the role of the court in the Japanese American episode of World War II was still one of the great failures in its history—comparable with its surrender to slavery in *Prigg* v. *Pennsylvania* and in *Dred Scott* v. *Sandford.*

In terms of procedure and substance—rather than of the deprivation of constitutional rights which the high judges condoned—the failure of the Supreme Court consisted in:

1. Its failure to apply the substantial-basis test to the question of whether the discriminatory curfew for Japanese American citizens was reasonably necessary and appropriate as a means of preventing espionage and sabotage in the circumstances.
2. Its refusal to pass upon and hold unconstitutional the program of detention.
3. That, with respect to evacuation, it either abandoned the Constitution to military fiat or, what amounts to the same thing, applied the substantial-basis test in such a way as to leave the test meaningless.
4. That it attributed to the military a conclusion that the war crisis justified evacuation at the time it was ordered, without requiring *(a)* evidence that this was in fact the judgment of the military and *(b)* evidence that the conclusion was reasonably founded.
5. That it sustained the discriminatory evacuation of Japanese Americans, aliens and citizens, without requiring the military to supply substantial evidence *(a)* that there was danger of sabotage and espionage from the group, *(b)* that such danger was not already detected and controlled by existing methods, including curfew, *(c)*

that the disloyal could not be separated from the loyal by other and less drastic methods than evacuation within the time limits.

6. That it apparently failed to realize and certainly failed to hold that a decision might be based on grounds so untenable and ridiculous —as that racial strains are determinants of national loyalty—that not only folly but bad motive is proved thereby, and the decision is thus constitutionally void as discriminatory in its purpose.
7. That it gave the most perfunctory scrutiny to a ruinously harsh discrimination based on race and ancestry which in moral terms deserves, and in constitutional terms requires, the most rigid scrutiny; and by this default the United States Supreme Court elevated racism to a constitutional principle.

In this way did the United States Supreme Court strike a blow at the liberties of us all.

14

The Radical Right: A Problem for American Democracy

Seymour Martin Lipset

During the early 1950s the tensions of the Cold War produced widespread charges of subversion in high places. Senator Joseph R. McCarthy was especially prominent in arousing fears of Communist infiltration into government. Although Seymour Martin Lipset views right-wing extremism from several vantage points, the concept of status politics occupies center stage in his analysis of McCarthyism. According to Lipset, McCarthyism was a mass movement that cut across class and party lines and was the result of irrational forces that had little to do with Cold War realities or major party politics.

In evaluating the activities of the radical right, this paper is divided into three sections: part I deals with continuing bases of extremist politics in America which have their sources in American history; part II analyzes the social groups which disproportionately comprise the support of the radical right today; and part III deals with the specific

From Seymour Martin Lipset, "The Radical Right: A Problem for American Democracy," British Journal of Sociology, *VI (June 1955), 176–201. Excerpted and reprinted without footnotes by permission of the author and the publishers.*

character of McCarthyism as the principal expression of radical right ideology on the current scene, as well as with some of its inherent weaknesses.

I. Sources of Right-Wing Extremism in American Society

Status and Class Politics Any analysis of the role of political extremism in the United States must be based in part on a recognition of two fundamental political forces operating under the varying historical conditions of American society. These forces may be distinguished by the terms status politics and class politics. Class politics refers to political division based on the traditional discord between the left and the right, between those who favor redistribution of income, and those favoring the preservation of the status quo. As used here, status politics refers to political movements whose growth is based on appeals to the not uncommon resentments of individuals or groups who desire to maintain or improve their social status.

In the United States, political movements or parties which stress the need for economic reform have traditionally gained strength during periods of depression. On the other hand, prosperity, especially periods when full employment is accompanied by inflation and many individuals are able to improve their economic position, fosters status politics. Receptive to status-oriented appeals are not only groups which have risen in the economic structure, who may be frustrated in their desire to be accepted socially by those who hold status, but groups already possessing status as well, who feel that various social changes threaten their own claims to high social position, or enable previously lower-status groups to claim equal status with them.

The political consequences of status frustrations differ considerably from those resulting from economic deprivation, in that there is no clear-cut political solution for the problem. There is little or nothing which a government can do to relieve these anxieties. It is not surprising, therefore, that the political movements which have successfully appealed to status resentments have been irrational in character, that they focus on attacking a scapegoat, which conveniently symbolizes the threat perceived by their supporters.

Historically, in the United States, the most common scapegoats have been the minority ethnic or religious groups. Such groups have repeatedly been victims of political aggression in periods of prosperity for it is precisely in these times that status anxieties are most pressing.

American political history from this perspective emerges as a fairly consistent pattern. Before the Civil War, there was considerable anti-Catholic and anti-immigrant sentiment in the nation. Such agitation often took the form of organized political parties, the most important of which was the Know-Nothing or American Party. And it was during a prosperous decade that these parties and movements were at their height. The Know-Nothings, who polled one-quarter of the total popular vote for President in 1856, reached their greatest power in a period of great prosperity and inflation, and practically vanished in the depression year of 1857.

The American Protective Association (APA), which emerged in the late 1880s, was the next major organized anti-Catholic movement, arising and winning strength in a period of renewed prosperity. . . .

A possible link between this mass organization and the desire of high-status, old family Americans to resist the upward mobility of the second generation Catholics is suggested by the fact that the publisher of many anti-Catholic APA works was also the publisher of the Social Register, which was first copyrighted in 1887, the year in which the APA was organized. A large number of individuals listed in the Social Register were among the important financial supporters of the APA, as well as of anti-immigration organizations. The late 1880s were also marked by the first overt efforts to bar wealthy Jews from participation in the social affairs of the American elite.

Still another prosperity-born movement directed against the rights of minority groups was the Ku Klux Klan. Expanding and reaching its height during the twenties, the KKK disappeared contemporaneously with the depression. Its decline cannot, of course, be blamed solely or even primarily on the depression. Nevertheless, the depression seems to have dealt the death-blow.

The Progressive movement, which flourished from 1900–1912, is yet another protest movement which attracted the interest and participation of large numbers during a period of high prosperity. This movement, while differing considerably from the other three, since it was concerned with liberal social reforms, may, nevertheless, be a reflection of status politics. Richard Hofstadter has suggested that the movement was in large measure based on the reaction of the Protestant middle class against threats to its values and status. On one hand, the rise of the "robber barons," the great millionaires and plutocrats of the late nineteenth and early twentieth centuries, served to threaten the status of many old families, upper middle-class Americans who had previously considered themselves the most important group in society. Their position was challenged by the appearance of the new millionaires who were able to outdo them in philanthropy and in their styles of life. On the other hand, this movement, like previous expressions of status politics, was opposed to immigration. It viewed the immigrant and the urban city machines based on immigrant support as a basic threat to American middle-class Protestant values. The Progressive movement had two scapegoats—the "plutocrat" millionaires, and the immigrants.

These four movements, Know-Nothing, APA, Ku Klux Klan, and Progressives, all illustrate the way in which American society has thrust up major protest movements in periods of prosperity, thereby confounding the general assumption that protest politics are primarily products of depressions. The prosperity movements are distinct from those groups which are responses to economic crises, because they attack their "scapegoat" for threatening the American value system rather than its economy. The Progressives were concerned with the way in which the nouveaux riches and the immigrants were corrupting American institutions, while the Klan focused on attacking the "cosmopolitanism" of Catholics, Jews, and the metropolitan elite, which undermined the middle-class Protestant virtues. And it is this concern with the protection of traditional American values that characterizes "status politics" as contrasted with the regard for jobs, cheap credit, or high farm prices, which have been the main emphasis of depression "class politics."

Assuming that this is a pattern in American politics, it is not surprising that the continuing prosperity of the late forties and early fifties should also have developed a political movement resembling the four discussed above. McCarthyism, like its predecessors, is characterized by an attack on a convenient scapegoat, which is defined as a threat to American institutions, and also involves an attempt to link "cosmopolitan" changes in the society to a foreign plot.

The State of Tolerance in America A second important factor to consider in evaluating present trends in American politics is the traditional attitude towards tolerance in American society. The historical evidence, some of which has been cited above, indicates that, as compared to the citizens of a number of other countries, especially Great Britain and Scandinavia, Americans are not a tolerant people. In addition to discrimination against ethnic and religious minorities, each war and most prewar situations have been characterized by the denial of minority rights, often even to minorities which were not opposed to the war. Abolitionists, for example, faced great difficulties in many areas, North as well as South, before the Civil War. Many were fired from schools and universities. During World War I, German-Americans and Socialists often experienced physical attacks, as well as economic discrimination. In the last war, the entire Japanese American population was denied the most elementary form of personal freedom.

Political intolerance has not been monopolized by political extremists or wartime vigilantes. The Populists, for example, discharged many university professors in state universities in areas where they came into power in the 1890s. Their Republican opponents were not loath to dismissing teachers who believed in Populist economics. Public opinion polls, ever since they first began measuring mass attitudes in the early thirties, have repeatedly shown that sizeable numbers, often a majority, of Americans oppose the rights of unpopular political minorities. In both 1938 and 1942, a majority of the American public opposed the right of "radicals" to hold meetings.

One important factor affecting this lack of tolerance in American life is the basic strain of Protestant puritanical morality which has always existed in this country. Americans believe that there is a fundamental difference between right and wrong, that right must be supported, and that wrong must be suppressed, that error and evil have no rights against the truth. This propensity to see political life in terms of all black and all white is most evident, perhaps most disastrous, in the area of foreign policy, where allies and enemies cannot be gray, but must be black or white. And it is also evident in domestic politics. . . .

Although Puritanism is probably one of the main sources of American intolerance, there are certainly many other elements which have contributed to its continuance in American life. The lack of an aristocratic tradition in American politics, which is related in large part to our early adoption of universal male suffrage, helped to prevent the emergence of a moderate rhetoric in political life. Almost from the start of democratic politics in America, the political machines were led by professional politicians, many of whom were of lower middle-class or even poorer origins, who had to appeal to a relatively uneducated electorate. This led to the development of a campaign style in which any tactic that would win votes was legitimate. Thus, Jefferson was charged with "treason," with being a French agent before 1800, and Republicans waved the "bloody shirt" against the Democrats for many decades following the Civil War. In order to involve the masses in politics, politicians have resorted to attempting to make every election appear as if it involved life or death for the country or specific strata.

Another factor which has operated to decrease tolerance in this country has been mass immigration. The prevalence of different cultural and religious ways of life has always constituted a threat to

American stability and cultural unity. In order to build a nation, it was perhaps necessary that men should be intolerant of the practices of newcomers, and should force them to assimilate. All through world history, the intermingling of people from different cultural backgrounds has resulted in strife. Such conflict is obviously not conducive to the emergence of a tradition of civic discipline, in which everyone has the right to live out his life as he sees fit, and in which minorities are protected.

It is interesting to note in this connection that the minority immigrant groups themselves have contributed to the support for conformity. One of the principal reactions of members of such groups to discrimination, to being defined as socially inferior by the majority culture, is to attempt to completely assimilate American values, to reject their past, and to overidentify with Americanism. They tend to interpret discrimination against their ethnic group as a consequence of the fact that it is foreign, that it behaves differently, that it is not, in short, American enough. Many of these who adopt the assimilationist solution attempt to enforce conformity within their own group, and are intolerant to those who would perpetuate foreign ways and thus earn the enmity of those of Anglo-Saxon origin. . . .

Americanism as an Ideology: Un-Americanism A third element in American life which is related to present political events is the extent to which the concept of Americanism is an ideology rather than simply a nationalist term. That is, Americanism is a creed in a way that "Britishism" is not. The notion of Americanism as a creed to which men are converted rather than born stems from two factors: first, our revolutionary tradition which has led us to continually reiterate the superiority of the American creed of equalitarianism, of democracy, against the old reactionary monarchical and more rigidly status-bound system of European society; and second, the immigrant character of American society, the fact that people may become Americans—that they are not simply born to the status. While foreigners may become Americans, Americans may become "un-American." This concept of "un-American activities," as far as I know, does not have its counterpart in other countries. American patriotism is allegiance to values, to a creed, not solely to a nation. An American political leader could not say, as Winston Churchill did in 1940, that the English Communist Party was composed of Englishmen, and he did not fear an Englishman.

Unless one recognizes that Americanism is a political creed, much like Socialism, Communism, or Fascism, much of what is currently happening in this country must remain unintelligible. Our national rituals are largely identified with reiterating the accepted values of a political value system, not solely or even primarily of national patriotism. For example, Washington's Birthday, Lincoln's Birthday, and the Fourth of July are ideological celebrations comparable to May Day or Lenin's Birthday in the Communist world. Only Memorial Day and Veteran's Day may be placed in the category of purely patriotic, as distinct from ideological, celebrations. Consequently, more than any other democratic country, the United States makes ideological conformity one of the conditions for good citizenship. And it is this very emphasis on ideological conformity to certain accepted common political values that legitimates the campaigns to locate the "un-Americans" in our midst.

The Inchoateness of Power in America While the emphasis on Americanism is an indicator of the great pressures towards an integrated social system in America, it is also a reflection of another aspect of the society, which is an important political factor, the inchoateness of power. The size and rapid growth of American society have prevented it from developing an integrated cultural or power structure such as exists in many smaller and older, more tradition-oriented European societies. It is impossible, for example, to speak of an American elite, whether economic, or political, or cultural. We have elites, elites which are differentiated regionally, ethnically, and culturally. There is constant friction and competition among the various elites, West against East, North against South, new rich versus old rich, Anglo-Saxons against minority ethnics, the graduates of leading eastern schools against those of schools in other sections of the country.

Political and social movements have in large measure been limited to specific regions of the country or to certain ethnic groups. This fact has operated both to facilitate the emergence of new social movements, religions, and cultural fads, but also, has usually prevented any one of them from sweeping the country. A large part of the elite, as well as the mass of the population, can be relied on to oppose each new movement. Thus Populism, the Ku Klux Klan, various efforts to organize labor or Socialist parties, the Progressive movement, the Know-Nothings, the Townsend Plans, have all had important regional and local successes but died away without coming to national power. It is difficult to build a movement on a single issue, or on an appeal to a single interest group, since such issues or groups never constitute more than a minority of the population. Perhaps the only exception to this rule was the prohibition movement.

While on one hand, the lack of coherence operates to prevent any intolerant group from coming to power, it also operates to facilitate the existence of large numbers of deviant and intolerant groups. Such groups can almost always find supporters both in the general population, and in sections of the elite. Anti-Catholicism or anti-Semitism will appeal to some groups, monetary reform to others, and so on. It is almost a maxim of American politics that any kind of movement can find some millionaires to back it, and it does not take many millionaires to provide enough money to set up an impressive-looking propaganda apparatus. Each of the various radical groups, the Socialist Labor Party, the Socialist Party, and the Communist Party, has had its millionaires. In recent decades, the Communists were more successful than others. . . .

The Background of the Current Disputes Three aspects of American society have been suggested as contributing to an understanding of current extremist political developments in the U.S., the recurrence of status politics focused on attacking scapegoats in periods of prosperity, the absence of a firm tradition of civic discipline or tolerance, and the definition of Americanism in ideological terms. A fourth background factor which is at least as important as these three is the way in which the swing of the political pendulum from the left to the right affects the vulnerability of different groups to extremist pressures.

The period from 1930 to 1945 was generally characterized by the predominance of liberal, or reformist, sentiments in American politics. This was the result of two main factors, the depression and the struggle against Fascism. The depression emphasized the need for socioeconomic reforms and threatened the legitimacy of conservative and business institutions. It was followed immediately by a war, which was defined as a struggle against fascism. Fascism was a rightist movement, and this fact tended to reinforce the political predominance of leftist or liberal sentiments among many Americans. During this period, the political dynamic in most democratic countries was in the hands of the left. The left or liberal groups, in addition to passing reform legislation, attempted to use their power to weaken the prestige of conservative forces. . . .

During this period, also, in the United States as in many other countries, the Communist left was able to make considerable headway in penetrating and manipulating the liberal or moderate left groups. The validity or legitimacy which the depression, or the war against fascism, gave to liberal and leftist ideas tended to facilitate united action by liberals and leftists against the right. The Communists, especially, by concealing their real objectives, by acting positively for liberal causes, by being the best organizers of the left against the conservatives, were able to penetrate into various liberal organizations in this country and into Socialist organizations in Europe.

The postwar period, on the other hand, has been characterized, at least since the Cold War began, by a resurgence everywhere of conservative and rightist forces. This has been the result of two factors, one, prosperity and full employment, and second, the fact that the ideological content of democratic foreign policy has changed. Instead of a war against fascism, identified with the "right," there is now a war against communism, identified with the "left." And while it is possible to validly argue that fascism and communism are much closer to each other in practice than either is to the democratic right or left, the fact remains that each is considered as an extreme version of conservatism or liberalism (leftism). Thus, the period from 1947–1948 to the present affords a very different picture from the decade and a half which preceded it. The conservatives and the extreme right are now on the offensive. Business which provides full employment is once more legitimate. Radical or liberal ideas can be identified with communism or with Russia.

It is important to note the similarities between the present situation and that of the thirties in this country. In the thirties and early forties, conservatives, business leaders, Republican Congressmen and Senators were criticized as having attitudes which were semifascist, or were charged with outright sympathy with fascism. If one looks into the source of this ideological attack on conservatism in that period, it came to a considerable extent from the Communists, even though it was picked up and supported by many people who had no connection with the Communist Party, and were unaware of the extent to which they had absorbed a Communist ideological war position. Similarly, in the last eight years or so, it has been the extreme, or the radical, right which has set the ideological tone for many of the conservatives, which has attacked liberals for being pro-Communist, or "creeping socialists."

In each period, the extremists on both sides have been able to capitalize on sympathetic predispositions, those of the liberals earlier, and the conservatives more recently. These ideological predispositions have not reflected sympathy with extremism, but rather led men to view sympathetically attacks directed against their principal political opponents. Consequently, the dynamic right or left extremists have been able to set the ideological tone for entire periods even though their actual numbers have been small. Today, the major background factor, which has structured the situation so as to permit repressive measures against liberal and left groups, has been the development of a conservative political climate. Once this atmosphere was established, various elements on the extreme right were able to secure influence far beyond that which they could gain during a period of liberal predominance.

II. The Radical Right Today

The Two Conservatives . . . The radical right, . . . refuses to accept the recent past, is radical in the sense that it rejects the status quo. It wants to turn the clock back all the way; it refuses to accept what has happened as something inevitable, or irreversible. In concrete terms, most though not all the sections of the radical right are opposed to: (1) the labor movement, preferring to see trade unions eliminated; (2) the income tax, the movement for the repeal of the sixteenth amendment is largely a movement of the radical right; (3) the welfare state and government planning, it would like a return to the days of limited government; World War II, the radical right sees the war as an avoidable mistake, and prefers in retrospect a policy of Russia and Germany fighting it out alone.

In a larger sense, the radical right views our entire foreign policy from the recognition of Russia to Potsdam as appeasement, treachery and treason. It is opposed to membership in the United Nations, and to entangling foreign commitments. It tends to be Asia-oriented, rather than Europe-oriented; it is especially suspicious of Great Britain as a Machiavellian power which has manipulated us into two wars, and now refuses to back us in our time of need. Since the radical right believes that both our domestic and foreign policies over the last twenty years have represented tremendous setbacks for the country, it looks for an explanation of these calamitous errors and finds it in the penetration of the government and the agencies of opinion formation by a subversive alien group, namely the Communist movement. In many ways the attitude of the American radical right towards the New Deal is similar to the attitude of many German conservatives towards the Weimar Republic and everything that followed the downfall of the Kaiser. . . .

What are the sources of the support of the radical right in this country? It is difficult to answer this question since a number of groups help to back its efforts to suppress the civil liberties of men with whom it disagrees, without themselves completely agreeing on all or even most issues. The only common denominator on which all the supporters of extremist action in the political arena agree is vigorous anticommunism.

This issue, today, has replaced anti-Catholicism or anti-immigrant sentiment as the unifying core for mass right-wing extremist action. It is possible to suggest a number of groups which play important roles in the anti-Communist crusade. These include groups reacting to the need for status policies, both the upward mobile ethnic population, and some of the downward mobile old American groups; groups responding to economic as well as status appeals; the nouveaux riches, and the insecure small businessmen; groups whose values or ties to groups in other countries make them especially vulnerable to anti-Communist appeals (such as the Catholics or people coming from countries occupied by the Communists); the traditionalist and authoritarian elements within the working class; and the traditional isolationists, especially those of German ancestry.

Status Politics and the Radical Right One traditional source of support for extreme conservatism in the United States has been those who derive status from a claim to American history—the people who need the status or activity secured from membership in organizations such as the Daughters of the American Revolution, the Colonial Dames, various veterans' organizations, groups which are organized to commemorate past historical events, and so forth. The point one must always recognize in considering such organizations is that none of them is actually what its name implies. The Daughters of the American Revolution are not *all* the female descendants of the Revolutionary soldiers, but only a minority of those who are eligible. The same point may be made about the membership of groups commemorating the War of 1812, the Civil War, the Confederacy, and other comparable situations. Further, in practice, the members who are active in these groups, who set policy, constitute an infinitesimal minority of the total membership.

Who is the minority deriving status and other gratifications from such membership? Various sociological insights may be of some help here although, unfortunately, there is little or no research on their membership. It has been suggested that individuals who participate in such societies tend disproportionately to be people who have little claim to achieved status. They may be members of families which once were important, but whose present position is such that on the basis of achievement alone they would have little right to social prestige. Alternatively, they may also come from backgrounds which never yielded any significant source of status, except for the fact that they or their ancestors participated in an important event in American history, usually a past war. Many such individuals tend to magnify the one claim to status which they have, a claim to history, a claim to lineage, an identification with an heroic American past, which other people cannot have. This is their defense against the newcomers, against the rising minority ethnic groups. And consequently, such individuals and their organizations make a fetish out of tradition and past styles of life, and tend to be archconservative. Thus the groups which have the greatest sense of status insecurity will oppose both economic reform and internationalism, both of which are viewed as challenges to tradition.

While on one hand, the status-threatened old-family American tends to overemphasize his identification with American conservative traditions, and thus be potentially or actually a supporter of the radical right, it is important to note that the new American, the minority ethnic, also now contributes his share to the groups fostering status needs. For while the old American desires to maintain his status, the new American wishes to obtain it, to become accepted. This is particularly true for those members of the minority groups who have risen to middle- or upper-class position in the economic structure. These groups, having initially entered at the bottom, tend to view the status ladder as paralleling the economic climb. That is, they believe that one need only move up the economic scale to obtain the good things of the society. However, as they move up economically, they encounter social resistance. There is discrimination by the old-family Americans, by the Anglo-Saxon, against the minority ethnics. . . .

. . . Status insecurities and status aspirations are most likely to appear as sources of frustration, independent of economic problems, in periods of prolonged prosperity. For such situations make it possible for individuals and groups to move up rapidly and constitute a visible threat to the established status groups; while at the same time the successfully mobile begin to search for means of improving their status. It is obvious that there are always many who do not prosper in periods of prosperity. And it is precisely members of the older prestigeful groups who are disproportionately to be found among the rentier class economically, with many living on fixed incomes, old businesses, and the like—sources of income which are prone to decline in their relative position. Thus clearly prosperity magnifies the status problem by challenging the economic base of the older groups, and accentuating the claim to status of the emerging ones. It may be suggested as a general hypothesis that the supporters of the radical right in the 1950s will come disproportionately from both the rising ethnic groups, and those old-family Americans who are oriented towards a strong identification with the past.

The Economic Extremists A second source of support for extreme right-wing activities, here as in other countries, is the important group of newly wealthy individuals thrown up by great prosperity. New wealth most often tends to have extremist ideologies, to believe in extreme conservative doctrines in economic matters. The man who makes money himself feels more insecure about keeping it than do people who possess inherited wealth. He feels more aggrieved about social reform measures which involve redistribution of the wealth, as compared with wealthy individuals who have grown up in an old traditionalist background in which they have learned the values conventionally associated with upper-class aristocratic conservatism. Consequently, the new millionaires, such as those concentrated in Texas, have given extensive financial support to radical right movements, politicians, and propaganda organizations, such as Facts Forum.

While the most important significance of the newly wealthy lies in the power which their money can bring, rather than their being part of a mass base, there is a mass counterpart for them in the general population, the small independent businessmen. Statistical data on social mobility in the United States indicates that there is a great turnover in the ranks of these groups. A large proportion, if not a majority of them, come from other social strata: the small storekeepers and businessmen often are of working-class origin; the small manufacturer often comes out of the ranks of executives, white collar, or government workers. These small businessmen, perhaps more than any other group, have felt constrained by progressive social legislation and the rise of labor unions. The latter, for example, often affects them more seriously than large business. Their competitive position cannot sustain increases in wages as readily as can big firms, and large unions tend to have more power in dictating the affairs of the industry than do the individual small concerns. . . .

The "Tory" Worker The previous sections have dealt with factors differentiating middle- and upper-class supporters of right-wing extremism from those who back more moderate policies. The fact remains, however, that every American study of attitudes toward civil liberties and McCarthy has indicated that the lower a person is in socioeconomic status or educational attainment, the more likely he is to be in favor of restrictions on civil liberties, and a "get tough" policy with the Communist states.

The lack of tolerance exhibited by large sections of the lower classes as compared with the middle classes is, of course, quite understandable. Support of civil liberties or tolerance for persons with whom one strongly disagrees requires, one would guess, both a high degree of material and psychic security, and considerable sophistication. As compared with the middle classes, the working class lacks these attributes. The consequences of these differences are manifest not only in the political arena, but in religion as well, for chiliastic evangelical religions have tended to draw their support from the lower classes, while liberal "tolerant" denominations have almost invariably been middle- and upper-class groups.

When one attempts, however, to go beyond the variables of economic status and education, in distinguishing between greater or less liberalism in civil liberties among the lower classes, the principal differentiating factor seems to be party allegiance. In the United States and Great Britain, the conservative workers, those who back the Tory or Republican parties, tend to have the most intolerant attitudes. Comparative impressionistic data suggest that these differences are not inherent in varying social strata, but rather are a consequence of partisan identifications and values. That is, the Democratic and Labour parties are more concerned with propagating a civil libertarian value system than are the conservative parties. Within the Democratic and Labour parties, however, the working class is more intolerant than the middle class.

The support which a large section of the American working class gives to right-wing extremism today may also be related to the greater sense of status deprivation felt by "failures" in periods of prosperity discussed earlier. Workers who fail to get ahead while some friends, classmates, and fellow war veterans do, are also likely to feel embittered. This prosperity-born bitterness should be greater in America than in Europe, since American workers, unlike European ones, do not have a socialist ideology which places the blame for individual failure on the operation of the social system, and consequently will be free to adopt more varied ideologies. . . .

The Isolationists A fourth source of strength of the radical right has developed out of the old isolationist-interventionist controversy. The traditional isolationists have become, in large measure, a base of the radical right. If one looks over the background of isolationism in this country, it seems largely rooted in ethnic prejudices or reactions, or ties to the homeland. Samuel Lubell, for example, suggests, "The hard core of isolationism in the United States has been ethnic and emotional, not geographic. By far the strongest common characteristic of the isolationist-voting counties is the residence there of ethnic groups with a pro-German or anti-British bias. Far from being indifferent to

Europe's wars, the evidence argues that the *isolationists are over-sensitive to them."*

For two wars now, the pro-German ethnic groups have been isolationists. They were opposed to fighting on England's side against Germany. In addition to the Germans and some midwestern Scandinavian groups tied to them by religious and ecological ties, the Irish also have opposed support of Britain in two wars. In large measure, however, in part because German influence was concentrated in the Midwest, in part because isolationist ideologies were part of the value system of agrarian radicalism, isolationism was centered in the Midwest, especially among once-radical agrarians. The radical agrarian character of isolationism, however, gradually began to change for at least two reasons: (1) numerically its mass Midwest base became less and less rural as the farm population declined, and more and more small-town, middle-class in character, that is, people who basically are economic conservatives; and (2) because interventionism was identified with the New Deal and social reform. Thus the small-town, midwestern middle class was anti-New Deal, conservative, and isolationist; this all added up to a fervent opposition to Roosevelt and his domestic and foreign policy. . . .

The common tie which binds the former isolationist with the economic radical conservative is on the one hand the common enemy, Roosevelt and the New Deal, and secondly, the common scapegoat with which they can justify their past position. Both can now suggest that they were right, right in opposing the foreign policy or correct in opposing certain economic policies because these past policies were motivated or sustained by communism or the Communist Party. Thus, both have an interest in magnifying the Communist plot, in identifying liberal and internationalist forces in American society with communism.

The Catholic Population A fifth base of mass support for the radical right in the recent period is the Catholic population. Catholics, independently of the other elements which have been discussed, such as their minority ethnic status or the particular problems of the Irish-Catholics as a national group, probably have a greater predisposition to fear communism, to accept notions of Communist plots, than any other population in America. This predisposition derives from the long history of Catholic opposition to socialism and communism, an organized opposition which has been perhaps more formalized in theological church terms than almost any other group. This opposition has, in recent years, been magnified by the fact that a number of countries taken over by the Communists in Eastern Europe are Catholic, and it is notable that those countries which are most in danger of Communist penetration are, in fact, Catholic.

Catholics, however, in the United States and other English-speaking countries, have been traditionally allied with more left-wing parties. For example, in Great Britain, Australia, and New Zealand, the Catholic tends to be identified as a supporter of the Labour Party. In the United States, he has been traditionally associated with the support of the Democratic Party, while in Canada he is often a supporter of the Liberal Party. . . . The rise of the Communist threat, however, and its identification with the left has created a conflict for many Catholics. Historically, this ideological conflict has developed just as the Catholic population in these countries has produced a sizeable upper and middle class of its own, which in economic terms is under pressure to abondon its traditional identification with the lower-class party.

The conservative party in the United States and in Australia as well, it is interesting to note, is suddenly given an opportunity to break the Catholics from their traditional political mores. The conservatives face the problem in the era of the welfare state, that welfare politics obviously appeal to lower-class people. Consequently, in order for the conservatives to gain a majority (and here I speak not only of the radical right but of the moderate conservatives as well), they must have some issues which cut across class lines, and which can appeal to the lower classes against the party of that class. Traditionally, nationalism and foreign policy issues have been among the most successful means for the conservatives to break through class lines. However, in this specific case, if the conservatives can identify the left with communism they have the possibility of gaining the support of many Catholics, both lower and middle class. This combination of the party desire to win elections plus the general desire of conservatives to dominate the society has led them to adopt tactics which normally they would abhor.

It is appropriate in this context to recall that the use of bigotry as a tactic by the conservatives to gain a political majority is not unknown in American history. The Whig Party before the Civil War was faced with the fact that increased immigration, largely Catholic, was constantly adding to the votes of the Democratic Party. This added to the likelihood that the Whigs could never win a majority. They were in much the same position for most of their existence that the Republican Party was from 1932 to 1952. The Whigs, led largely by the so-called aristocratic elements in American society, upper-class Protestants both north and south, supported mass movements which were anti-Catholic and anti-immigrant, because of the belief that this would be the only way to win elections against the party of the "Demagogues," as they described the Democratic Party.

The upper-class Whigs hoped to break lower-class white Protestants from their support of the Democratic Party by identifying that party with the immigrants and with the Catholics. Today, of course, the position is reversed. The attempt is not so much to break Protestants from the Democrats, but to win the Catholics from the Democrats. The Republicans wish to break the Democratic allegiance of the Catholics, rather than use them as a scapegoat. . . .

Today the Catholics face the Communist issue as the Jews did Nazism. Even unscrupulous anticommunism, the sort which is linked to motives and policies unrelated to the problem of fighting Communists, can win support within the Catholic community. And just as the Communists were able to press forward various other aspects of their ideology among the Jews in the 1930s, so the radical right, stressing the anti-Communist issue, is able to advance other parts of its program. The radical right uses the anti-Communist issue to create or sustain hostility among the Catholics against the New Deal, against social reform, at the same time identifying liberalism with communism.

It is, therefore, impossible to analyze the impact of the radical right on American life without considering the vulnerability of the Catholics to the Communist issue, and the effect of this Catholic sensitivity on the political strategy of both Republican and Democratic politicians in their reactions to the radical right. For political reasons many existing analyses of the radical right in this country have found it convenient to ignore the Catholics, and attempts have been made to interpret the problem in terms of other variables or concepts, some of which, like the minority ethnic's reaction to status deprivation, have been suggested in this paper as well. While such processes are important, it should not be forgotten that the majority of Catholics are still proletarian, and not yet in a position to make claim to high status. The role of the Catholic vulnerability to the radical right today, like the similar reaction of the Jews to the Communists a decade ago, must be considered independently of the fact that both groups have also reacted to the situation of being an ethnic minority.

The Catalytic Elements One additional important group comprise the catalytic element—the organized extremists—the members of Fascist, neo-Fascist, and so-called borderline organizations. These groups and individuals have been advocating various extremist right-wing ideologies for a long time. They remain a constant in the situation, though their number may vary and their strength fluctuate. During the thirties, there were many such crack-pot organizations, in fact, there were many more openly fascist or racist organizations at that time than there are at present. Fascism, Nazism and racism, at least in the form of anti-Semitism, lost whatever appeal it had following World War II. But a new scapegoat has appeared for those who have a need for one, in the form of communism. It is probable that all neo-fascist groups which survived the war, or have been created since, now use the anti-Communist issue instead of anti-Semitism. Here again, the analogy may be made with the role of the Communist Party in the thirties. That movement, in a period of ascending liberalism and antifascism, was able, as was indicated earlier, to initiate campaigns which appealed to large sections of the population.

While there is no right-wing conspiracy equivalent to that of the Communist party (the various organizations and groups are disunited and often conflict with each other), nevertheless, in a general sense, there is a radical right extremist movement which exists without discipline and receives the support of many who are not open members of extremist organizations. These may be termed the fellow travelers of the radical right. In sociological terms, these groups should come disproportionately from the categories discussed earlier, that is, from the status-threatened or the status-aspiring, from the nouveaux riches, from the small businessman, from the ardent Catholics. However, it may be suggested that some of the research findings of studies such as the *Authoritarian Personality* are relevant in this context. The *Authoritarian Personality* and similar studies suggest that for a certain undefined minority of the population, various personality frustrations and repressions result in the adoption of scapegoat sentiments. Prejudice directed at a weak minority acts as a means of satisfying personal frustrations, suggesting that there is a certain personality type which regards discipline and order as conducive to its needs. Such individuals are probably to be found disproportionately among the members of various patriotic and anti-Communist societies, in the crack-pot extremist groups, and significantly in the committees of various organizations which are engaged in Communist-hunting, for example, in the un-American activities committees of local Legion posts, in the equivalent committees of the American Bar Association, and other groups. . . .

Before concluding this review of general tendencies, one interesting and important contradiction between radical right ideology in the United States and the consequences of its promulgation should be stressed. Many political observers often overlook the fact that the ideology of the radical right is a libertarian, civil-liberties-oriented value system. If one reads the *Freeman,* one might think at times that he is reading an anarchist magazine, at least philosophically anarchist. One of the traditional criticisms which the radical right has launched against the New Deal ever since the early thirties is that it has increased the power of the state, that is, has reduced the civil liberties of individuals, that it has improved the power position of certain private governments, such as trade unions. The ideology of extreme conservatism in this country is laissez faire. Writers for the *Freeman* often attack the tariff. This ideology may be found even in the books of some of the major critics of heresy in American culture. For example, James Burnham continually argues that one important reason for war against communism, internal and external, is the need to defend civil liberties. McCarthy's young intellectual spokesman, William Buckley, is a devotee of Adam Smith. In a real sense, the radical right is led by the Frondists of American society, those who want to turn the clock back to a golden age of little government.

III. The Radical Right and McCarthyism

McCarthyism: The Unifying Ideology Extreme conservatism cannot ever hope to create a successful mass movement on the basis of its socioeconomic program alone. Except during significant economic crises, the majority of the traditional middle- and upper-class conservative elements are not likely to support extremist movements and ideologies, even when presented in the guise of conservatism, and the lower classes do not support movements in defense of privilege. The problem of the radical right is to locate a political philosophy which will have appeal to its traditionally rightist support, and will also enable it to win a mass base in the body politic. Nazism was able to do this in Germany by combining a strong nationalist appeal to the status-threatened German middle and upper classes, together with an "attack on Jewish international capitalism" designed to win over those most concerned with economic reform. As a number of European political commentators have suggested, anti-Semitism has often been the extreme rightist functional equivalent for the socialist attack on capitalism. The Jewish banker replaces the exploiting capitalist as the scapegoat.

In the United States, the radical right had to find some equivalent method of appealing to the groups which have a sense of being underprivileged, and McCarthy's principal contribution to the crystallization of the radical right in the 1950s, has been to hit on the key symbols with which to unite all its potential supporters. McCarthy's crusade is not just against the liberal elements of the country, cast in the guise of "creeping socialists"; he is also campaigning against the same groups midwest Populism always opposed, the eastern conservative financial aristocracy. In his famous Wheeling, West Virginia, speech of February 9, 1950, McCarthy began his crusade against internal communism by presenting for the first time an image of the internal enemy:

> The reason why we find ourselves in a position of impotency is not because our only potential enemy has sent men to invade our shores, but rather because of the traitorous actions of those who have been treated so well by this nation. It is not the less fortunate, or members of minority groups who have been selling this nation out, but rather those who have had all the benefits the wealthiest nation on earth has had to offer—the *finest homes,* the *finest college educations,* and the *finest jobs* in the government that we can give. This is glaringly true in the State Department. There the *bright young men who are born with silver spoons in their mouths are the ones who have been worse.*

This defense of the minority groups and the underprivileged, and attack on the upper class, has characterized the speeches and writings of McCarthy and his followers from the beginning. In this McCarthy differs considerably from other anti-Communist investigators. He is rarely interested in investigating or publicizing the activities of men who belong to minority ethnic groups. The image which recurs time and again in his speeches is one of an easterner, usually of Anglo-Saxon Episcopalian origins, who has been educated in schools such as Groton and Harvard, and who is a member of the intelligentsia, the educated classes, not simply the intellectuals. . . .

Over and over again runs the theme, the common men in America have been victimized by members of the upper classes, by the prosperous, by the wealthy, by the well-educated, and when it is necessary to list names, these are almost invariably individuals whose names and backgrounds permit them to be identified with symbols of high status. Since he could attack other individuals and groups, this concentration on the Anglo-Saxon elite is no accident. What are the purposes it serves?

Initially McCarthy, coming out of a state, Wisconsin, which for over forty years had elected the two La Follettes with their isolationism and attacks on eastern business and Wall Street, may have been searching for an equivalent to the La Follette appeal. Much of the electorate of Wisconsin, and other sections of the Midwest, the German-Americans and those who were sympathetic to their isolationist viewpoint, *have been smarting under the charge of disloyalty*. McCarthy has argued that it was not the isolationists but rather those who favored our entry into war with Germany who were the real traitors, because by backing Great Britain in World War II they had played into the hands of the Soviet Union and had been dupes as well as servants of communism. The linkage between the attacks on Anglo-Saxon Americans and Great Britain may be seen in McCarthy's infrequent speeches on foreign policy, which invariably wind up with an attack on Great Britain, sometimes with a demand for action (such as economic sanctions, or pressure to prevent her from trading with Red China). Thus McCarthy is in fact attacking the same groups in the United States and on the world scene, as his liberal predecessors.

On the national scene, McCarthy's attacks are probably much more important in terms of their appeal to status frustrations than to resentful isolationism. In the identification of traditional symbols of status with procommunism the McCarthy followers, of non-Anglo-Saxon extraction, can gain a feeling of superiority over the traditionally privileged groups. Here is a prosperity-born, functional equivalent for the economic radicalism of depressions. For the resentments of prosperity are basically not against the economic power of Wall Street bankers, or Yankees, but against their status power. An attack on their loyalty, on their Americanism, is quite clearly also an attack on their status. And this group also not only rejects the status claims of the minority ethnics, but also snubs the nouveaux riches millionaires. . . .

Anticommunism: The Weakness of a Single Issue In spite of its seeming successes in intimidating opponents, and gaining widespread support behind some of its leaders, the radical right has not succeeded in building even one organization of any political significance. And without organizing its backing, it cannot hope to secure any lasting power. This failure is not accidental, or a result of inept leadership, but rather stems from the fact that the only *political* issue which unites the various supporters of radical right politicians is anticommunism. It is only at the leadership level that agreement exists on a program for domestic and foreign policy. The mass base, however, is far from united on various issues. For example, as McCarthy well knows, the dairy farmers of Wisconsin want the government to guarantee 100 percent parity prices. But this policy is an example of "creeping socialism" and government regimentation to some of the extremist elements on his side.

The Catholic working class still remains committed to the economic objectives of the New Deal, and still belongs to CIO trade unions. While McCarthy and other radical rightists may gain Catholic support for measures which are presented under the guise of fighting communism, they will lose it on economic issues. And should economic issues become salient again as during a recession, much of the popular support for McCarthyism will fall away. As a result any attempt to build a radical right movement which has a complete political program is risky, and probably will not occur.

The radical right also faces the problem that it unites bigots of various stripes. Although there is little available evidence, it seems true that most anti-Semites have become McCarthyites. In the South and other parts of the country, fundamentalist Protestant groups which are anti-Semitic and anti-Catholic back the radical right in spite of the fact that McCarthy is a Catholic. . . .

Perhaps the greatest threat to the political fortunes of the radical right has been the election of the Republican Party in 1952. As long as the Republican Party was in opposition the radical right could depend upon the covert support, or at worst the neutrality, of most moderate conservative sections of the Republican Party. Republicans, even when they viewed the methods of the radical right with distaste, still saw the group as potential vote gainers for the Party. The frustration of twenty years in opposition reduced the scruples of many Republicans, especially those who were involved in party politics. The differences between the radical right and the moderate right are evident indeed and open factionalism existed in the party long before the election of Eisenhower. Nevertheless, the evidence is quite clear that a large proportion, if not the majority, of the moderate Republicans did not view McCarthy or the radical right as a menace to the party, until he began his attack upon them. Walter Lippman once persuasively argued that when the Republicans were in office they would be able to control the radical right, or that the radical right would conform for the sake of party welfare. Most Republicans probably at the time agreed. However, the program of Eisenhower Republicanism has not been one of turning the clock back, nor has it fed the psychic needs of the radical right in domestic or foreign policy. . . .

It is extremely doubtful that the radical right will ever secure more power or influence than it has in the past. It has reached its optimum strength in a period of prosperity, and a recession will probably cripple its political power. It cannot build an organized movement. Its principal current significance, and perhaps permanent impact on the American scene, lies in its success in overstimulating popular reaction to the problem of internal subversion, in supplying the impetus for changes which may have lasting effects on American life, e.g., the heightened security program, political controls on passports, political tests for school teachers, and increasing lack of respect for and understanding of the Constitutional guarantees of civil and juridical rights for unpopular minorities and scoundrels. Whether these changes become institutionalized, however, depends on political developments of the next decade. And if the Cold War and prosperity continue, the radical right, although organizationally weak, may play a decisive role in changing the character of American democracy. It is, therefore, a tendency in American life about which we need to know much more than we do.

15

McCarthyism and Mass Politics

Michael P. Rogin

Rejecting Lipset's analysis, Michael Rogin argues that McCarthyism was not the result of popular passions flowing from irrational sources. McCarthyism, Rogin says, "reflected the specific traumas of conservative Republican activists—internal Communist subversion, the New Deal, centralized government, left-wing intellectuals, and the corrupting influences of a cosmopolitan society." Republican leaders shrewdly exploited popular concern over the Cold War and the Korean conflict, seeing in McCarthy "a way back to national political power after twenty years in the political wilderness." Rogin's work, along with that of Walter Nugent, challenges the interpretations of writers such as Talcott Parsons, Peter Viereck, and Edward Shils who argue that a direct connection exists between the agrarian radicalism of the Populists and twentieth-century extremist movements, especially McCarthyism.

From 1950 through 1954, Joseph McCarthy disrupted the normal routine of American politics. But McCarthyism can best be understood as a product of that normal routine. McCarthy capitalized on popular concern over foreign policy, communism, and the Korean War, but the animus of McCarthyism had little to do with any less political or more developed *popular* anxieties. Instead it reflected the specific traumas of conservative Republican activists—internal Communist subversion, the New Deal, centralized government, left-wing intellectuals, and the corrupting influences of a cosmopolitan society. The resentments of these Republicans and the Senator's own talents were the driving forces behind the McCarthy movement.

Equally important, McCarthy gained the protection of politicians and other authorities uninvolved in or opposed to the politics motivating his ardent supporters. Leaders of the GOP saw in McCarthy a way back to national power after twenty years in the political wilderness. Aside from desiring political power, moderate Republicans feared that an attack on McCarthy would split their party. Eisenhower sought for long months to compromise with the Senator, as one would with any other politician. Senators, jealous of their prerogative, were loath to interfere with a fellow senator. Newspapers, looking for good copy, publicized McCarthy's activities. When the political institutions that had fostered McCarthy turned against him, and when, with the end of the Korean War his political issue became less salient, McCarthy was reduced to insignificance.

Politics alone does not explain McCarthyism; but the relevant sociopsychology is that which underpins normal American politics, not that of radicals and outsiders. Psychological insights are not relevant alone to the peculiar politics of the American Right. Equally important, the ease with which McCarthy harnessed himself to the everyday workings of mainstream politics illuminates the weaknesses of America's respectable politicians.

Attention to sociology and psychology must be concentrated within the political stratum, not among the populace as a whole. It is tempting to explain the hysteria with which McCarthy infected the country by the hysterical preoccupations of masses of people. But the masses did not levy an attack on their political leaders; the attack was made by a section of the political elite against another and was nurtured by the very elites under attack. The populace contributed to McCarthy's power primarily because it was worried about communism, Korea, and the cold war.

The analysis of McCarthyism presented here focuses on political issues, political activists, and the political structure. As an alternative to this interpretation of McCarthyism, the pluralists have suggested an analysis that goes further beneath the surface of American politics. To be sure, unlike La Follette and Hitler, McCarthy mobilized no cohesive, organized popular following. Nevertheless, for the pluralists the concept of mass politics captures both the flavor of McCarthy's appeals and the essence of his threat to American institutions.

In the first place, they argue, McCarthyism drew sustenance from the American "populist" tradition. "Populists," suspicious of leadership, seek to register the unadulterated popular will at every level of government. Giving McCarthyism as his example, Lipset writes,

> American and Australian egalitarianism is perhaps most clearly reflected in the relative strength of "populist" movements through which popular passions wreak their aggression against the structure of the polity. . . . Conversely, in Canada as in Britain such problems have been handled in a much more discrete fashion, reflecting in some part the ability of a more unified and powerful political elite to control the system. . . .
>
> The values of elitism and ascription may protect an operating democracy from the excesses of populism . . . whereas emphasis on self-orientation and anti-elitism may be conducive to right-wing populism.

In this view, McCarthy had to go outside the "political stratum" to obtain support; his power came from his ability to exploit mass resentments.

The alleged mass character of McCarthyism flows, in the second place, from the character of the popular resentments he exploited. He is said to have mobilized feelings of uneasiness over a sophisticated, cosmopolitan, urban, industrial society. He focused these vague discontents, the argument continues, on such specific symbols as intellectuals, striped-pants diplomats, homosexuals, and effete eastern aristocrats. McCarthyite status politics was thus radical in its rejection of industrial society as well as in its suspicion of responsible political leadership.

The third perceived mass characteristic of McCarthyism flows from the first two. McCarthyite appeals, it is argued, were not rooted in the traditional cleavages between the major political parties and groups in America. Like other mass phenomena, McCarthyism split apart existing political coalitions. Talcott Parsons sees it as

> . . . not simply a cloak for the "vested interests" but rather a movement that profoundly splits apart the previously dominant groups. This is evident in the split, particularly conspicuous since about 1952, within the Republican Party. . . .
>
> But at the same time the McCarthy following is by no means confined to the vested-interest groups. There has been an important popular following of very miscellaneous composition. . . . The elements of continuity between western agrarian populism and McCarthyism are by no means purely fortuitous. At the levels of both leadership and popular following, the division of American political opinion over this issue *cuts clean across the traditional lines of distinction between conservatives and progressives*. . . .

For the pluralists, then, McCarthy disrupted the traditional group basis of politics by exploiting popular resentments over changes in American society. In the view adopted here, McCarthy exploited popular concern over foreign policy, structured by existing political institutions and political cleavages. Four subjects provide evidence relevant to these alternative contentions. The first is the political and social background from which McCarthy rose to power. Did the Wisconsin Senator disrupt political alliances? Did he transform traditional conservative politics? If McCarthy was merely a traditional conservative, why did he achieve so much more notoriety than other conservatives?

Second, we will look at McCarthy's ideology. Was this ideology new for a conservative Republican? Did it exploit populistic resentments and moral indignation? Whom was it likely to attract?

Third, we will investigate the evidence bearing on McCarthy's popular support. What social groups supported the Wisconsin Senator? What psychological characteristics and political attitudes led to sympathy for him? What was the relationship between approving of McCarthy in a public opinion poll and voting for him in the election booth? Was McCarthy's popular support sufficient to explain his influence?

The final inquiry will be directed at the response to McCarthy by political institutions and elites. Did the "political stratum" defend the "rules of the game" against this outsider? Did the education and political sophistication of elites insulate them from susceptibility to McCarthy? Were there important differences among elites in this respect? Do the varying fortunes in the war between elite pluralism and mass populism successfully account for the rise and fall of Joe McCarthy?

The Context

The entry of the Senator from Wisconsin onto the political stage did not split apart a previously united Republican Party. The split in the GOP between the East and the western Middle West goes back decades before McCarthyism. In Populist and progressive days, the West North Central states were the center of liberal opposition to an eastern-dominated Republican Party. During the New Deal and World War II, the two wings of the Republican Party switched places. On "traditional economic issues" as well as on foreign policy, midwest Republicans had been more conservative than their eastern counterparts for a decade before McCarthyism. The midwest wing of the party had been more isolationist for perhaps half a century.

It was this wing that mobilized itself behind McCarthy. It supported him on the censure resolution in the Senate, and Republican businessmen in the Middle West were more sympathetic to McCarthyism than those in the East. McCarthy did not split apart an elite, the parts of which had been equally conservative before him. He rather capitalized on an existing liberal-conservative split within the existing Republican elite.

Former centers of agrarian radicalism, like the plains states, sent right-wing Republicans who supported McCarthy to the Senate. But McCarthy was not the agent who disrupted the traditional agrarian radical base. Before these states supported McCarthy, they had already undergone an evolution from agrarian radicalism to extreme conservatism. . . .

The decline of agrarian radicalism increased conservative power in the trans-Mississippi West, but there have been important continuities in the conservative outlook. An ambiguity about the state of the country continues to plague these conservatives; in some ways they are satisfied and in others they are not. The right wing of the Republican Party reveals an uneasiness about cosmopolitan values and styles of life, about large cities and big bureaucracies. In this sense it seeks to change American institutions, not to conserve them. At the same time, it profoundly wishes to preserve the status quo in its own areas —not simply in terms of rural virtues but in terms of the local prestige and economic power of the elites that have since the decline of agrarian radicalism controlled the Republican Parties of the rural and small-town Middle West. This ambiguity—complacency at home and fear of the outside world—is nothing new for midwest conservatism.

Half a century ago, it motivated midwestern conservative opposition to agrarian radical movements, which were perceived as alien imports from the bureaucratized and hostile outside world. McCarthy sprang from this conservative background.

For Leslie Fiedler, McCarthy's support among local newspapers indicated his populist roots. Anyone could get the support of a millionaire or two, Fiedler explained, but the

> resolutely anti-intellectual small-town weeklies and . . . the professionally reactionary press . . . continue to say in [McCarthy's] name precisely what they have been saying now for thirty-five years. To realize this is to understand that McCarthyism, generally speaking, is the extension of the ambiguous American impulse toward "direct democracy," with its distrust of authority, institutions, and expert knowledge; and that more precisely it is the form which populist theory takes when forced to define itself against such a competing "European" radicalism as Communism.

The "resolutely anti-intellectual" small-town newspapers, however, led the opposition to every agrarian radical movement from Populism to La Follette to the contemporary Farmers Union. The Populists and the Non-Partisan League, for example, had to start their own newspapers because the existing local press would not give them a fair hearing in their news columns, much less support them on the editorial page. The small-town press may be suspicious of certain authorities and institutions, but it is supported by others—particularly local business interests. The role of this press provides evidence for McCarthy's conservative inheritance, not his "populist" roots.

There are important continuities between nineteenth century conservatism and the contemporary variety, but several new developments have had their impact. There has, first, been a change in the character of eastern conservatism. As the industrial giants of the East become more established and bureaucratized, they become less militantly conservative. Taft blamed Eisenhower's victory over him in 1952 on eastern financial interests. This Populist-sounding charge hardly reflects Taft's Populist roots; the Taft family has always opposed agrarian radicalism. It reflects rather a change in the politics of "Wall Street."

The New Deal created a balance of forces more opposed to midwest conservatism than this country had seen since the Civil War. Social legislation and trade unions became prominent, and the power of the national government increased. It is quite true, as Parsons argues, that McCarthy directed little fire against trade unions and the New Deal. Indeed, much of McCarthy's genius lay in his ability to concentrate on the single issue of communism—so pressing and popular an issue in the early 1950s—and not raise other, more divisive appeals. But the activists around the Senator supported him so enthusiastically just because they knew he was attacking their enemies. McCarthy's attacks on foreign policy were often framed as attacks on Roosevelt and the New Deal, and his attacks on Britain were generally tied to its Socialist leadership. A writer for *Fortune* who conducted a survey of business opinion about McCarthy wrote, "Among businessmen who approve of McCarthy's war on subversion there is a satisfaction, subconscious perhaps but very strong, over his incidental licks at all longhairs, eggheads, professors, and bright young men of the 1930s and 1940s."

This support, so important to McCarthy, explains why he did not develop an overtly statist appeal. The activists around McCarthy were traditional conservatives, rejoicing in McCarthy's attack on the party of Roosevelt. Like the businessmen in the *Fortune* study, they would have deserted the Senator had he developed a demagogic "liberal" economic program. . . .

The international situation brought the frustrations of midwest conservatism to a head and at the same time seemed to offer a political issue and a way out. The new long-term importance of foreign policy reinforced an already powerfully moralistic political approach. Much as some progressives at the turn of the century had reacted with defensive moralism to the waves of immigrants, so conservatives now reacted to the Communist threat. There had not yet been time to become accustomed to the new situation.

Traditionally, the Middle West has been isolationist for both ethnic and geographic reasons. Many of the region's political leaders thought Roosevelt had forced the country into a war against Germany; now Truman seemed afraid to fight a much worse enemy. Communism represented to them the epitome of an alien world—atheism, immorality, destruction of the family, and socialism. But far from defeating this enemy or withdrawing from the outside world that it contaminated, the Democratic Party dealt in an ambiguous atmosphere of international involvement, limited war, and compromise with evil.

Communism in the abstract was threatening enough. The danger became concretized and symbolized by two traumatic events. The first of these was the "loss of China." The right wing insisted with a stridency born of inner doubt that only a failure to apply traditional

American values and tactics could have caused this defeat. The loss of China was a loss of American potency; it could only cease to be frightening if those responsible were identified.

Following hard upon the loss of China came the Korean War. Wars in America often produce superpatriotism, and this in turn claims victims. Those suspected of opposing wars have often been the victims of 100 percent Americanism. But during the Korean War the superpatriots perceived the very prosecutors of the war as the ambivalent ones. This again was something new and reinforced right-wing Republican fears that the centers of power in the society were working against them. If Woodrow Wilson had not approved of all the excesses of the superpatriots during and following World War I, he at least approved of the war. In the Korean War, the powers that be seemed unenthusiastic; one had to seek support for superpatriotism elsewhere. This was fertile ground for McCarthy.

If China preoccupied conservative elites, the Korean War attracted the attention of the population as a whole. Here real fighting brought to a head amorphous cold war anxieties and intensified concern over communism. McCarthy's prominence coincides with the years of the Korean War. He made his famous Wheeling speech in February 1950, and as its impact appeared to be ending the Korean War began in June. Three years later a truce was signed, and a year after that the Senate censured McCarthy.

Less than 1 percent of a national sample interviewed in the early 1950's volunteered communism as something they worried about. Many more, however—34 percent—checked it off a checklist of things they had recently talked about. In addition, almost all families knew someone fighting in Korea. The poll data did not suggest a mass political uprising over the question of communism, but no more did it suggest the issue's political irrelevance.

Of the authors of *The New American Right,* only Parsons placed foreign policy at the center of his analysis, and even he did not mention the Korean War. But Parsons, although he saw the importance of foreign policy, seriously underestimated the role of elites in shaping McCarthyism. Parsons knew that at the popular level "liberal" attitudes about domestic and foreign policy did not go together. He therefore concluded that since the focus of McCarthyism was foreign policy, it cut across the Left–Right cleavage on domestic politics. This analysis failed to comprehend that McCarthyism was the product less of attitude syndromes at the mass level than of the character of political leaders whom the people supported. Parsons failed to see that fear of communism was generally most salient among those who already voted conservative. He overlooked the fact that McCarthy and anti-communism were far more salient to the conservative elite—from precinct workers to national politicians—than to the mass of voters. If the attitude structure at the popular level was not coherent, those whom the people supported did have a coherent set of attitudes. McCarthyism fed into an existing conservative tradition at the elite level, very conservative on both domestic and foreign questions. (Similarly, Parsons found evidence for the "mass" character of McCarthyism in its strength in former agrarian radical territory because he missed the intervention of conservative elites in the political evolution of those states.) This underestimation of the role of political elites in structuring McCarthyism recurs in pluralist analysis, and we will return to it.

Those who did not stress foreign policy in explaining McCarthyism had additional difficulties. They rightly saw that their analysis had to explain why some people supported McCarthy and others did not; presumably everyone was anti-Communist. Therefore they examined the American social structure to find groups particularly prone to status political appeals of the type McCarthy employed. In this view, McCarthy's concern with communism and foreign policy was only the immediate condition which enabled status seeking and populist groups to act out their frustrations. For example, Lipset wrote, "On the national scene, McCarthy's attacks are probably more important in terms of their appeal to status frustrations than to resentful isolationism."

Those who took this approach still had to explain why McCarthyism should be so powerful in the early 1950s and not at some other time. They had to explain why those with personal and status concerns were seeking a political outlet. Bell wrote, "A peculiar change, in fact, seems to be coming over American life. While we are becoming more relaxed in the area of traditional morals . . . we are becoming moralistic and extreme in politics." Bell explained the growing ideological character of American politics by such factors as the prominence of large, symbolic groups like labor, business, and government.

Whatever the plausibility of this interpretation, Bell himself implicitly rejected it a few years later. Entitling a collection of his essays "The End of Ideology," he argued that ideological politics was on the way out in America. He now viewed McCarthyism as an exception to this general trend. In thus contradicting his earlier effort to explain why McCarthyism flourished in the early 1950s, Bell had nothing else to offer. But the aim here is more basic than simply to catch Bell in a contradiction. Pluralist analyses failed to explain the appearance and meaning of McCarthyism because they overlooked the political context in which McCarthy appeared. They underestimated his roots in an already existing conservative faction inside the GOP— a faction even more concerned about communism, the Cold War, and Korea than was the country as a whole. McCarthy came out of an old American right. What was in part new was the intensity and hysteria he provoked. This in turn is largely explained by changes in American society and politics that agitated the conservatives and by the new importance of foreign policy. Analysis of McCarthy's ideology and of his popular following reveals the role foreign policy and conservative Republicanism played in his power. . . .

To his most devoted followers McCarthy was fighting more than the Communists. . . . Speaking in eulogy of the Senator from Wisconsin, Congressman Smith of Kansas said, "In a world which has lost its understanding of the concepts of right and wrong, truth and error, good and evil, and seeks only to adjust itself to what is expedient, a man like Senator McCarthy is a living contradiction of such Machiavellianism." This sentiment was reiterated in newspaper obituaries. A study of McCarthyism in a Wisconsin county found the same emotion among McCarthy supporters at the grass roots.

That McCarthy should be so widely viewed as a moral figure is no paradox to the pluralists. It is just in his cultivation of a political concern with good and evil that they find his relation to agrarian radicalism. But McCarthy attacked the traditional devils of the conservatives. Just as traditional conservatives had feared the intrusion of alien bureaucrats, alien social legislation, and alien agrarian radicals into their stable world, so McCarthy attacked communism. Godless radicals, intellectuals, and bureaucrats were targets of American conservatism many decades before McCarthyism. If he was more extreme than many conservatives, he was extreme within that tradition.

Moreover, one cannot counterpose McCarthy's moralism to a healthier American pragmatism. For one thing, by McCarthy's use of the document-filled briefcase and the elaborated and detailed untruth, he was able to play upon the devotion of Americans to concrete detail. He promised always to "name names"; he always knew of a specific number of Communists; he had lists, affidavits, reports, right in his hand. McCarthy's "fact-fetishism" played upon our attention to the "real world." Had McCarthy not capitalized on the American weakness in the face of the practical and concrete, he would have been far less effective.

Nor was McCarthy's appeal an alternative to the corrupt but safer image of the ordinary politician. In many ways, such as his insistent friendliness with men he had just pilloried, McCarthy was a caricature of the ordinary politician. He was deliberately crude and liked to be thought of as a "guts fighter," a tough guy. There was something quite prurient in his atmosphere. As a punishing figure, he could immerse himself in the evil around him—loving both the immersion and the punishing in good sadistic fashion. Perhaps his supporters, turning their guilt at their own illicit desires into anger at the corruption of the outside world, could permit themselves to experience McCarthy's lasciviousness vicariously, since he was wreaking vengeance against their external enemies. In any case, dichotomies between a politics of purity and one tolerant of human corruption hardly do justice to the seaminess of McCarthy's appeal.

McCarthy's rhetoric was hardly principled; what principles there were had traditional conservative antecedents. Yet did not McCarthy attack traditional conservative institutions and defend the virtues of the plain people? How is this part of a traditional conservative approach? . . .

A gigantic rally called in honor of McCarthy sang "Nobody Loves Joe but the People," suggesting that if political leaders and institutions could not be relied on, the people could. Other alleged examples of McCarthy's "populism," such as his calling for telegrams against Eisenhower, are examples less of "populism" than of traditional American political practice. Nevertheless, the antielitist flavor of McCarthy's rhetoric is clear.

This fact alone, however, does not remove McCarthy from the conservative tradition. Since the decline of the Federalists, American conservatives have used "populist" rhetoric; in American politics this rhetoric is essential. "Populist" rhetoric does not necessarily reflect a reality of popular enthusiasm and power; often it disguises the power resting in the hands of local and national elites. "Populism" is often an ideological formula used to gain legitimacy, not a factual description of reality.

Moreover, nothing in McCarthy's rhetoric would have frightened several conservative elite groups away. Insofar as McCarthy's appeal transcended anticommunism, its roots were in groups disturbed about cosmopolitanism and about the prestige given to the educated and the established families and businesses of the East. Success in their own bailiwick did not insulate the political and economic elites of the Middle West from these concerns any more than prosperity per se insulated the population at large. The nouveaux riches, however wealthy, could still be upset about those born with silver spoons in their mouths. The midwest political elite, however long established, was still upset about striped-pants diplomacy, intellectuals in the State Department, Harvard intellectuals, and British "pinkos." These were McCarthy's targets, and in the Middle West attacks on such targets did not frighten the elite. Furthermore, McCarthy and other midwestern conservatives never went beyond rhetorical attacks on eastern corporate patricians. They never proposed to injure the vital interests of eastern businessmen, who were, like their midwestern business counterparts, members of the moneyed classes.

Nevertheless, there was in McCarthy's rhetoric a heightened sense of betrayal by the rich and well-born. In part this reflected the growing anxiety of midwestern conservatism in the face of the New Deal and the "liberalism" of Wall Street. Equally important, McCarthy himself was personally very different from other midwestern conservatives. Far from being a man of dangerous principles, McCarthy was a thoroughgoing nihilist. Other conservatives—Goldwater is the prime example—believe in something; he believed in nothing. Whatever the psychological roots of McCarthy's political approach, its sociological roots lay in his one-man struggle for power and prestige, handicapped by a background of relative poverty most unusual in a successful American politician.

McCarthy's personal and social makeup fitted him for the role of destroyer. Perhaps his destructiveness found a sympathy denied his more righteous conservative colleagues. Certainly his outrageous gall catapulted him to a position of power he could exploit.

But McCarthyism is alleged to be more than the exploits of a single man; it is said to reveal the stresses and strains of the American social structure. Analysis of the Senator and of the ideology he employed tells us little about his reception. Did McCarthy's rhetoric in fact embolden the masses to an attack on modern industrial society? Did his "populist" rhetoric in fact attract exradicals, or even ex-Democrats? Did the danger from McCarthyism in fact flow from popular passions?

In January 1954, a majority of the American population approved of Senator McCarthy. For the next eleven months, one third of the total population consistently supported him; eliminate those with no opinion, and the figure rises to 40 percent. . . . This man, terribly dangerous in the eyes of sophisticated observers of American politics, had obtained the backing of millions of American people.

McCarthy's popularity in the polls reenforced a growing belief among intellectuals that the mass of people could not be relied on to defend civil liberties and democratic rights. The Stouffer study of popular attitudes toward communism and civil liberties, published the year following the censure of McCarthy, seemed to demonstrate the willingness of the mass of people to deny civil liberties to socialists and atheists, much less Communists. Community leaders, on the other hand, were much more tolerant of divergent and unpopular points of view. Leaving issues of democratic rights up to the people was apparently a dangerous business; better if they could be decided among political leaders without resort to popular passions. McCarthy had apparently achieved his successes by taking questions of communism and civil liberties out of the hands of the political elite.

In a simplified form, this theory of McCarthy's power ran into trouble. There is evidence to suggest that mass attitudes are not so different in other countries, such as Britain, without producing anything like McCarthyism. Therefore Lipset has suggested that one must look beyond popular attitudes to the political structure that mobilizes and channels those attitudes. This is an important argument, which could have led the pluralists to question the association between popular attitudes and McCarthy's power. But the pluralists contented themselves with pointing to two elements in the American political structure that *fostered* the translation of popular attitudes into political programs. First, it is alleged that McCarthy supporters lacked group ties to the institutions of modern industrial society. Second, Americans are said to lack deference for political leaders; they are not willing to permit a sufficient amount of elite autonomy. With this "populist" outlook, they will be more willing to trust their own (anticivil libertarian) views than the views of their elected representatives.

Pluralist explanations focused on the "mass" character of McCarthy's appeal, challenging political leaders and cutting across party lines. But perhaps the single most important characteristic of supporters of McCarthy in the national opinion polls was their party affiliation; Democrats opposed McCarthy, and Republicans supported him. In April 1954, Democrats outnumbered Republicans more than two to one among those having an unfavorable opinion of McCarthy; 16 percent more Republicans than Democrats had a favorable opinion of the Senator. Totaling support for McCarthy in a series of Gallup Polls in the early 1950s reveals that 36 percent of the Democrats favored McCarthy while 44 percent opposed him. The comparable Republican figures were 61 percent for and 25 percent against. Democrats were 8 percentage points more against McCarthy than for him. Republicans 36 points more for him than against him. The total percentage point spread by party was 44 points. In these polls, as in the data reported by Polsby, no other single division of the population (by religion, class, education, and so forth) even approached the party split.

Similarly, in October 1954 respondents were asked whether they would be more or less likely to vote for a candidate endorsed by McCarthy. The strong Republicans split evenly, the strong Democrats were five to one against the senator, and the weak and independent Democrats divided four to one against McCarthy. By that date, only hard-core Republicans were actively sympathetic to the Wisconsin senator; even the weak and independent Republicans strongly opposed him.

As Lipset suggests, there is evidence that pro-McCarthy sentiment influenced party preference as well as vice versa. Nevertheless, the great disproportion in support for McCarthy along the lines of previous party commitment was not predicted by the pluralist approach. Pluralism stressed McCarthy's roots in the social structure but not his roots in the existing political structure.

Support for McCarthy was also reasonably close to attitudes on political and economic questions of the day. On a whole range of foreign policy issues, McCarthy adherents had right-wing preferences. . . .

Perhaps more surprising, "McCarthy also drew disproportionately from economic conservatives. Measures of such attitudes as position on liberalism in general, laws to prevent strikes, a federal health program, and support of private development of national resources all indicate that the conservative position on these issues was associated with greater support for McCarthy. . . .

Clearly McCarthy drew support from the traditional constituency and traditional attitudes of the Republican right wing. However, he also received considerable backing in the polls from traditional Democratic ethnic and social groups. The relevant survey data comes from a variety of different sources, and although the pattern of support for the Senator is consistent, the degree of cleavage varies. Without holding the influence of party constant, religion and occupation best distinguish opponents of McCarthy from supporters. . . . Professional people were more anti-McCarthy than any other occupational group. On five of six reported polls they were the most anti-McCarthy group, and on four of these polls they were far more anti-McCarthy than any other group. Wealthy businessmen were also apparently anti-McCarthy, although there is less evidence about them. Unskilled workers and small businessmen were the most consistently pro-McCarthy groups. However, union membership significantly increased the opposition to McCarthy among laborers. Apparently the liberal impact of the union leadership reached significant numbers of workers who would otherwise have been neutral or ignorant about McCarthy.

Farmers also tended to be pro-McCarthy, but their degree of support varied sharply from poll to poll. Perhaps this provides further evidence of farmer political volatility. In one combined group of polls, farmers were clearly the most pro-McCarthy group; in other polls they were no more for McCarthy than were unskilled workers and small businessmen.

The occupational impact on support for McCarthy is clear. In several polls, occupational differences at the extremes equaled or exceeded the party differences. The size of both party and occupational differences is particularly striking since these usually worked against each other. Professionals tended to belong to the pro-McCarthy party, workers to the anti-McCarthy party.

Like occupation, the impact of religion also cut across party loyalties, with the exception of the heavily anti-McCarthy, pro-Democratic Jews. Lipset does not report religious data except within the political parties. Other studies demonstrate that in spite of Catholic and Protestant party affiliations, Catholics were significantly more pro-McCarthy than Protestants. . . .

Within the parties the influence of religion was even more apparent. The percentage point spread in attitudes toward McCarthy between strong Democratic Protestants and Catholics was 33. The difference between strong Republican Catholics and Protestants was 21. On the other hand, for strong party identifiers party seems to have been even more important than religion. Strong Democratic Protestants differed in their attitudes from strong Republican Protestants even more than they did from strong Democratic Catholics. And Republican Catholics were closer to Republican Protestants than to Democratic Catholics. Since workers tend to be Catholics, religion and class reinforced each other. Either factor might have declined in importance if the other had been held constant.

Ethnic data also cut across party lines to some extent. Irish and Italian Catholics, traditionally Democratic, were highly pro-McCarthy. However, the influence of party may explain the greater support McCarthy received from German than Polish Catholics, as the latter are strongly Democratic. Among Protestants, differences by ethnic background were small and inconsistent, although Germans were clearly more pro-McCarthy than British.

Finally, level of education was of great significance in explaining support for McCarthy. Without holding party constant, differences are apparent, but they are less significant than occupational influences. However, when party is held constant the effect of education upon support for McCarthy is truly pronounced. The percentage point spread between graduate-school Democrats and grade-school Republicans was 65, the largest spread in all the poll data. However, college-educated

Republicans were no more anti-McCarthy than grammar-school Democrats.

The polls provide us with considerable evidence about support for McCarthy, and reveal a broadly consistent pattern. When the influence of party is eliminated and often even when it is not, the lower socio-economic groups, the more poorly educated, and the Catholics tended to support McCarthy, the big business and professional classes, the better educated, and the Protestants to oppose him. These differences cannot be dismissed as small or insignificant.

There is also clear evidence linking support for McCarthy to the "authoritarian personality." The evidence does not suggest a very strong relationship, however, particularly compared to the impact of party, political issues, and demographic variables. . . . In a national sample, there was a slight relationship at all three levels, but it reached substantial proportions only among the college-educated. As Lipset writes, "Among the less educated, a high authoritarian score reflects in some part attitudes common to the group, which are also subject to modification by more education. If someone is well educated and still gives authoritarian responses, then the chances are that he really has a basic tendency to react in an authoritarian fashion." Where authoritarianism is simply an artifact of low education, it may reflect broad cultural values that lack psychological or political relevance. . . .

At the national level, there was . . . no relationship between ethnocentrism and pro-McCarthy sentiments. Nor has it been possible to establish any relationship between social mobility and support for McCarthy. However, one community study has demonstrated that those with felt status incongruities (that is, those who felt they got less money than their education entitled them to) did support the Senator. This is perhaps the best evidence that McCarthy's appeals tapped generalized discontent.

The data, in sum, do not suggest intense, active, mass involvement in a McCarthyite movement. Efforts to relate status frustrations and psychological malformations to McCarthyism have not proved very successful. Party and political issue cleavages structured McCarthy's support far more than pluralist hypotheses predicted. But the ignorant, the deprived, and the lower classes did support McCarthy disproportionately. Were they expressing their animus against respectable groups and institutions?

To answer this question, we must ask two others: Why did McCarthyism attract a large popular following of this character, and what impact did support for the Senator have on political behavior?

Most people supported McCarthy because he was identified in the public mind with the fight against communism. In June 1952, a national sample was asked whether, taking all things into consideration, they thought committees of Congress investigating communism, like Senator McCarthy's, were doing more good than harm. In a period when less than 20 percent of the population had a favorable personal opinion of the Senator, 60 percent were for the committees and only 19 percent against them. The more McCarthy's name was identified with anticommunism, the more support he got from the population. Perhaps because they themselves feared the Communist menace, the pluralists underplayed the anti-Communist component of McCarthy's appeal. . . .

McCarthy's stress on communism may have suggested "the weakness of a single issue" for building a right-wing mass movement, but by the same token it explained the strength of McCarthyism.

Popular concern over communism could have symbolized a basic uneasiness about the health of American institutions. So it did for McCarthy and his most vociferous supporters, who saw a government overrun with dupes and traitors. For them, the Communist issue was the issue of Communists in government; internal subversion was the danger. For the American people, however, communism was essentially a foreign policy issue. In the 1952 election, less than 3 percent expressed concern over Communists in government—fewer than referred to the Point Four program. Foreign policy, on the other hand, was an extremely salient issue, and those concerned over foreign policy were more likely to vote Republican. The external Communist threat and the fear of war benefited the GOP at the polls in the 1950s: the internal Communist danger, salient to committed Republicans alone, did not. Moreover, mass concern about foreign policy did not appear over the loss of China, which the right-wing invested with such peculiar moral significance. It was only when American soldiers went to Korea that foreign policy became salient at the mass level. And the desire there—as expressed in the election of Eisenhower—was for peace not for war.

Why then, if McCarthy's appeal had specifically to do with foreign policy and the Korean War, did he receive greater support among the poorer and less-educated groups? Had the working class been actively concerned about McCarthy, we might expect this support to overcome the relative lack of political knowledge among those of low socioeconomic status. But asked to name the man who had done the best job of fighting communism, the less-educated and poorer strata volunteered McCarthy's name no more than did the better-educated and rich. Highly conscious pro-McCarthy sentiments were as prevalent among the upper as the lower classes. (Those of higher socioeconomic status, with more political information and sophistication, were more likely to name McCarthy as someone who had done a particularly bad job.) Disproportionate working-class support for McCarthy thus only manifested itself when his name was actually mentioned in the polls; it was not powerful enough to emerge when workers had to volunteer his name on their own.

The evidence does not suggest that the Communist issue preoccupied the lower classes, or that they were using that issue to vent general grievances about their position in society. More likely, they simply had less information about McCarthy's methods, a less sophisticated understanding of their nature, and less concern in the abstract about possible victims of the Senator's techniques. Therefore, when the pollsters specifically mentioned McCarthy's name, it tapped among the middle-class revulsion over McCarthy's crudities and opposition to his infringements of individual rights. Among the working class, it tapped an anticommunism relatively less restrained by these concerns.

Still, lack of sophistication on matters of civil liberties can have as dangerous consequences as the political mobilization of status anxieties and anti-industrial hostilities. It can, that is, if it becomes politically mobilized. But sympathy for McCarthy among the less politically sophisticated was not translated into action. To many Americans, especially those in the lower classes who were not actively in touch with events in the political world, McCarthy was simply fighting communism. Support for McCarthy meant opposition to Communists. This was a long way from being willing to break traditional voting patterns, or vote against other interests, in order to support the Wisconsin Senator. In fact, the issue of McCarthyism was more salient to its opponents than to its sympathizers—precisely because McCarthy's opponents were more concerned with political events. . . .

Analysis of electoral data confirms both the minimal impact McCarthy had on actual political behavior and his greater salience to opponents than supporters. In Connecticut in 1952, McCarthy made a particular effort to unseat William Benton, but Benton's support was virtually identical to that given the rest of the Democratic ticket. The Eisenhower landslide defeated Benton; McCarthy did not. In Wisconsin and particularly in the Dakotas, McCarthy's impact on the regular party vote was also minimal. There is some evidence that he hurt Republican senators in states where he campaigned for them. . . .

One need not assume the worst about the motivations for conformity, or about its consequences, or about the aspects of the American tradition that inspire conformity. Compulsive Americanism may have produced Catholic support for Eisenhower. That hardly makes it look like a dangerous source of political extremism. In our society, those with severe personal problems are likely to turn their back on politics. Status anxieties may find an outlet in political moderation. One must not too readily identify personal anxieties or status politics with political extremism. No particular political consequences follow from nonpolitical attitudes such as status anxieties. The intervening political and organizational structures and attitudes are crucial.

The McCarthy years were also the Eisenhower years. Far from demonstrating their discontent with respectable political leadership, the mass of Americans responded to the political anxieties of the cold and Korean wars and whatever social and personal anxieties may also have been relevant by electing Eisenhower. Eisenhower's personal and political appeal depended on the belief that he could be trusted to take care of things without disrupting the society. Eisenhower politics was the politics of deference to responsible leadership, of apolitical moderation. Support for Eisenhower indicates more about the mood of the populace in the America of the 1950s than does support for McCarthy. And McCarthy became prominent in the vacuum of popular apathy and moderation, not on a wave of radical mass mobilization.

What are we to conclude, then, about McCarthy's "mass" appeal? McCarthy's popular following apparently came from two distinct sources. There was first the traditional right wing of the midwestern Republican Party. Here was a group to whom McCarthy was a hero. He seemed to embody all their hopes and frustrations. These were the militants in the McCarthy movement. They worked hardest for him and were preoccupied with his general targets. To them, communism was not the whole story; their enemies were also the symbols of welfare capitalism and cosmopolitanism. These militants were mobilized by McCarthy's "mass" appeal. Yet this appeal had its greatest impact upon activists and elites, not upon the rank-and-file voters. And while McCarthy mobilized the Republican right wing, he did not change its traditional alliances. This was not a "new" American Right, but rather an old one with new enthusiasm and new power.

McCarthy's second source of popular support were those citizens mobilized because of communism and the Korean war. Concern over these issues throughout the society increased Republican strength, although this increase in popular support accrued not so much to McCarthy as to Eisenhower. McCarthy's strength here was not so much due to "mass," "populist," or "status" concerns as it was to the issues of communism, Korea, and the Cold War. At the electoral level, there was little evidence that those allegedly more vulnerable to "mass" appeals were mobilized by McCarthy to change their traditional voting patterns.

McCarthy had real support at the grass roots, but his was hardly a "movement in which popular passions wreaked their aggression against the structure of the polity." In a period in which the populace gave overwhelming support to Eisenhower, it can hardly be accused of failing to show deference to responsible political leadership. In so arguing, I by no means wish to minimize the danger of McCarthyism. But the pluralists, writing in a context of fear of the masses, have misunderstood both the source and the nature of that danger. They see a rebellious populace threatening the fabric of society. In fact, McCarthy did immense damage to the lives and careers of countless individuals. He exercised an inordinate influence over policy making. But popular enthusiasm for his assault on political institutions simply cannot explain the power he wielded. Insofar as McCarthy challenged political decisions, political individuals, and the political fabric, he was sustained not by a revolt of the masses so much as by the actions and inactions of various elites.

16

The McCarthyism of the Left

James Hitchcock

The founding of organizations such as the John Birch Society and the Christian Anti-Communist Crusade in the late 1950s clearly reveals that the appeal of right-wing anticonspiracy movements have not lost their appeal in some sectors of American society. As some of the articles in this book make clear, however, fears of conspiracy are not associated exclusively with the radical right. In the piece that follows James Hitchcock argues that the "extreme segments" of the present-day New Left view the world in a conspiratorial vein. Despite "great differences in political ideology," Hitchcock contends, the character and spirit of New Left extremism is comparable to that of McCarthyism.

The experience of McCarthyism in the early 1950s was a trauma from which American liberalism has never recovered; the badly healed scars and the nerve endings still close to the surface help explain feel-

James Hitchcock, "The McCarthyism of the Left," South Atlantic Quarterly, *LXIX (Spring 1970), 171–185.*

ings and perceptions of liberals and radicals today. McCarthyism has acted like a cumulative poison, nearly fatal in its time and never wholly expelled from the system. The trauma for liberals was on three levels, distinct from a logical point of view but nonetheless irrationally connected. The first was the liberals' awareness, stated publicly and excessively by some and passionately denied by others, that Senator McCarthy's charges against them were built around a kernel of truth —a whole generation of liberals had been dupes, to a greater or lesser degree, of the "international Communist conspiracy." This fact, and the burden of guilt which it imposed, caused many liberals to behave in bizarre and irrational ways, ranging from fanatic reaction against all their former opinions to stubborn insistence that no sin had been committed. The second level was that of betrayal. Most liberals recognized the distortions and gross excesses of McCarthy's movement, yet many not only failed to resist him with vigor and courage but actually adopted a prudent attitude of watchful waiting and in a few cases of active cooperation in the persecution of friends and colleagues. This imposed a different kind of guilty burden, but one which has been equally real and wounding. The final trauma was the relatively more simple and bearable one of public humiliation and attack, in which for the most part the victims could at least take satisfaction in their own innocence, although few people probably ever wholly recover from pilloryings of the kind to which many liberals were exposed more than fifteen years ago.

From the Senate's censure of McCarthy in late 1954 until the emergence of the New Left about 1965 liberals enjoyed a period of general peace and modest triumph. Intellectuality became fashionable, and intellectuals moved from a condition of being despised for their impracticality and uselessness to one of being very much in demand by government and private agencies. Under President Kennedy and in the early years of President Johnson liberal ideas were implemented to a degree not dreamed possible a few years before. Many wounds healed over, and something like an era of good feelings seemed to be forming, as black leaders, elected officials, nuns, and even a few enlightened businessmen joined hands and sang together in public.

Yet the past five years have been in their way as traumatic for liberal intellectuals as the era of the first Senator McCarthy. Many of the old wounds have been aggravated and the same traumas are being suffered, and even if liberalism survives its second life-and-death struggle in twenty years, it is inevitable that the invisible effects will be felt for a long time. It will be the burden of this essay to argue that in character and spirit McCarthyism was, despite the great differences in political ideology, quite similar to the extreme segments of the New Left.

Both McCarthyism and the New Left gained a public hearing in the wake of certain political happenings, especially certain sensational exposés which gave credibility to the idea that liberals were involved in unwholesome conspiracies to betray both American liberties and the rights of certain foreign peoples. In the postwar period the fall of so many nations to communism, especially China, led to the belief that the State Department acquiesced in these events. A few actual Communists, even a few bona fide Russian spies, were discovered. A larger number of individuals were revealed to have had Communist connections in their past or to have spoken and written favorably about communism over the years. They could be plausibly designated fellow travelers or even crypto-Communists. In time the right wing discovered that in fact the whole ideology of the American Left for decades had been sympathetic to Communists and to the Russian experiment and that many American liberals had excused even the excesses of Stalin and most had not felt a compulsion to denounce them.

During the second half of the 1960s the New Left discovered that certain respected members of the liberal establishment and certain respected liberal institutions like the National Student Association and the magazine *Encounter* had been subsidized or otherwise "co-opted" by the Central Intelligence Agency. Numerous other liberals, especially professors, had relations, in proximate or remote degree, with other government agencies or with the defense establishment and could be fairly designated the equivalent of fellow travelers. Turning to the ideas of liberalism itself, the new radicals discovered that much of this ideology, even that deemed subversive by the Right, actually supported "the System" in subtle and crucial ways. Just as the McCarthyites discovered that liberal agitation for reform from 1933 on prepared the way, intentionally or otherwise, for the imposition of communism in America, the New Left discovered that for decades the liberals and the Old Left had built up an intellectual climate favorable to American corporate imperialism and that liberals were, knowingly or unknowingly, part of a conspiracy to delay crucial reforms at home and suppress "people's revolutions" in places like Vietnam and the Dominican Republic.

Two lesser parallels between McCarthyites and New Leftists are worth noting. One is a certain cavalierness about political categories. For the McCarthyites there was no essential difference in the positions of Adlai Stevenson and Gus Hall, and the New Left persists in labeling the Vietnam conflict a "liberals' war," despite the fact that before

1964 at least, few people considered Lyndon Johnson a liberal and the liberalism of McGeorge Bundy, Dean Rusk, Henry Cabot Lodge, and other men in charge of policy is highly questionable.

A second parallel is the New Left's unwillingness to acknowledge early and severe liberal opposition to the war and to racism and poverty, or the fact that it has been liberal agitation primarily which has made these issues real in American politics. (It is official New Left doctrine that its own activities are what has made the war unpopular, although quite clearly it was the respectable dissent of men like Eugene McCarthy which did the most in this regard.) The fanatic cannot acknowledge that others, working in different ways, can possibly be sincere or effective. Thus the first Senator McCarthy managed to convey the impression that he had uncovered a large number of Communists in the government and was a lone wolf in this mission, whereas in actuality he uncovered not a single one; those few who were discovered were discovered by others. Similarly, although the New Leftists paint a picture in which all liberals have been C.I.A. dupes or agents, it was the liberal, hawkish, now defunct magazine the *Reporter* which first exposed some of the C.I.A. involvements, although *Ramparts* managed to claim credit. In McCarthy's time liberals who had repudiated earlier pro-Soviet enthusiasms or had ever had them were dismissed as serving the Red cause in subtler and more sinister ways—the same kind of charge that the new radicals now bring against liberals who have been dissenters for years.

In fanatic politics the enemy is not merely he who opposes the cause but, even more culpable, he who claims to be an ally but who fails to support the cause wholeheartedly. (Thus in the eyes of the McCarthyites a man like President Eisenhower, who was anti-Communist, was still denounceable because he was not anti-Communist enough.) There is a certain validity in this attitude, but it is enormously dangerous. Since almost no one ever does enough, this principle can be the basis for endless purges and witch hunts.

The inability of the liberals to satisfy their critics as to their integrity and their trustworthiness has much to do with the fact that conspiratorial beliefs of the Right and the Left, which are originally stimulated by specific political events and can be measured against these events, soon become cosmic in scope and are revealed to be deeply rooted in a whole tangle of irrational fears and expectations which go far beyond politics. In the McCarthy era liberals were bewildered by the fact that the fanatic hatred of communism which affected the Right soon came to include such diverse objects as homosexuality in the State Department, atheism on the campus, the power of labor unions, modern art, pornography, fluoridated water, the decline of small-town America, etc., etc. The most extreme rightists believed that a conscious conspiracy linked all these together, promoting the single end of weakening "American moral fiber," thus insuring the triumph of the Reds. The less fanatic believed that the degeneracy of the liberals merely made them susceptible to the whole range of subversions—political, moral, and cultural—that objectively served the same end.

The New Left's notion of a "revolution in consciousness" is a mirror image of this earlier view. "The System" is seen as a coordinated whole, and whether this coordination is believed to have been purposely built, or merely the evil flowering of the sick capitalist-imperialist structure, the result is the same. Unrepressed sex, mind-blowing drugs, hippie clothes, psychedelic art, etc., etc., are seen as almost as important as the revolution itself. Not just the political and economic system but the entire culture, including such apparently innocent aspects of it as short hair and coats and ties, are seen as bolstering reactionary policies.

Like McCarthyism, the more extreme manifestations of the New Left have arisen not only in a time of bewildering political disorders (parallel to the fall of eastern Europe and China to communism in the forties) but in a time of accelerating cultural change as well. (The war economy of 1941–1945 probably dealt the fatal blow to free-enterprise, isolationist, small-town America.) In periods of severe change men's psyches are stretched in strange and painful ways, and one method of maintaining some kind of balance is to find concrete scapegoats, usually politicians, who are blamable for all that is menacing in society. Here, however, Old Right and New Left diverge sharply. The former implacably opposed these manifestations, which they believed a liberal conspiracy fostered; the latter embraces them ecstatically but believes with equal fervor that a liberal conspiracy retards them and produces a repressive atmosphere.

Naturally education then becomes a crucial focus of antiliberal attack, because so many professional educators are liberals and because the educational system, at least vaguely, has a liberal veneer over it. The McCarthyites believed that on every level of school, from primary grades to graduate schools, a burgeoning conspiracy existed in which teachers attempted to infect students with collectivist ideas. The new radicals not only declare that the school system is a vast conspiracy to make students docile and conservative but now speak regularly of "cultural genocide." (The next stage, already being reached, is for affluent middle-class youths to discover that their own educations, and not merely those of ghetto blacks, have been murderous.) Teachers are not even credited with sincere ineptitude; they are seen as engaged in a semideliberate effort to destroy the minds of the young.

The remedy for this situation is inevitably "community control" in some form. Since the professionals are profoundly untrustworthy—enemies of the students they are supposed to be educating—there is no alternative except to allow pure-minded amateurs to regain direction of the educational process. For the right wing these are the healthy, correct-thinking suburban parents, who will purge libraries, censor textbooks, and fire subversive teachers. For the left it is black parents, saved from the degeneracy of the American middle class, who will perform the same function. The universities must also be purged, but although the Right has usually reserved this function for outside agencies, the Left will entrust the responsibility to the students themselves, or at least selected cadres of them.

The attack on education and on liberal professional educators closely parallels the attack on government and social-welfare bureaucrats, also mainly liberals, who are seen by Right and Left as similarly infected with pernicious ideas, sometimes reaching conspiratorial proportions, which make them, at least "objectively," enemies of the people. Power must be taken from them by force, if necessary, and radicals of all stripes look forward to the day when, as George Wallace said, the bureaucrats and their brief cases will be thrown into the Potomac.

Perhaps the essence of fanatic politics is precisely the fact that political and economic issues come to be joined in the radical's mind with pervasive cultural issues. This is the root of totalitarianism—the belief that political means should be used to force cultural change in society or, conversely, that culture must be forcibly changed to serve certain political ends. Since these beliefs are almost always irrational, they always portend fanatic politics and violence.

The extremists' hostility to educators and bureaucrats goes far beyond their dissatisfaction with what these men think and do and becomes an implacable hostility to what they are. On one level it is anti-intellectualism—the liberal is dangerous because of his theories, either leftist and subversive or rightist and imperialist, which have corrupted him. He is also dangerous because he thinks so nimbly and can thus rationalize his indefensible beliefs and actions in the face of criticisms by blunter and more honest persons, who in order to withstand the liberals' endless rationalizings must simply assert heartfelt truths with increasing forcefulness, refusing to debate, because debate gives the liberal a tactical advantage. Thought itself soon becomes suspect. Certain intellectuals, like Frederick Hayek or Herbert Marcuse, whose theories are useful to the cause, will be cited and their ideas employed, but most of the radicals will hold even these intellectuals in contempt, and those who do not nonetheless respect them only because their ideas are useful, not because they feel any necessity to engage in rigorous theorizing. Although a work of scholarship may rarely be cited which lends support to a radical belief, for the most part scholarship is regarded as totally irrelevant. Painstaking, detailed research designed to establish the true facts of a political or economic situation is either dismissed a priori as unreliable or held to be invalid because it is not informed by passion and a desire to meet crucial political emergencies. (A common form of this argument is that since most scholars are liberals, all their work is inherently untrustworthy.)

The ultimate source of the liberal intellectual's perniciousness is finally recognized as the fact that he is cut off from "the people" and, except for those liberals who are conscious participants in a Communist or C.I.A. conspiracy, from the "real world" as well. He lives in a world of theory, trying vainly to understand all sides of the question, and hence cannot empathize with the urgent feelings and needs of either the "true American" (on the right) or the blacks and the workers (on the left). The right-wing businessman's contemptuous remark that liberal professors have "never had to meet a payroll" and hence have no right to criticize capitalism, has its equivalent in his left-wing son's belief that the professors have nothing to teach him, since they have never lived in a black ghetto. The appeal which conspiracy theories have is easily understandable in this context. Since the people are basically pure and right-thinking, society can be corrupted only through the manipulations of the few, who hold all power. (Both left and right must therefore hold that ordinary electoral democracy is mere sham; otherwise the people would have to be held responsible for the misdeeds of their rulers.)

An unstated theme of radical politics is also that of a return to fundamentals—those things which appear to be simple, elemental, and human. For it is precisely through the complexities and compromises of liberal thought and the modern liberal state that betrayal has entered. Fanatic politics naturally feeds on everyone's mistrust of complexity and everyone's longing for renewed simplicities. Strong feelings, and actions informed by strong feelings, thus become almost self-validating, and while thought is not abandoned altogether, the worst evil is thought without feeling, the liberal intellectual ideal of "objectivity." Since it is easy to show that liberals who think they are being objective are really susceptible to prejudices, it is easy to dismiss thought itself as fundamentally illusory. It is also antilife and furthermore antidemocratic—since not all people are intelligent in the educators' meaning of the term. And since few have access to superior formal schooling, these things can have no relevance to real human needs or to "life."

The disgruntled radical, whether of the Right or the Left, soon begins to champion a counterculture that subverts the official high culture which is the monopoly of liberal intellectuals. Most theoretical learning and high culture are dismissed as effete and irrelevant. Students are urged to study subjects which can be put to use, like business (on the Right) or (on the Left) guerrilla tactics or actual ghetto conditions. Education comes to have no value unless its effects are immediate and measurable. The radical then begins to cultivate a self-conscious style of living which demonstrates his contempt for the official culture. He adopts folksy ways (the McCarthyites' "plain American talk" and "buy American" and the New Leftists' affectation of denim clothes and folk music) and, in given circumstances, blunt and aggressive, even obscene words as the only appropriate means of telling the truth. (The McCarthyites did not often use obscenity in public, but many of them were said to be very fond of it in private. It is, after all, barracks-room talk, and a sign of a real man, in the right-wing sense.) Eventually this impatience with intellectuality and this exaltation of feeling end in a glorification of action, almost for its own sake. Even though the radical knows that his actions—a physical assault on an enemy, a violent demonstration, perhaps even the caching of guns—will probably have counterproductive effects, he nonetheless feels compelled to assert his commitment and his manhood.

The radical also begins to develop a messianic complex, at unacknowledged variance with his desire to be at one with "the people." When McCarthy began to lose his popular support and when the myth of a silent reactionary majority in the United States was laid to rest in the 1964 election, the true believers responded sadly that these events merely showed the extent of brain-washing to which the American people had been subjected. This is precisely the response of the New Leftists when they need to explain the antagonism of "the workers" to progressive movements. The McCarthyites and the extreme New Leftists both consider themselves saving remnants of the nation, authorized to pass absolute and unquestionable moral judgments on their fellow citizens and justified in taking whatever actions are necessary to resist evil and enforce virtue, even, in extreme cases, guerrilla warfare.

During the 1950s liberals placed themselves in the hardly tenable position of seeming to argue that civil liberties are the only absolutes in society, not to be violated for any reason whatsoever. This belief is untenable for a number of reasons, among them the fact that no one really believes it. Everyone is willing to see civil liberties curtailed at some point; the debate is always over where to locate the point. The fanatic temperament naturally scorns civil libertarianism with a special passion, since it seems like a classic type of sacrificing the greatest good to middling goods, or like classic hypocrisy, in which the liberal uses an idealistic argument to justify an illiberal position. The McCarthyites believed fervently that since the Communist movement literally aimed at the enslavement of the world, it was criminal folly to observe the niceties of the Bill of Rights in prosecuting Reds. An exaggerated concern for the rights of the subverter would result in the loss of all rights by everyone. The classic New Left argument also rests on the idea that civil liberties objectively favor the oppressor in society and need not therefore be respected. Both Right and Left add that civil liberties are merely a sham, since a small group of corrupted individuals virtually control government, education, and the mass media, effectively stifling real dissent.

Both attitudes depend on a strong sense that a dire emergency exists in society—the McCarthyites' belief that the timetable of the international conspiracy was being realized, the New Leftists' belief that the time is ripe for revolution, which liberal reforms delay. The frenetic, passionate, often hysterical moods of Right and Left are psychologically necessary to sustain the sense of crisis which justifies the suspension of ordinary rules of speech, thought, and behavior.

The denouncers on both left and right of civil libertarianism also face an inevitable criticism which they refuse to answer adequately. While proposing that civil liberties can be temporarily curtailed in the interest of achieving greater liberty for all people, both groups admire certain foreign regimes (notably Spain and Nationalist China for the Right and Cuba and Mao's China for the Left) where civil liberties have either never existed or have long been curtailed. It is therefore legitimate to suspect that the triumph of the alleged friends of liberty, right or left, would very likely see an enduring police state in America, even after the immediate menace of communism or imperialism had been eliminated.

The similarities of attitude and program of Old Right and New Left are quite obvious and also probably inevitable—fanaticisms of whatever kind tend to merge in style and forms of thought, although not in ideology. There are, however, certain similarities also between the ways in which McCarthyism functioned in American society seventeen years ago and the ways the New Left functions now. The most obvious difference is that at the height of his influence Senator McCarthy had considerable popular support among "average Americans," which the New Left does not have and cannot gain by any conceivable means. However, this does not mean that the New Left is powerless. As more and more college students are "radicalized," there may come to be a substantial number of active, articulate younger citizens who are at least partially sympathetic to the New Left's goals and methods. More important, there are signs that the split between white and black radicals is being healed, and blacks may in time form a kind of constituency for New Left programs. Most important, on some leading campuses the New Left seems to enjoy at least the passive support of a majority of the students.

Both Senator McCarthy in his time and now the New Left are maverick phenomena, outsiders who are highly antagonistic to that elusive reality, the Establishment. The Senator from Wisconsin almost made "The East" a dirty word in the rest of the country, and his biggest guns were directed at Ivy League alumni in government and in major corporations, who he charged were the people most susceptible to the Communist line. The New Left blames primarily these same people for the corruption of the American dream; even the obvious racism of the police and union laborers is attributed ultimately to the cynical manipulations of the Establishment.

Yet a curious feature of both the McCarthy era and our own day is the degree to which the Establishment has given the marauders a measure of legitimacy and support and has failed to defend itself as vigorously as it might. Although McCarthy assaulted the eastern, moderate wing of the Republican party quite forcefully, there were few from that quarter who were willing to counterattack and some who were willing to give at least mild approval to the Senator's actions. Today the official establishment line on the New Left, insofar as one exists, seems to be that old chestnut from the McCarthy era, "We sympathize with many of their goals, but we disapprove of their methods." Beyond this, such establishment figures as Robert Finch, secretary of Health, Education, and Welfare, former President James A. Perkins of Cornell, John D. Rockefeller III, and Tom Wicker, chief of the *New York Times* Washington bureau, continually alert Americans to the good aspects of the New Left's program and proportionately distract attention from its extremists. This inevitably gives radical tactics a legitimacy they would not otherwise have.

The reasons for the cooperation of certain establishment figures in what could be their own destruction (President Perkins had to resign at Cornell, and at Columbia the S.D.S. has reportedly taken to attacking its own faculty supporters, on the grounds that it is these men who by their benign presence legitimize the System) are difficult to discern. For most it is probably simple prudence—the Establishment, such as it is, always prefers to deal with problems quietly and with a minimum of blood; hence there is probably a feeling that volcanic movements should not be met head on but should be left to spend themselves. For others it is probably cynical self-interest—all conservatives benefited from the black eye which Senator McCarthy gave liberalism, and establishmentarians like McGeorge Bundy (who is involving the Ford Foundation in some radical neighborhood projects) can be seen as forging a power alliance with new militant groups, against old-line liberal organizations like labor unions. Some perhaps even think the radicals may win and wish to be on their side in case they do, and on many campuses the road to prominence and political success is clearly marked out as along radical paths. And there is finally the phenomenon of upper-middle-class guilt feelings, the fascinating disarray and loss of self-confidence which Malcolm Muggeridge loves to dwell on in the British ruling classes and which affect our own as well.

Fifteen years ago in moderate and conservative political circles the accepted line on Senator McCarthy was that he was an undoubtedly crude, potentially dangerous, demagogic, and distasteful person who nonetheless was performing a valid and necessary task, a task too dirty for conventional methods. Thus few respectable people criticized the senator publicly, and ardent anti-McCarthyites were regarded even by unfanatic people as soft on communism. The assumption was that since the liberals had failed to halt the advance of communism they had forfeited the right to criticize those who tried harsher methods. Today, as the New Left is subjected to vigorous criticisms from liberal quarters, the standard counterattack is to assert that since liberals have allowed the society to get into a mess, they have no right to snipe at those who try to right the situation. Apologists for the extreme Left, while admitting apprehension over some of its ideas and programs, nonetheless assert that conventional methods and a scrupulous respect for civil liberties are not sufficient, and rougher methods must be used. Often this is accompanied by a sneer directed at liberals who are too "civilized," effete, or cowardly to do the dirty work revolution requires. So far the full effects of the New Left have not been felt much outside the universities, but within them their impact has been considerable. In America the university is the easiest of all institutions to attack, because it tolerates and even invites criticism, it is reluctant to use force in its own defense, and the majority of people in society are suspicious of the institution and are not anxious to defend it.

One of the most pernicious aspects of McCarthyism was its effective suspension of the principle of presumed innocence—many people were put in the untenable position of having to prove that they were not Communists. On the more advanced campuses of today, and even some not so advanced, a similar atmosphere seems to have developed, in which charges of "racism," "C.I.A. dupe," "reactionary," etc., are hurled with such indiscriminate abandon that professors and administrators find themselves on the defensive against charges which have never been specified or documented. The familiar technique of the big lie is employed, by which an assertion, if repeated often and vigorously enough, will be believed by a substantial number of people. (At Columbia the S.D.S. accuses President Andrew Cordier of complicity in the murder of Patrice Lumumba, although no proof is offered.) While insisting on free speech for themselves (vowing, like Senator McCarthy, never to be muzzled), the radicals tend to inhibit free and candid speech in the university, since professors' published writings, and sometimes their private correspondence as well, are combed for statements which indicate ideological deviations, and these deviations are publicized and become the basis for denunciations of the university and demands for radical change, sometimes even of physical harassment of professors. (At the University of Chicago, history graduate students circulated a document detailing the political sins of a number of the history faculty, both their actions and their ideas.)

The atmosphere on certain campuses today and the prevailing sentiments of many liberals are a familiar recapitulation of the response of many people to the Red Scare in the early part of the fifties. The intensity of the radicals' passions, the persistence and forcefulness of their recriminations, the broad tolerance accorded them by many moderates, lead to a mood of despair with respect to scrupulosity about civil liberties. The prevailing attitude comes to be something like this: Admittedly the radicals (either left or right) are extreme and demagogic. Admittedly some innocents are being hurt. Admittedly an atmosphere of fear and distrust is being built up. Nonetheless the radicals care deeply, in a way in which moderates do not. Furthermore it seems impossible to silence them either by intimidation, rational argument, or partial concessions. Hence it no longer seems of the first importance whether any particular charge, directed against any particular person, is valid, or whether any particular demand, based on any particular grievance, is legitimate and well conceived. For the sake of restoring peace, for the sake of paying dues to a movement which seems both physically irresistible and morally compelling, despite its obvious failings, the radicals must be allowed their conspicuous victories.

There are now innumerable university administrators and some faculty who have been forced to resign merely as scapegoats for the general failings of the whole academic community, or because they were attacked with such vehemence that scarcely anyone would defend them or because of the general impression that they were simply incapable of handling the situation. Some of these people no doubt deserved what they got, but it is the essence of an era of hysteria like this one that it begins to make little difference, even to men of good will, whether the victims deserved their fate or not. They are merely symbols of something deeper.

Many liberals are now frankly bored with the whole subject of civil liberties, which seems (as it did to the McCarthyites) an effete parlor game. It is distressing to recall that although many liberals are now exhilarated or amused by the "confrontations" arranged by the New Left, they were not long ago outraged when Adlai Stevenson was mobbed in a Dallas hotel lobby. (This incident was later resurrected to explain the assassination in 1963.) Publications of the kind called "hate sheets" when put out by the Right are praised as "the underground press" on the Left. While the McCarthyites were considered worse than despicable for the methods they used to gather "evidence," the radical students are considered ingenious for their ability to rifle files and publish the contents. The term "racist" is used as loosely and as murderously as the term "Red" once was. In 1954 certain professors were denounced by McCarthy for their Communist affiliations fifteen years before, and fifteen years later they were denounced by the radicals for their cooperation with the investigators at that time.

The liberal Catholic magazine *Commonweal,* which valiantly fought McCarthy and McCarthyism, now publicizes charges that a black astronaut was deliberately murdered by the C.I.A. to keep him from attaining glory in space and that a C.I.A. plot, "computerized from Washington," has been responsible for the death of Malcolm X and many other black leaders. The journal does not endorse this charge, but an associate editor gives the clear impression he would like to believe it. It is one of the agonies of a time like this, and a time like McCarthy's, that one cannot entirely dismiss such conspiracies as impossible; there could have been a Communist cadre in the State Department in 1952, there could be a C.I.A. conspiracy against blacks now. But it is the essence of a principled liberalism not to join in rank hysteria, but to demand proof for all charges, however sincere the accusers seem to be. Above all it is the liberal's duty, and the true radical's as well, not to mistake character assassination and frenetic hatreds for real political action.

17

Anxiety in Politics

Franz Neumann

The last three selections in this book are largely theoretical studies illustrating the conceptual models and approaches used by some scholars to explain the origins, significance, and effects of fears of conspiracy in politics. In the first, Franz Neumann analyzes the interplay among historical, sociological, and psychological factors in an attempt to explain the success of demagogues in winning mass support.

How does it happen that the masses sell their souls to leaders and follow them blindly? On what does the power of attraction of leaders over masses rest? What are the historical situations in which this identification of leader and masses is successful, and what view of history do the men have who accept leaders?

The extraordinary difficulty in the comprehension of group-psychological phenomena lies first of all in our own prejudices; for the experiences of the last decades have instilled in us all more or less strong prejudices against the masses, and we associate with "masses" the epithet "mob"—a group of men who are capable of every atrocity.

From Franz Neumann, "Anxiety in Politics," Dissent, *II (Spring 1955), 133–143. Excerpted and reprinted by permission of the publishers.*

In fact the science of group psychology began with this aristocratic prejudice in the work of the Italian Scipio Sighele, and Le Bon's famous book is completely in this tradition. His theses are familiar. Man in the mass descends; he is, as it were, hypnotized by the leader *(operateur)* and in this condition is capable of committing acts which he would never commit as an individual. As the slave of unconscious—i.e., for Le Bon, regressive—sentiments man in the mass is degraded into a barbarian: "Isolated, he may be a cultivated individual; in a crowd, he is a barbarian—that is, a creature acting by instinct. He possesses the spontaneity, the violence, the ferocity, and also the enthusiasm and heroism of primitive beings." Critics of Le Bon, among them also Freud, have pointed out that his theory, which rests on Sighele and Tarde, is inadequate in two aspects: the answer to the question, What holds the masses together? is inadequate, for the existence of a "racial soul" is unproved. In addition, in Le Bon the decisive problem—the role of the leader-hypnotist—remains unclarified. As is frequently true in socialpsychological studies, the descriptions of psychological states are adequate, the theoretical analyses inadequate.

From the outset, Freud sees the problem as that of the identification of masses with a leader; an identification which becomes of decisive significance particularly in an anxiety situation. And he sees in the libido the cement which holds leader and masses together, whereby—as is known—the concept of libido is to be taken in a very broad sense, to include the instinctual activities, which "in relations between the sexes . . . force their way toward sexual union," as well as those which "in other circumstances . . . are diverted from this aim or are prevented from reaching it, though always preserving enough of their original nature to keep their identity recognizable (as in such features as the longings for proximity, and self-sacrifice)." The cement which holds the mass together and ties them to the leader is thus a sum of instincts that are inhibited in their aims.

Since the identification of masses with the leader is an alienation of the individual member, identification always constitutes a regression, and a twofold one. On the one hand, the history of man is the history of his emergence from the primal horde and of his progressive individualization. Thus the identification with a leader in a mass is a kind of *historical* regression; this identification is also a "substitute for a libidinal object tie," thus a *psychological* regression, a damaging of the ego, perhaps even the loss of the ego.

But this judgment is valid only for the libido-charged, i.e., affective, identification of an individual in a mass with a leader; and not as a matter of course (and perhaps not at all) for that of lovers and of small groups. Nonaffective identification too, cannot be simply considered as regressive. For identification with organizations (church, army) is not always libidinally charged.

It is thus necessary to make distinctions. There are affect-less identifications, in which coercion or common material interests play an essential role, either in bureaucratic-hierarchic or in cooperative form. It seems to me incorrect, above all for recent history, to see in the identification of the soldier with the army, i.e., in the loyalty to an organization, an actual identification of the soldier with the commander-in-chief. Surely there are examples of this—Alexander, Hannibal, Caesar, Wallenstein, Napoleon. But the commander-in-chief of the twentieth century is much more the technician of war than the leader of men, and the libidinal tie of the soldier is, if I may coin the phrase, essentially cooperative, namely with the smallest group of comrades with whom he shares dangers.

Thus I would like to establish two fundamental types of identification: a libido-charged (affective) and a libido-free (affect-less); and maintain generally that the nonaffective identification with an organization is less regressive than the affective identification with a leader. Nonaffective loyalty is transferable, personal loyalty is not. The former always contains strong rationalist elements, elements of calculability between organization and individual, and thus prevents the total extinction of the ego.

But I believe that one must also distinguish two types within affective identification. One may call them: cooperative and caesaristic. It is conceivable (and it has probably happened in short periods in history) that many equals identify themselves cooperatively with one another in such a manner that their egos are merged in the collective ego. But this cooperative form is rare, limited to short periods or in any case operative only for small groups. The decisive affective identification is that of masses with leaders. It is—as I have said—the most regressive form, for it is built upon a nearly total ego-shrinkage. It is the form which is of decisive significance for us. We shall call it caesaristic identification.

Caesaristic Identification and False Concreteness: The Conspiracy Theory in History

Caesaristic identifications may play a role in history when the situation of masses is objectively endangered, when the masses are incapable of understanding the historical process, and when the anxiety activated by the danger becomes neurotic persecutory anxiety through manipulation.

From this follows, first of all, that not every situation dangerous to the masses must lead to a caesaristic movement; it follows further, that not every mass movement is based on anxiety, and thus not every mass movement need be caesaristic.

Thus it is a question of determining the historical conditions in which a regressive mass movement under a Caesar tries to win political power.

However, before we describe these historical situations, I may perhaps point to a clue which will frequently permit us an early diagnosis of the regressive character of such a mass movement. This clue is the view of history which the masses and the leaders employ. It may be called the conspiracy theory of history, a theory of history characterized by a false concreteness. The connection between caesarism and this view of history is quite evident. Just as the masses hope for their deliverance from distress through absolute oneness with a person, so they ascribe their distress to certain persons, who have brought this distress into the world through a conspiracy. The historical process is personified in this manner. Hatred, resentment, dread, created by great upheavals, are concentrated on certain persons who are denounced as devilish conspirators. Nothing would be more incorrect than to characterize the enemies as scapegoats, for they appear as genuine enemies whom one must extirpate and not as substitutes whom one only needs to send into the wilderness. The danger consists in the fact that this view of history is never completely false, but always contains a kernel of truth and, indeed, must contain it, if it is to have a convincing effect. The truer it is, one might say, the less regressive the movement; the falser, the more regressive.

It is my thesis that wherever affective (i.e., caesaristic) leader-identifications occur in politics, masses and leader have this view of history: i.e., that the distress which has befallen the masses has been brought about exclusively by a conspiracy of certain persons or groups against the people.

With this view of history real anxiety, which had been produced by war, want, hunger, anarchy, is to be transformed into neurotic anxiety and is to be overcome by means of identification with the leader-demagogue through total ego-renunciation, to the advantage of the leader and his clique, whose true interests do not necessarily have to correspond to those of the masses. . . .

It may perhaps be useful to discuss a fundamental model of conspiracy theories, one which shows the sequence: intensification of anxiety through manipulation, identification, false concreteness. . . .

The most important example—if only because of its immense political influence—is the theory of the *conspiracy of the Jews* according to the Protocols of the Elders of Zion. These contain the secret plans of Jewish leaders, supposedly formulated in the year 1897, for achieving Jewish world domination by force, terror, corruption, the disintegrating influence of liberalism, freemasonry, etc. This world domination was to be a mock-democracy, through which the Jewish leaders were to operate. That the *Protocols* are a forgery, prepared by Czarist Russians, was definitely established by the Bern trial of 1934–1935.

But if the *Protocols* represent a forgery, and if the plans for a Jewish world conspiracy belong in the realm of mythology, where then does that kernel of truth lie which according to my view is necessary to make possible the influence which anti-Semitism and the *Protocols* have had? I shall confine my analysis to Germany, but the German situation can be understood only when one becomes aware of the fact that in Germany before 1933 *spontaneous* anti-Semitism was extremely weak.

The element of truth (if one may call it that) is first of all a religious one: the catechistic representation of the crucifixion and with it the blood guilt of the Jews. But this is a thoroughly ambivalent element: for it is precisely the crucifixion of Christ which makes possible the salvation of Christians (and all men); and the spiritually Semitic origin of Christianity is acknowledged by the Church. While thus the historical-religious defamation of the Jews forms the basis without which anti-Semitism could hardly be activated, the catechistic representation of the crucifixion is not sufficient by itself. The existence of a total anti-Semitism can perhaps be better understood if we start from the policy of National Socialism and seek to understand the role of anti-Semitism within the political system. Germany of 1930–1933 was the land of alienation and anxiety. The facts are familiar: defeat, a tame unfinished revolution, inflation, depression, nonidentification with the existing political parties, nonfunctioning of the political system—all these are symptoms of moral, social, and political homelessness. The inability to understand why man should be so hard-pressed stimulated anxiety which was made into neurotic anxiety by the National Socialist policy of terror and its propaganda of anti-Semitism. The goal of National Socialism was clear: the welding together of the people with the charismatic leader, for the purpose of the conquest of Europe and perhaps of the world, and the creation of a racial hegemony of the Germans over all other peoples.

But how was the people to be integrated—despite all cleavages of class, party, religion? Only through hatred of an enemy. But how could one settle on the enemy? It could not be Bolshevism, because it was too strong; the Catholic Church could not be so designated because it was needed politically and loyalties to it were anchored too securely. The Jews remained. They appeared in the public consciousness as powerful—but were in reality weak. They were relative strangers, and at the same time the concrete symbols of a so-called parasitical capitalism—through their position in commerce and finance they incarnated a supposedly decadent morality through their *avant garde* position in art and literature; they seemed to be the successful competitors sexually and professionally. With all this the thesis of the Jewish conspiracy had the element of truth necessary to permit this view of history to become a frightful weapon. It would be mistaken to want to construe a connection between the socioeconomic status of a person and his anti-Semitism; that is, to claim that the academically educated person is more immune than the uneducated, or the poorly paid more immune than the better paid. What is correct, however, is that there exists a connection between loss of social status and anti-Semitism. The fear of social degradation thus creates for itself "a target for the discharge of the resentments arising from damaged self-esteem."

This leads us to the analysis of the historical situations in which anxiety grips the masses.

Situations of Collective Anxiety, Identification, Guilt

We have distinguished three strata of alienation. The psychological stratum remains no matter what social institutions man lives in, creating potential anxiety which man in the mass attempts to overcome through ego-surrender. This affective identification with a leader is facilitated by the view of history of false concreteness, the theory of conspiracy.

But so far we have not yet said when such regressive mass movements are activated; that is, when potential anxiety can be activated in such a manner that it can become a cruel weapon in the hands of irresponsible leaders.

In order to get at this problem we must take into account the two other strata of alienation: the social and political.

1. Alienation of labor: it is the separation of labor from the product of labor through hierarchical division of labor which character-

izes modern industrial society. Probably no one doubts that the division of labor as well as the hierarchical organization of labor have shown a steady rise since the industrial revolution of the eighteenth century. German romantic psychology of labor calls this the "desouling of labor" *(Entseelung der Arbeit)*. This concept as well as the various remedies are dangerous—for they cover up the inevitability of this process of alienation which must be admitted, understood, and accepted. If this does not happen, if one refuses to take account of the inevitability of the division of labor and of the hierarchical ordering of the process of labor and attempts to make dependent labor "soul-full" instead of restricting it to a minimum, then social anxiety is deepened. The attitude of the so-called new middle class (salaried employees) can exactly be understood from this.

While this new middle class does labor which—to remain with the language of German psychology of labor—is "more desouled" than that of the industrial worker, and although his average income probably lies below that of the industrial worker, he yet holds fast to his middle-class ideology and customs. Thus he refuses to take account of the inevitability of the social process and—as in Germany before 1933—becomes the social stratum most susceptible to caesarism.

2. In a society which is constituted by competition, the competitor is supposed to be rewarded for his effort when he is competent; that is, when he exerts himself, is intelligent, and accepts risks. There is little doubt that the principle of competition dominates not only the economy but all social relations. Karen Horney, a representative of Freudian revisionism, claims that the destructive character of competition creates great anxiety in neurotic persons. Now this is not convincing when genuine competition really prevails, that is, competition in which more or less equally strong persons fight with fair methods; that is, the kind of competition which Adam Smith defines in his *Theory of Moral Sentiments* as follows: "One individual must never prefer himself so much even to any other individual as to hurt or injure that other in order to benefit himself, though the benefit of the one should be much greater than the hurt or injury to the other." And again, "In the race for wealth and honors and preferments, each may run as hard as he can and strain every nerve and every muscle in order to outstrip all his competitors. But if he jostle or throw down any of them, the indulgence of the spectator is entirely at an end. It is in violation of fair play, which they cannot admit of." I cannot here undertake a social analysis to show that this ethically circumscribed competition does not exist and perhaps never has existed, that in

reality a monopolist struggle hides behind it, that, in other words, the efforts of the individual, his intelligence, his vision, his readiness to take risks, are easily shattered by the constellations of power.

In fact, behind the mask of competition, which is supposed to have no destructive effects when it rationally organizes a society, there hide relations of dependence which make up reality. To be successful in present-day society, it is much more important to stand in well with the powerful than to preserve oneself through one's own strength. Modern man knows this. It is precisely the impotence of the individual who has to accommodate himself to the technological apparatus which is destructive and anxiety-creating.

But even where fair competition is effective, no effort will help if crises ruin the merchant. The inability to understand the process of crises, and the frequent need to ascribe blame for them to sinister powers, is an additional factor in the destruction of the ego. This psychological process operated in the so-called old middle class of Germany before 1933.

3. In every society that is composed of antagonistic groups there is an ascent and descent of groups. It is my contention that persecutory anxiety—but one that has a real basis—is produced when a group is threatened in its prestige, income or its existence; i.e., when it declines and does not understand the historical process or is prevented from understanding it. The examples are too numerous to be possibly mentioned here. German National Socialism and Italian Fascism are classical examples.

But not only social classes resist their degradation by means of such mass movements—religious and racial conflicts, too, frequently produce similar phenomena. The conflict between Negroes and whites in the southern states of the U.S., the contemporary struggle of the South African government against the natives, takes place in accord with the following scheme: the anxiety of a dominant white minority that it will be degraded through the economic and political rise of Negroes is used in propagandist fashion for the creation of affective mass movements, which frequently take on a fascist character.

4. Social alienation; i.e., the fear of social degradation, is not adequate by itself. The elements of political alienation must be added. As a rule one is satisfied with defining abstention from voting at elections as political apathy. But I have pointed out elsewhere that the word "apathy" describes three different political reactions: first, the lack of interest in politics, say the opinion that politics is not the business of the citizens because it is after all only a struggle between small

cliques and that therefore nothing ever changes fundamentally; then, the Epicurean attitude toward politics, the view that politics and states only have to supply the element of order within which man devotes himself to his perfection, so that forms of state and of government appear as secondary matters; and finally, as the third reaction, the conscious rejection of the whole political system which expresses itself as apathy because the individual sees no possibility of changing anything in the system through his efforts. Political life can, for example, be exhausted in the competition of political parties which are purely machines without mass participation, but which monopolize politics to such an extent that a new party cannot make its way within the valid rules of the game. This third form of apathy forms the core of what I characterize as political alienation. Usually this apathy, if it operates within social alienation, leads to the partial paralysis of the state and opens the way to a caesarist movement which, scorning the rules of the game, utilizes the inability of the citizen to make individual decisions and compensates for the loss of ego with identification with a Caesar.

5. The caesaristic movement is compelled to institutionalize anxiety in two cases: if its coming into power is delayed and after it has actually seized control of the state. The institutionalization of anxiety is necessary in the first case because it can never endure a long wait for power. This is precisely what follows from its affective basis. While the nonaffective mass-organization—like a normal political party—can exist for a long time without disintegrating, the caesarist movement must hurry precisely because of the instability of the cement that holds it together: the libido-charged affectivity. After it has come to power it faces the need of institutionalizing anxiety as a means of preventing the extinction of its affective base by its bureaucratic structure.

The techniques are familiar: propaganda and terror—i.e., the incalculability of sanctions. I do not need to discuss this here. Montesquieu, building on Aristole and Machiavelli, distinguished between three constitutional and one tyrannical governmental and social systems. According to him, monarchy rests on the honor of the monarch; aristocracy, on the moderation of the aristocrats; democracy, on virtue (i.e., with him, patriotism); but tyranny, on fear. It must, however, not be overlooked that every political system is based on anxiety. But there is more than a quantitative difference between the anxiety which is institutionalized in a totally repressive system and that which is the basis of a half-way liberal one. These are qualitatively different states of affairs. One may perhaps say that the totally repressive system institutionalizes depressive and persecutory anxiety, the halfway liberal system, real anxiety.[1]

Who does not here think of Dostoyevsky's *The Possessed,* when Stavrogin gives the following piece of advice: "All that business of titles and sentimentalism is a very good cement, but there is something better; persuade four members of the circle to do for a fifth on the pretence that he is a traitor, and you'll tie them all together with the blood they've shed as though it were a knot. They'll be your slaves, they won't dare to rebel or call you to account." This famous passage in Dostoyevsky is important not only because it verifies our psychological theory, but also because it shows at the same time that the leader activates anxiety through guilt for his own advantage, not for the sake of the led.

If one examines the Spartan example, Stavrogin's advice, the Fehme-murders, and the collective crimes of the SS, one may perhaps undertake the following psychological analysis:

There are anxiety and an unconscious feeling of guilt.

It is the task of the leader, by creating neurotic anxiety, to tie the led so closely to the leader that they would perish without identification with him. Then the leader orders the commission of crimes; but these are—in accord with the morality that prevails in the group—with the Lacedaemonians, the Nihilists, the SS—not crimes, but fundamentally moral acts. Yet the conscience—the super-ego—protests against the morality of the crimes, for the old moral convictions cannot simply be extirpated. The feeling of guilt is thus repressed and makes anxiety a nearly panicky one, which can be overcome only through unconditional surrender to the leader and compels the commission of new crimes.

This is how I see the connection between anxiety and guilt in a totally repressive society. Hence this anxiety is qualitatively different from the anxiety that is the basis of every political system.

It is time to summarize our results:

1. Psychological alienation—the alienation of the ego from the instinctual structure, or the renunciation of instinctual gratifications—is inherent in every historical society. It grows with the growth of modern industrial society, and produces anxiety. Anxiety can be protective, destructive, or cathartic.

---

[1] One has to be clear about the fact that a totally repressive system is held together not by neurotic anxiety alone—it depends on keeping this anxiety alive in significant groups—but that material advantages and prestige are equally important.

2. Neurotic, persecutory anxiety can lead to ego-surrender in the mass through affective identification with a leader. This caesaristic identification is always regressive, historically and psychologically.
3. An important clue for the regressive character is the view of history of false concreteness—the conspiracy theory. Its peculiar danger lies in the kernel of truth that is contained in this view of history.
4. The intensification of anxiety into persecutory anxiety is successful when a group (class, religion, race) is threatened by loss of status, without understanding the process which leads to its degradation.
5. Generally, this leads to political alienation, i.e., the conscious rejection of the rules of the game of a political system.
6. The regressive mass movement, once it has come to power must, in order to maintain the leader-identification, institutionalize anxiety. The three methods are: terror, propaganda, and, for the followers of the leader, the crime committed in common.

18

Demagogy

Gordon W. Allport

Marked similarities exist between the approaches used by Franz Neumann and Gordon W. Allport to explain the effects of anticonspiratorial rhetoric in politics. In contrast to Neumann, however, Allport centers his attention on the manipulative techniques used by successful demagogues to sway their followers.

Demagogues play up false issues to divert public attention from true issues. Not all of them select the alleged misconduct of minority groups as their false issue—but a great many do so. . . .

It has been estimated that there are ten million followers of racist demagogues in the United States. The estimate is, however, hazardous and probably too high, for not everyone who attends an agitator's meeting is a follower. However that may be, in the year 1949 there were, according to Forster, forty-nine anti-Semitic periodicals in the United States, and over sixty organizations with an anti-Semitic

---

From Gordon W. Allport, The Nature of Prejudice, *1954, Addison-Wesley, Reading, Mass. Pp. 410–423. Excerpted and reprinted by permission of Addison-Wesley Publishing Company, Inc.*

record. Add to this array periodicals and organizations that specialize in anti-Catholicism and in anti-Negroism—and the total, in spite of overlapping, is impressive.

Sample Materials

The outpouring from the agitator's tongue and pen has a curiously constant quality, though this quality defies easy definition. The following excerpts from a "Christian Nationalist" meeting in 1948 are typical:

> We're gathered together from the corners of America for the sole purpose of taking the steps necessary to beat back the wave of materialism, the tidal waves of the evil force that threaten to engulf our beloved nation, the United States of America. We have assembled under the banner of Jesus Christ and the banner of our American Republic, the Cross, and the Flag, to demonstrate to the international financiers of Wall Street, the international Communists of Moscow and the international Jewish terrorists throughout the world, that they have failed. The political party that we are creating is a monument to the fact that resistance to evil, resistance to slavery, resistance to godless communism still lives in the world.
>
> Why were not the American people told that 90 million dollars of Marshall Plan funds were to be paid to the international banking houses to feed and fatten the purses of the black marketeers and the socialist racketeers who are destroying Christianity throughout Europe and who would destroy it here if we give them a chance? Under the bipartisan foreign policy we were burdened with the secret deals and the secret promises of our now dead former dictator, Franklin Delano Roosevelt! Under the bipartisan foreign policy we became guilty of allowing the satanic Morgenthau policy to be imposed upon the German people. Millions of Christian women and children being deliberately starved. Now why were not the American people told that this Morgenthau policy was invented by a group of power-mad, sadistic, pro-Communist Jews who wanted to destroy the German people so that the Soviet armies could occupy and enslave all of Christian Europe?
>
> In searching the platforms of the old political parties for a solution to the problems of international Jewish conspiracy, and the problem of Communist Jewish treason, and the problem of Zionist Jewish terrorism, the only words we found was a wailing cry of sympathy because of the work that the old political parties had done in creating the so-called Jewish state in Palestine. We saw no mention of the Jewish gestapos in America that coerce and smear

American citizens who stand and speak for Christian Americanism. We saw no mention of the Communist Jews who have infiltrated our government for the purpose of preparing the way for regimentation and slavery in a Communist America. We saw no condemnation of the dual allegiance practiced by the Zionist Jews who milk America to arm a foreign army. We saw no condemnation of the Jewish terror gangs that stalk the streets of America for the purpose of depriving Christian Americans of their rights of free speech and assembly.

It's the purpose of the Christian Nationalist Party to outlaw the Communist Party in America, as a crime against all that is decent, as a crime against the American government, and as a crime against all things that we Christian Nationalists hold dear. We intend to throw into the jails of the United States every member of the Communist party, every member of the Communist brotherhood, and every person who puts the love of Josef Stalin ahead of his love for the stars and stripes of American and the Constitution of the United States.

Now all of these people that are being exposed in Washington were students of Felix Frankfurter. I think it's about time we find out what he's teaching these fellows at Harvard University if they all turn out to be Communist spies when he gets through with them. And he sits on the Supreme Court of the United States. Now how can our government be safe when these people remain in positions of power and importance in Washington, D.C. It's time that we have a cleansing of the government in the United States and we're organizing the Christian Nationalist Party to clean out the rats who have taken over our government.

Now we're not demagogic about the Negro problem. We're going to speak the truth, we're going to speak what we believe, we're going to speak what is the only solution of the problem of black and white mixture in the United States. We advocate a Constitutional amendment making segregation of the black and white races a law of the United States of America. And we advocate making it a federal crime for intermarriage between the black and the white races!

I shall tell a little story I heard the other day when I was down in Jackson, Mississippi, meeting with some of my good friends there. A Negro had been up to St. Louis and married a white woman and he came back to Jackson, Mississippi and the boys cornered him on the street and said, "Mose, you can't stay here in this town with that white woman. We don't allow niggers to go around with white women, to marry white women, you know." And he said, "Boss, you is wrong as wrong can be, that woman is half Yankee and half Jew, she ain't got a drap of white blood in her."

Communists on the right, Communists on the left, out to liquidate Father Coughlin, Charles Lindbergh, Martin Dies, Burton Wheeler, Gerald Smith. Threaten, incite them, persecute them, ridicule them, DESTROY them, take them out of circulation, and by the Grace of God I refuse to go out of circulation. I was right on the Dies Committee, I was right on Alger Hiss, I was right on Stettinius, I was right on the United Nations, I was right . . . on Eleanor Roosevelt!

Never have business men been ruined, never have more men and women been abused, shaken down, trampled on by the presidential household, equal with what has been practised over the last fifteen years by that family of cutthroats, charlatans, Stalin appeasers, warmongers, known as the Roosevelts! God save America from the Roosevelts!

At first sight, this concoction seems to defy analysis.

The obvious motif is hatred. Mentioned as hated villains in this relatively short tirade are: materialism, international financiers, Jews, Communists, black marketeers, socialists, Morgenthau, Soviet armies, Zionists, Felix Frankfurter, Harvard University, Negroes, Alger Hiss, the then Secretary of State Stettinius, former President Roosevelt, Mrs. Roosevelt, and the Roosevelt family. The leading devil seems to be the Jews, who are mentioned more often and in more combinations than any other malefactors. There is, in addition, a peculiarly fierce venom reserved for the Roosevelts. Catholics are not condemned—for in a large urban gathering there might be many Catholics in the audience, and the demagogue may be bidding for their support. . . .

We learn from this diversified animus . . . that hatred for minority groups does not stand alone. The hatred is generalized. Whatever is sensed as a threat is hated.

The threat is never clearly defined. But underlying the abuse appears one fairly evident theme—namely, fear of liberalism or social change. The Roosevelts are above all else a symbol of change—threatening especially conservative patterns of economic life and race relations. Intellectualism (the symbol here being Harvard University) is hated, for it too brings about change, and at the same time intensifies the inferiority feelings of anti-intellectuals. Socialism and communism bring about change. An improvement in the condition of the Negro would do so likewise. Jews have always been associated with venture, risk, and fringe values. . . . Authoritarian personalities cannot face all this indefiniteness, unconventionality, and loss of familiar anchorage. . . .

Their symbols of security are no less interesting than their symbols of dread. Mentioned as idols are: Jesus Christ, the banner of the American Republic, the Cross and the Flag, Father Coughlin, Charles Lindbergh, Martin Dies, Burton Wheeler, Gerald K. Smith. In portions of the speech not printed here, there were favorable references to Paul Revere, Nathan Hale, Lincoln, and Lee, and to George Washington—"the mightiest Christian Nationalist of all time." As perceived by the speaker and auditors, these idols are all symbols of conservatism, standing for nationalism, isolationism, anti-Semitism, or a conventional religion which serves as the ultimate island of safety for institutionalists. . . .

Having learned from this sample speech what some of the negative and positive symbols are, and how they reflect above all else the theme of dread and insecurity, let us consider the appeal in more detail. One demagogic speech is much like another. It is the pattern that is important.

The Program of the Demagogue

In their volume *Prophets of Deceit,* Lowenthal and Guterman have analyzed a large number of similar speeches and tracts. There is a sameness of protest and hatred in all of them. What the demagogue is saying seems to boil down to the following points:

You've been cheated. Your social position is insecure because of the machinations of Jews, New Dealers, Communists, and other agents of change. Sincere and plain folk like us are always dupes. We must do something.

There is widespread conspiracy against us. It is being engineered by devils—by Wall Street, Jewish bankers, internationalists, the State Department. We must do something.

The conspirators are sexually corrupt too. They "roll in wealth, bathe in liquor, surround themselves with the seduced daughters of America." "Oriental erotics debauch youth for the purpose of wrecking gentile morale." Aliens enjoy all the forbidden fruit.

Our present government is corrupt. The two-party system is a sham. Democracy is a "trick word." "Liberalism is anarchy." Civil liberties are "silly liberties." We cannot be universalistic in our ethics. We must look out for ourselves.

Doom is just around the corner. Look at the "Nudeal communistic confiscatory taxation," at the CIO and radical AF of L unions. They and the Jews are rapidly taking power. There will be immediate revolutionary violence. We must do something.

Capitalism and communism both threaten us. After all, atheistic communism was originally spawned in Jewish capitalism and Jewish intellectualism.

We can't trust the foreigners. Internationalism is a threat. But we can't trust our own government either. Alien termites bore within. Washington is a "Bolshevik's rat's nest."

Our enemies are low animals: reptiles, insects, germs, subhuman. Extermination is called for; we must do something.

There is no middle ground. The world is divided. Those who are not for us are against us. It is a war between haves and have-nots; between true Americans and "foreigners." "The Talmudic philosophy of Europe-Asia-Africa and Nudeal is directly opposite that of Christian."

There must be no polluting of blood. We must keep racially pure and elite. Vile contamination comes from dealing at all with the moral lepers of liberalism.

But with disaster around the corner what can you do? Poor, simple, sincere people need a leader. Behold I am he. It isn't the American nation that is wrong; it is the corrupt men in office. Change the personnel. I am available. I'll change the whole smelly mess. You'll have a happier and safe life.

The situation is too urgent to permit the luxury of thought. Just give me your money, and I'll tell you later what to do.

Everybody is against me. I am your martyr. The press, the Jews, the stinking bureaucrats are trying to shut me up. Enemies plot against my life, but God will protect me. I'll lead you. And I'll ignite the public mind everywhere. And I'll liquidate millions of bureaucrats and Jews.

Maybe we'll march on Washington. . . .

Here the program trails off. For there are laws against inciting violence and advocating the overthrow of the government by force. The excitement is left dangling with a vague promise of a Utopia where milk and honey shall flow, and a hint that some legal or extralegal way will be found to enter this New Jerusalem. In various countries of Europe this demagogy has, of course, translated itself into action. Whole governments have been swept away by the mobs that have been swayed by a similar set of appeals.

The demagogue makes a dramatic but erroneous diagnosis of the causes of the dissatisfaction and malaise that his followers suffer. That they are frustrated, bitter, on the outs with themselves and society, there can be no doubt. True issues are not stated; they would point to flaws in economic structure, to the failure of men to find a cure for war, to neglect of basic principles of human relations in schools, industries, and community life, and—above all—to inner lack of mental health and ego-firmness.

This true causation, being complex, is entirely avoided. The sufferers are assured that they are not to blame. Their precarious self-esteem is protected by comforting assurance that they are Christians, true patriots, the elite. They are even told that to hate the Jews is not a sign of anti-Semitism. At every turn their extropunitiveness is justified and their ego-defenses strengthened.

While the demagogue never offers a rational program for the relief of social anomie and personal malaise, neither does he, in a country with a firm governmental structure, offer a clear-cut program of violence. A tottering social structure, such as has existed in Germany, Spain, Italy, and in Russia, is needed before the agitator can safely incite to revolution. Prosperity and stability are poor soil for agitators.

Sometimes, however, even in an otherwise stable nation, he may gain a measure of political power on a local basis—in cities or states.

Whether successful or not, the demagogue is at bottom advocating a totalitarian revolution following the pattern of fascism. In America certain face-saving devices are required in order that the historical values of the nation shall not be too obviously violated. Demagogues usually protest that they are not anti-Semites and that they are opposed to fascism just as they are opposed to communism. It has been remarked that if fascism comes to the United States it will take the guise of an anti-fascist movement. But the earmarks are nevertheless clearly visible. The program is essentially alike in all countries.

In a memorandum entitled "How to recognize an American Pro-Fascist," the Friends of Democracy, Incorporated, has listed the following characteristics:

1. *Racism* is common to all groups. In fact, it is a cornerstone of the profascist movement everywhere. In this country it takes the form of White Supremacy.
2. *Anti-Semitism* is a common denominator of all profascist and "one-hundred percent Americans" groups. *Anti-Catholicism* sometimes is substituted for anti-Semitism in predominantly Protestant areas, but the demagogues have found anti-Semitism to be the most effective political weapon.
3. *Antialienism, antirefugeeism, and anti-everything foreign* is a

major characteristic. Fascism all over the world professes strong "nativism" and invariably is opposed to "foreigners" and people of other nations.

4. *Nationalism* is the key. The extreme nationalist claims that his own country is "the master country," just as he asserts that his own people are "the master race." Power is the keynote.
5. *Isolationism* is a distinct part of the pattern. Isolationists take the position that this country is secure behind the impregnability of two great oceans.
6. *Anti-internationalism* is also a part of the pattern. This anti-internationalism includes opposition to the United Nations and all other efforts to arrive at international understanding and cooperation for peace.
7. *Red-baiting* indiscriminately labels all opponents as communists and bolsheviks. Communism is used as a bugaboo to frighten people into accepting fascism. Liberals and progressives, Jews, intellectuals, international bankers, and foreigners are described as communists or "fellow travelers" by the profascists.
8. *Antilabor,* particularly antiorganized labor, is a predominant characteristic, though often masked.
9. *Sympathy for other fascists* is common among the profascists. In pre-Pearl Harbor days, this sympathy included a defense of Hitler and Mussolini as "the great bulwarks" against communism. During the war, it was directed to sympathy for Petain, and his Vichy government. Later it took the shape of sympathy and defense of the Franco and Perón regimes.
10. *Antidemocracy* is another common denominator. "Democracy is decadent," fascists everywhere declare. In the United States, the favorite theme is that our country is a "Republic," not a "democracy." A "Republic" is the rule of the elite, while democracy is virtually a synonym for communism.
11. *The glorification of war, force, and violence* is a major theme. War is regarded as creative activity, and military heroes are glorified. One of the profascist slogans maintains "Life is struggle, struggle is war, war is life."
12. *The one-party system* is a distinct feature of the fascist pattern. Totalitarianism is applauded under the slogan, "One people, one party, one State."

American democracy has a remarkable resiliency, for it has withstood such demagogy for decades, in fact, since before the founding of the nation. But today, the aggravating of strains, the cultural lag (i.e., the failure of social skills to keep pace with technological) have made the appeal greater than ever before. It is not a movement that is born overnight. Its seeds are always present, and its growth may be gradual and imperceptible up to a point, and then sudden and alarming. It waxes and wanes with the rise and fall of particular demagogues. But sometimes its roots gain a firm hold in congressional committees, in local and state political groups, in certain newspapers, and among certain radio commentators.

On the whole, the democratic tradition seems still in the ascendancy. Each fascistic movement generates a strong countercurrent. Yet the mounting of social strain and the acceleration of social change in our day create a precarious condition. The question is whether realistic diagnoses and policies can be evolved to ameliorate domestic and international ills and to improve men's outlook before panic and fear drive them in larger numbers to embrace demagogic nostrums.

The Followers

People who follow demagogues have no precise idea of the cause to which they are devoted. There is vagueness both about the objective and about the means for reaching the objective. The demagogue may not know them himself or, if he does, he finds it expedient to keep attention riveted only on himself. He has learned that concrete images (leaders) are more firmly held in mind than are abstractions.

Since there is no way out of the predicament (except the distant and vague possibility of unspecified violence) followers are forced to trust the demagogue for guidance and devote themselves to him blindly. He provides them with channels for protest and hate, and these pleasures of indignation are diverting and temporarily satisfying. There is comfort in the tautological assurance that Americans are Americans and that Christians are Christians and that these are the best people, the truly elite. One is a Christian because one is not a Jew, an American because not a foreigner, a simple fellow because not an intellectual. The comfort may seem thin, but it bolsters self-esteem.

We need a comprehensive, scientific study of the membership of nativist organizations. Observers have reported that members seem to be people who have obviously not succeeded in life, mostly over 40 years of age, uneducated, bewildered, grim in facial expression. The presence of many rigid-appearing women suggests that some may be loveless creatures ready to find in the demagogue a fantasied lover and protector.

It may well turn out that followers are nearly all individuals who have felt themselves to be somehow rejected. Unhappy home life, unsatisfactory marriage, may be frequent among them. Their age suggests that they have lived long enough to sense a hopelessness about their vocations and social relations. Because they have little backlog in terms of personal or financial resources, they dread the future and gladly ascribe their insecurity to the malignant forces that the demagogue singles out. Deprived of realistic gratifications and subjective safety, they have a nihilistic view of society and indulge in fantasies of fury. They need an exclusive island of security where their frustrated hopes may yet be fulfilled. All liberals, intellectuals, deviates, and other agents of change must be excluded. To be sure, they too want change of a sort, but only the change that will provide personal security and bolster their own weakness.

Every character-conditioned source of prejudice . . . helps to explain the followers of demagogues. Demagoguery invites the externalization of hatred and anxiety; it is an institutional aid to projection; it justifies and encourages tabloid thinking, stereotyping, and the conviction that the world is made up of swindlers. It bifurcates life into clear-cut choices: follow the simple fascist formula or disaster will occur. There is no middle ground, no national solution. While the ultimate objective is vague, still the need for definiteness is met by the rule, "Follow the Leader." By declaring that every social issue is the result of out-group misconduct, the demagogue consistently avoids focusing his followers' attention upon their own painful internal conflicts. Their repressions are thus safeguarded and all the mechanisms of ego defense are bolstered.

One small-scale experimental study gives us a certain amount of insight into the nature of people who are susceptible to the appeals of demagogues. The subjects of this experiment were a selected sample of war veterans in Chicago who had been previously interviewed and whose opinions and history were known. To them were mailed two pieces of anti-Semitic propaganda. Two weeks later these men were reinterviewed. It was found that some had accepted and agreed with the message; some had rejected it. The former group was composed of men who had previously shown intolerance or who had given mere lip service to tolerance. They were not among the veterans who had strong protolerance convictions. Furthermore, they perceived the tracts as coming from an authoritative, reliable, and unbiased source. Finally, they were men who found the literature reassuring; it alleviated their anxieties and aroused no new fears or conflicts. Summing up this evidence, so far as it goes, the demagogic appeal builds on previous attitudes and beliefs in harmony with the appeal; it appears to the consumer as authoritative; it reduces his anxiety. If it does all these things it is likely to be accepted.

The Demagogue as a Person

Agitators flourish because the authoritarian type of personality needs them. Their motives, however, are not altruistic. They have axes of their own to grind.

In many instances, demagogism is a lucrative racket. Dues and gifts, the purchase of shirts and other insignia, may keep the leaders in clover. Small fortunes have been made at the game, and by the time the movement fails—through mismanagement, legal complications, or the desire of followers for novelty—a tidy sum has been salted away.

Political motives are also common. Extravagant if vague promises (spiced with hate-appeals) have elected senators and congressmen, as well as candidates for local offices. The techniques are melodramatic enough to make good headline stories or to invite radio comment. The result is that the demagogue becomes well known by name, and this prominence he finds an asset in reelection. His technique is one of arousing hope (e.g., "share the wealth") and also of arousing fear. "Vote for me, or the Reds (Negroes, Catholics) will get control of the government." Both techniques—used with skill—lifted Hitler into power within a short time.

But the motives of demagogues are likely to be still more complex. They too have character-conditioned prejudice. Rarely does one find a completely cold and calculating politician who uses anti-Semitism and related tricks only for gain.

Consider Hitler's anti-Semitic strategy. Some of its roots probably lay in his own inferiority and sexual conflicts. . . . But it seems unlikely that he would carry out anti-Semitism as a state policy merely to satisfy his personal feelings. Perhaps he and his henchmen wanted Jewish money and property. Straight expropriations of Jewish wealth may be a contributing factor, although here again it is questionable whether the gain actually offset the capital loss in the Reich through a disruption of business and markets. The chief motive lay in offering to the German people a scapegoat for the defeat of 1918 and for the subsequent inflation. Nationalism and unity were intensified by fixing blame in this way. All these motives probably existed, along with another. Hitler tried, not only in Germany but in the world at large, to gain favor for himself by posing as St. George slaying the dragon.

Since anti-Semitism is widespread in all countries, he wished to be seen as a friend to all. In many lands one heard people say they liked Hitler for one reason only, because he was against the Jews. He counted on this bid for sympathy to carry him through his many rough dealings with foreign countries. That he gained some sympathy cannot be doubted; but in the long run he overestimated the value of this particular trump.

Demagogues who are already in power may use antiminority appeals as a diversion. Occupied with plots of their own, they keep telling people of the peril they are being saved from. They use minority groups much as the Roman emperors used bread and circuses.

Agitators cannot succeed unless there is large-scale malaise in the population. They fail if their intended followers are people with strong inner security and mature ego-development. But usually there is a sufficiently large potential population of followers (someone has called them "propageese") to reward their efforts. The masses are necessary to the demagogues. When there is no demagogue the population is not likely to become inflamed. McWilliams lays the blame for the treatment of the Japanese-Americans after Pearl Harbor upon certain professional patriots and witch-hunters. Whether the violence of World War II and the persecution of the Jews in Germany would have been avoided if Hitler had never existed is a question that will never be answered. It seems likely, however, that a demagogue is essential to the occurrence of the catastrophe. But when times are ripe, if one agitator does not arise, another probably will.

All in all, the motives of demagogues are likely to be a complex mixture. But many agitators, if not all, are themselves authoritarian personality types, endowed with verbal fluency. While some seek power and money, most of them are character-conditioned, especially the small-time fellows who have neither money nor political power to win by their printed tracts and soap-box oratory. Perhaps they are gratifying some exhibitionistic tendency, but they would not take this particular avenue of display unless their own bigotry was intense. Some of them—like many of the big-timers—seem close to the borderline of paranoid insanity.

Paranoid Bigotry

Kraepelin, in the course of classifying mental diseases, defined *paranoid ideas* as "erroneous judgments not subject to correction by experience." According to this rather broad definition, many ideas, including prejudice, would be paranoid.

The true paranoiac, however, has an impenetrable rigidity. His ideas are delusional, disconnected from reality and not subject to any influence.

> A paranoid woman had the fixed delusion that she was a dead person. The doctor tried what he thought was a conclusive logical demonstration to her of her error. He asked her, "Do dead people bleed?" "No," she answered. "Well, if I pricked your finger, would you bleed?" "No," answered the woman, "I wouldn't bleed; I'm dead." "Let's see," said the doctor, and pricked her finger. When the patient saw the drop of blood appearing she remarked in surprise, "Oh, so dead people *do* bleed, don't they."

A peculiarity of paranoid ideas is that they are usually localized. That is to say, the sufferer may be normal in all matters excepting in the region of his disordered conviction. It is as though all the preceding misery of his life—all his conflicts—had condensed into a single limited delusional system. . . . Rejective home life is characteristic of most paranoiacs. It is as though all their diffused early misery were caught up and rationalized in a single set of ideas—usually to the effect that the sufferer is being persecuted, perhaps by his neighbors, or by Communists, or by Jews.

Paranoid ideas are sometimes mixed up with other forms of mental disease, but often they seem to constitute an entity in themselves called "pure paranoia." And sometimes the affliction is mild enough to warrant only a diagnosis of borderline condition—a "paranoid tendency."

The theory held by most psychoanalysts and by many psychiatrists is that paranoia, of any degree or type, is a consequence of repressed homosexuality. There is some clinical evidence to support this claim. The explanation goes something like this: many people, especially if they have been sternly punished for any sex activity as children, cannot face homosexual impulses in themselves. They repress them, saying to themselves in effect, "I do not love him, I hate him." . . . This conflict becomes externalized. Complementary projection comes into play. "The reason I hate him is that he hates me. He has it in for me. He is persecuting me." A final step in this tortuous series of rationalizations is displacement and generalization. "It is not only he that hates me and has designs against me, but it is the Negro, Jewish, communistic group that is after me." (These may be regarded as substitute sexual symbols, or merely as convenient, socially sanctioned scapegoats who to the sufferer account for his feeling that *someone* is persecuting him.)

Whether or not this elaborate theory is altogether sound, the formula for paranoid thinking seems always to have a history consisting of the following steps: (1) There is deprivation, frustration, inadequacy of some sort (if not sexual, then something else of a highly personal order). (2) The cause, due both to repression and projection, is seen as lying wholly outside oneself. (The paranoiac utterly lacks insight in the region of his disorder.) (3) Since the external cause is seen as an acute threat, this source is cordially hated and aggression is generated against it. In extreme cases the sufferer may attack or eliminate the "guilty" party. Some paranoiacs are homicidal.

When a true paranoiac becomes a demagogue, disaster may result. The demagogue's success will, of course, be greater if he is normal and shrewd in all other phases of his leadership. If so, his delusional system will be reasonable, and he will attract followers, especially among those who themselves have latent paranoid ideas. Combine enough paranoiacs, or enough people with paranoid tendencies, and a dangerous mob may result.

The paranoid tendency explains why the compulsive drives of the anti-Semite and the communist-phobe never seem to relax. The sufferer is keyed up all the time. Even public disapproval, ridicule, exposure, or jail do not deter him. Although he may stop short of inciting his hearers to violence, he has an intensity, a humorlessness, and aggressiveness that nothing can shake. Neither argument nor experience will change his views. If contradictory evidence is offered him he will twist it to serve his previous conviction, as did the "dead" woman.

It is especially important for our purposes to note that paranoia may exist in otherwise normal individuals, also that all gradations of the paranoid tendency occur. The mechanism of projection is central in paranoia, but it is also present in normal people. It is not always possible to say where normality leaves off and pathology begins.

Paranoia represents the extreme pathology of prejudice. At present it seems impossible to prescribe a cure. Whoever invents a remedy for paranoia will be mankind's benefactor.

One approach to the problem of cancer control has been to study conditions that make for healthy organisms and that prevent the malignant growth of cells. Similarly, we may hope to learn something about the control of paranoia, projection, and prejudice from a study of tolerant personalities, where these forms of mental functioning have failed to take root. What makes for a tolerant personality?

19

Another Look at Nativism

John Higham

John Higham argues that future research on conspiracy fears generated by nativistic movements must explore new approaches. He finds the fascination of historians and social psychologists with ideology inadequate as a means for explaining "the total complex of ethnic tensions in American society." Such an approach, Higham maintains, is useful only for understanding "the extreme and fanatical manifestations of ethnic discord." It tends to obscure the fact that ethnic antagonisms are an integral part of the American social structure and have not usually produced conspiracy fears, hysteria, and hatred. In Higham's view, scholars should now search for the concrete social realities that lie behind ethnic and religious stereotypes. Although such a quest "transcends the dimensions of nativism," it should place the history of nativism in a more meaningful perspective.

Research on the conflicts associated with foreign elements in American society should take a new line. The nativist theme, as defined

From John Higham, "Another Look at Nativism," The Catholic Historical Review, *XLIV (July 1958), 147–158. Excerpted and reprinted with most of the footnotes omitted by permission of the author and the Catholic University of America Press.*

and developed to date, is imaginatively exhausted. Scholars who would do more than fill in the outlines of existing knowledge must make a fresh start from premises rather different from those that have shaped the studies of the last twenty years. To explain what I mean will require some consideration of the literature on nativism that is now extant. . . .

The very term "nativism" has influenced profoundly our angle of vision in studying antiforeign and anti-Catholic forces. The word is an "ism." It came into being in the middle of the nineteenth century to describe the principles advanced by a political party. Etymologically and historically, therefore, it refers to a set of attitudes, a state of mind. In contrast to words like assimilation, segregation, marginality, and the like, "nativism" does not direct attention primarily to an actual social process or condition. Those who study the phenomenon want to know why certain ideas emerge when and where they do, and how those ideas pass into action. Consequently, the histories of nativism have not tried, except incidentally, to clarify the structure of society. Instead, they trace an emotionally charged impulse.

While the word itself almost inevitably pulls our interest toward subjective attitudes, our contemporary culture has pushed us further in that direction. Since the 1930s the intellect and the conscience of America have been in revolt against what is called "prejudice," viz., the ill-treatment of ethnic and religious minorities. Now, prejudice is by definition subjective—a prejudgment not grounded in factual experience. Nativism, of course, commonly qualifies as prejudice; and students regard it not only as a state of mind but as one which badly distorts the true nature of things. A good historian will certainly not consider nativism entirely as a set of prejudices; but since no one writes about it unless he shares the current revulsion against ethnic injustice, the subjective irrationality of nativism leaps to the historian's eye. He wants to know how we have mistaken one another and, perhaps too, he wishes to assure us that the mistakes were, indeed, mistakes in the sense that they arose from no compelling social need.

Along with the crusade against prejudice, another aspect of modern thought has affected the study of nativism. We live in an age that has an almost superstitious awe and distrust of ideologies. That is to say, we dread the power of ideas that are weapons in the hands of "hidden persuaders." Karl Mannheim, George Orwell, and others have taught us to see, behind the inhumanity of our day, the coercion of ideas which interpret life in terms functional to someone's bid for power. Disseminated by the agitator and the propagandist, ideologies distort reality, attack the foundations of belief, and threaten the independence and integrity of the human mind.[1] Historians and social scientists alike have been fascinated by ideologies and have labored to expose their dynamics. There is a consequent tendency to fix upon ideology as the critical factor in many a social problem, in the perhaps tenuous hope that the problem will yield to a reasonable solution once the ideological magic is exorcised.

The relevant consideration here is that the concern over ideologies reflects, more systematically, the same assumption that underlies the concept of prejudice. Both owe a great deal to our distinctively modern emphasis on the irrational depths of human nature. The modern mind dwells on the unconscious savagery lurking in its own dark corners. At the springs of human action the irrationalist historian, novelist, or social psychologist is not likely to find realistic motives of solidarity or calculated self-interest; nor is he likely to find high ideals. Instead, he discovers a fog of myths, prejudices, stereotypes, and power-hungry ideologies. If he looks at the American past he may notice this miasma overhanging many scenes, but nowhere does he find it more densely exhibited than in nativism. Nativism displays all the terrors that beset his own sensibility. It is an ideology: a rigid system of ideas, manipulated by propagandists seeking power, irrationally blaming some external group for the major ills of society. It mobilizes prejudices, feeds on stereotypes, radiates hysteria, and provokes our outrage against ethnic injustice.

I have said enough, I hope, about the general frame of reference within which nativism is studied to indicate that interpretation of it almost inevitably stresses subjective, irrational motives. Whenever a contemporary point of view gives so much encouragement to a certain historical approach, should we not suspect that our angle of vision screens out a good deal? Specifically, should we not suspect that the nativist theme does little justice to the objective realities of ethnic relations? To answer this question concretely, let me turn to my own experience in studying the subject.

Nativism, I felt sure, would not submit to effective analysis unless it could be identified consistently as an idea. Its meaning must inhere in a set of beliefs protean enough to apply to a variety of adversaries yet definite enough to show the form and direction of its history. To unravel the strands of nativist ideology became, therefore, a central problem. I discovered that the main strands ran more or less inde-

---

[1] In using the elusive term "ideology" in the hostile sense in which Mannheim employed it, I intend to designate a point of view toward ideas, not to endorse that point of view.

pendently of one another. There were, in fact, several nativisms, each of which fixed upon some internal alien influence as a gravely divisive threat to national unity. Generically, nativism was a defensive type of nationalism, but the defense varied as the nativist lashed out sometimes against a religious peril, sometimes against a revolutionary peril, sometimes against a racial peril. Although on occasion nativists rallied against other kinds of disloyalty too, these persistent anxieties provided a framework for studying the nativistic mentality.

Notice what I was *not* doing by pursuing the subject in this way. I was not trying to explain the total complex of ethnic tensions in American society. I was not focusing upon the institutional rivalries of Protestant and Catholic or upon their religious beliefs. I was not dealing fundamentally with the living standards of Italian and Yankee or with the party affiliations of Irish and German. All these crowded the background, for all of them helped to shape the nativist temper. Yet such basic components of the American ethnic scene could not occupy the foreground of my picture without blurring the clarity and significance of nativism as an idea. The bad habit of labeling as nativist any kind of unfriendliness toward immigrants or Catholic values had to be resisted. If nativism is not a mere term of derogation, it can embrace only antagonisms that belong within the ideologies of a passionate national consciousness.

As I studied the main nativist traditions, I discovered that over a long span of time they had not changed conceptually as much as an historian of ideas might suppose. Except on the subject of race (and in related forms of anti-Semitism), the kind of accusations which nativists leveled against foreign elements remained relatively constant. Antiradical and anti-Catholic complaints in the twentieth century sounded much like those bruited in the eighteenth. The big changes were not so much intellectual as emotional. The same idea might be mildly innocuous at one time and charged with potent feelings at another. For the history of nativism, therefore, emotional intensity provided the significant measurement of change. If nativism was an ideological disease, perhaps, one might best diagnose it by observing when the fever raged and when it slackened.

The outlines of an overall interpretation now became visible. During four scattered intervals in American history (only two of which I studied in detail) nativism erupted powerfully enough to have an immediate impact on national development. In the late 1790s it produced the notorious Alien Acts. In the 1850s it contributed to the breakup of the party system. In the decade from 1886 to 1896 it magnified a host of social problems associated with unrestricted immigration. And in the period of World War I nativism unleashed repressive orthodoxies on a grand scale. In each of these four periods the United States was undergoing a major national crisis. In the 1790s international conflict intensified the cleavage between political parties. Sectional cleavage came to a head in the 1850s, class cleavage in the 1890s. World War I confronted an unprepared nation with the shock of total war. In each of these crises, confidence in the homogeneity of American culture broke down. In desperate efforts to rebuild national unity men rallied against the symbols of foreignness that were appropriate to their predicament.

My appraisal was more complex than this sketchy outline suggests, of course. And I have no doubt that nativist ideas deserve still further study, particularly to elucidate their relation to our traditions of individualism and Puritanism. What bothers me most, however, is that the concept of nativism has proved serviceable only for understanding the extreme and fanatical manifestations of ethnic discord. It illuminates the frenzies of the mob, the nightmares of the propagandist, the repressive statute, and the moments of national frustration. Nativism owes its significance to this intensity of feeling; and historians, fascinated by the men of passion and the moods of alarm, have neglected the less spectacular but more steadily sustained contentions imbedded in the fabric of our social organization.

In order to have a shorthand designation for such underlying stresses, we may call them status rivalries. By this I mean all of the activities—political, religious, economic, and associational—through which men of different ethnic backgrounds have competed for prestige and for favorable positions in community life. Status rivalries have not arisen from irrational myths but rather from objective conditions; they have not usually reached the point of hatred and hysteria; they have not depended upon ideological expression; they have not risen and fallen in cyclical fashion. Instead, they are part of the slow processes of ethnic integration, and they have shaped profoundly the course of our social development.

For a generation historians and even most social scientists interested in the jostling of Protestant and Catholic, of Christian and Jew, of old and new Americans, have not wanted to understand these tensions as basic structural realities. To do so is to recognize that our divergent and unequal backgrounds are causes—not just results—of our difficulties. It is more comforting to think that everyone is pretty much alike and that our differences are foisted upon us by myths and stereotypes. Attributing ethnic cleavage to nativism or racism takes the curse off the fact of inequality.

By the same token, the nativist approach validates our sympathy with the out-group. Nativism is primarily a one-way street, along which the native American moves aggressively against the outsider. Thus, the history of nativism inevitably portrays minorities as victims rather than partcipants. It permits us to assume their relative innocence. We need not ask too closely why the Irish were the shock troops of the anti-Chinese movement in California, how the American Protective Association could attract a following among Negroes, or why the Scots in America brought so much wrath upon themselves during the Revolution.

At this point you may concede that many peripheral frictions do occur outside the orbit of nativism, but you may still insist that it explains the more persistent difficulties, such as those which Catholics and Jews have met. At times, of course, irrational myths have played the decisive part in these encounters, but not as commonly or exclusively as historians have suggested. The real issues of faith which set religious groups apart can not fairly be reduced to nativist terms. Moreover, struggles for status underlie much that we attribute too easily to irrational prejudice, and I suspect that the question of status has touched the daily life of most Americans more intimately than any ideological warfare.

Consider for a moment the situation of the Irish Catholic in the late nineteenth or early twentieth century. Did he suffer much from nativist visions of popish conspiracies? It seems unlikely. He worshipped freely and had no legal disabilities; the most extravagant propaganda against him circulated in completely Protestant rural areas remote from his own urban habitations. The great handicap he faced was his social and economic subordination to the older Americans, who treated him partly as a joke, partly as an underling, and partly as a ruffian. And when he compensated in politics for his inferiority in other spheres, all the forces of Yankee respectability mobilized in Republican ranks against him. In scores of communities throughout the North both political parties were essentially ethnic coalitions. Even the American Protective Association was, perhaps, chiefly effective as an instrument for ousting the Irish from the municipal jobs which they held to the disadvantage of their ethnic rivals. In the western cities where the A.P.A.'s greatest strength lay, Yankees, Scandinavians, and British used it to get control of school boards, police forces, and fire departments.

Similarly, the Jews came up against actual conflict situations which affected them at least as seriously as did the slanders of anti-Semitic ideology. The evidence seems clear that the social discriminations which began to limit the opportunities of American Jews in the late nineteenth century owed little to nativist sources, in the sense in which I have used the term. Discrimination developed where and when Jews participated heavily in a general middle-class scramble for prestige; it developed where and when a hectic pace of social climbing made the guardians of distinction afraid of being "invaded." It grew in eastern summer resorts, fraternities, and urban real estate offices, not in the South and the West where farmers were beginning to murmur about the shadowy power of the international Jew.

The decisive significance of reality situations as opposed to anti-foreign propaganda may also be gauged from the very favorable reception which English immigrants have always enjoyed. If nationalist ideas dominated American ethnic relations as much as we sometimes suppose, English immigrants should have been among the most unpopular minorities at least until the 1870s. When Britain was our historic adversary, when Anglophobia was an editorial habit and twisting the lion's tail a political pastime, the English in America escaped opprobrium. In spite of their identifiable accent, their disinterest in naturalization, and their proud retention of British loyalties, the English did not differ enough from native Americans, socially and culturally, to seem outsiders. Since they had no status as ethnic rivals, the nativist crusade passed them by.

How, then, are we to explain those ethnic relations which are not simply nativist, and which rest on broader or deeper foundations? We must assume, I think, that in a competitive society everything which differentiates one group from another involves a potential conflict of interest, and we must proceed to analyze the historical composition of American society in ethnic terms. The little work so far done along these lines is not only fragmentary. It is also inadequate because the historians of immigration have focused too narrowly on the problem of cultural assimilation. Treating each group separately, they have weighed the effects of its old world culture against its Americanization. *Cultural* assimilation, however, does not necessarily involve *social* assimilation, as the history of the Negro clearly demonstrates. Ethnic identity affects men's position in the social structure long after their ancestral culture has largely disappeared.

Since we know very little about the stratification of our society in any period, particularly in its ethnic aspects, I can offer only a few suggestions for inquiry. Probably one of the crucial determinants of ethnic status has simply been the order of arrival. In the founding of communities, in the settlement of new areas, and in the development of new industries, the first-comers secured a preferential position. Groups arriving later have usually had to enter on terms acceptable to their predecessors, who owned the land, offered the jobs, provided the credit, and controlled the sources of power and prestige. In these circumstances the new group had to accept or to struggle for a long time against a subordinate status.

Immigrants have generally had such a disadvantage in America, since most of them were not pioneers. Sometimes, however, foreign groups did arrive at a sector of American society during its formative stage, thereby establishing a local respect that was not easily upset, particularly if they filled a vital need in the community. In many western communities the Irish met far less resistance than they did in New England, where the social system had congealed long before their arrival. Although the Protestant Irish on the eighteenth-century frontier are the most striking example of the prestige to be derived from an early arrival, the Catholic Irish did not wholly miss comparable benefits in the new West of the first half of the nineteenth century. Their religion, far from carrying a universal stigma, might even prove a social asset in the fairly numerous localities where the Catholic Church established the first and (for quite a while) the best academies and colleges. High status Protestants in Cincinnati, Terre Haute, and elsewhere not only welcomed the schools created by Jesuits, Sisters of Mercy, and other religious orders; they also enrolled their children to mingle on equal terms with Catholic students.

Similarly, the Jews have found a relatively secure niche in places where they contributed significantly to the establishment of the community. In San Francisco, Jews acquired an especially favorable status from their large share in molding the basic institutions of the city. On the other hand, they have endured a particularly bad situation in Minneapolis where they arrived late in the city's development. The same relationship applied to the Japanese in two adjacent California towns in the early twentieth century. In one the Japanese settled first and were accepted in the civic life of the American society that grew up around them; in the other they came later and met bitter persecution as their numbers grew.

How swiftly a group advances after its arrival also affects very strongly the reception it meets. Americans have expected immigrants to move toward cultural homogeneity but not to crowd the social ladder in doing so. When a new group, relatively depressed at the outset, pushes upward rapidly in the status system, conflict almost surely ensues. This happened in the late nineteenth century in the cases of the Irish and the Jews. Both came up against cruel social discriminations designed to retard the large proportion of each group who were getting ahead quickly.

Contrarily, a group that stayed put might escape opprobrium, once the older Americans had become accustomed to its presence, even if it retained a good deal of its cultural distinctiveness. The Germans, who did not bear the stigma attached to the more rapidly Americanized Irish, are a case in point. Although measuring relative rates of social mobility is obviously difficult, the census of 1890 offers an illuminating comparison between the Irish and the Germans. By comparing, for each nationality, the proportion of the first generation in various occupations with the proportion of the second generation in the same occupations, it becomes evident that the Irish were climbing the social ladder rapidly while the Germans were remaining relatively static, the sons being more content to occupy the stations of their fathers. The proportion of Irish in professional occupations almost doubled between the first and the second generation; the proportion of Germans did not change. The Irish entered other white-collar jobs and fled from common labor at twice the rate of the Germans. Here is an important reason why the ambitious Irish provoked a resistance which the more phlegmatic Germans did not face.

To explain such differentials between ethnic groups, historians must not shrink, finally, from studying their respective national or social characters. Surely the boisterous, free-and-easy manners of the Irish, the humble patience of the Chinese, and many ethnic inclinations we have not yet learned properly to define have shaped the relations between our various peoples. Instead of washing all of the specific color out of our ethnic fabric in our fear of propagating stereotypes, let us look for the realities behind them.

What I miss, in the most general way, is any serious effort to study historically the structure of American society—to work out, in other words, the interrelations between classes and ethnic groups, taking account of regional and local differences. This task transcends the dimensions of nativism. It transcends a preoccupation with conflict and discord, and urges us to confront our involvements with one another in comparative terms. But as this is done, the history of nativism itself should fall into a truer perspective.

Suggestions for Further Reading

A brief survey of the history of the fear of conspiracy is found in the title essay of Richard Hofstadter's *The Paranoid Style of American Politics* (1965). Gustavus Myers' indignant *History of Bigotry in the United States* (1943) deals entirely with religion. A recent study that emphasizes the social background of conspiracy fear is Seymour M. Lipset and Earl Raab, *The Politics of Unreason: Right-Wing Extremism in America, 1790–1970* (1970). Nathaniel Weyl accepts the reality of many conspiracies and spy scares and presents his findings in two works, *Treason, The Story of Disloyalty and Betrayal in American History* (1950), and *The Battle Against Disloyalty* (1951). David B. Davis, ed., *The Fear of Conspiracy: Images of Un-American Subversion from the Revolution to the Present* (1971) contains a splendid collection of documents on the fear of conspiracy. Two other useful collections are Seymour Mandelbaum, *The Social Setting of Intolerance* (1964), and Roland Delorme and Raymond McInnis, *Anti-Democratic Trends in Twentieth Century America* (1969).

Anti-Catholicism in the colonial period may be studied in Sr. Augustina Ray, *American Opinion of Catholics in the 18th Century* (1936). A vivid example of its use by American revolutionaries will be found in Fr. C. H. Metzger, *The Quebec Act* (1936). Bernard Bailyn's two works *The Ideological Origins of the American Revolution*

(1967) and *The Origins of American Politics* (1968) explore the English background and American adaption of fear of power, a theme endemic to anticonspiratorial rhetoric. Philip Davidson, *Propaganda and the American Revolution, 1763–1783* (1941) is useful, especially chapter eight.

Fears of conspiracy during the Federalist period are well-handled in two essays by Marshall Smelser, "The Jacobin Phrenzy: The Menace of Monarchy, Plutocracy, and Anglophilia, 1789–1798," *Review of Politics,* 21 (January 1959), and "The Jacobin Phrenzy: Federalism and the Menace of Liberty, Equality, and Fraternity," *Review of Politics,* 13 (October 1951). Vernon Stauffer, *New England and the Bavarian Illuminati* (1918) is the standard account of the origins of this often repeated conspiracy fear. The Alien and Sedition Acts have received definitive treatment in James M. Smith, *Freedom's Fetters: The Alien and Sedition Laws and American Civil Liberties,* (1956), and John C. Miller, *Crisis in Freedom: The Alien and Sedition Acts* (1951) contains excellent examples from newspapers of anticonspiracy rhetoric.

The best work on anti-Catholic polemics in the ante-bellum period is Ray A. Billington, *The Protestant Crusade: 1800–1860* (1938). Other works include G. M. Stephenson, "Nativism in the Forties and Fifties, with Special Reference to the Mississippi Valley," *Mississippi Valley Historical Review,* 9 (December 1922); W. Darrell Overdyke, *The Know-Nothing Party in the South* (1950); and David B. Davis, "Some Ideological Functions of Prejudice in Ante-Bellum America," *American Quarterly,* 15 (Summer 1962). One effect of the Know-Nothing movement is studied in Charles G. Hamilton, *Lincoln and the Know-Nothing Movement* (1954). A useful summary of the anti-Masonic movement is Charles McCarthy, "The Anti-Masonic Party: A Study in Political Anti-Masonry in the United States, 1827–1840," *Annual Report of the American Historical Association for the Year 1902,* 1 (1903). A recent analysis of the political significance of the movement can be found in Lee Benson, *The Concept of Jacksonian Democracy: New York as a Test Case* (1961).

Intolerance toward abolitionists in the North is examined in Russel B. Nye, *Fettered Freedom* (1963), and in the South in Clement Eaton, *Freedom of Thought in the Old South* (1940). John Hope Franklin, *The Militant South* (1956) suggests some of the intellectual conditions behind conspiracy fears in the South. Northern fears of southern conspiracies are revealed in Chauncey S. Boucher, "*In re* That Aggressive Slavocracy," *Mississippi Valley Historical Review* (June–September 1921); Harvey Wish, "The Slave Insurrection Panic of 1856," *Journal of Southern History,* 8 (1939); and David B. Davis, *The Slave Power and the Paranoid Style* (1969).

During the Civil War excessive fears of subversion led to strong governmental repression, which can be studied in James G. Randall, *Constitutional Problems Under Lincoln* (1951), and Harold Hyman, *Era of the Oath* (1954). Wood Gray, *The Hidden Civil War* (1942) accepts the reality of a conspiracy. As a counterbalance to Gray, see Frank Klement's *The Copperheads in the Middle West* (1960), and *The Limits of Dissent: Clement L. Vallandingham and the Civil War* (1971). See also the relevant articles in James A. Rawley, ed., *Lincoln and Civil War Politics* (1969).

Fear of anarchism and labor movements thought to be influenced by alien ideologies can be seen in Wayne C. Broehl, *The Molly Maguires* (1964). Henry David, *The History of the Haymarket Affair* (1936) is a definitive study of this event, but the national response to anarchism and labor agitation in the late nineteenth century needs further study.

Anti-Semitism, an ingredient of much conspiracy fear, has been extensively studied. Melvin Tumin, *An Inventory and Appraisal of Research on American Anti-Semitism* (1961) contains summaries and discussions of books and articles. Some important works are John Higham, "Anti-Semitism in the Gilded Age: A Reinterpretation," *Mississippi Valley Historical Review,* 43 (March 1957); Oscar Handlin, "American Views of the Jew at the Opening of the Twentieth Century," *Publications of the American Jewish Historical Society,* 40 (June 1951); and Donald Strong, *Organized Anti-Semitism in America* (1941), dealing with the 1930s.

One of the most hotly disputed issues in recent historiography is the question of paranoid fears and anti-Semitism among the Populists. The theme is most fully developed in Richard Hofstadter, *The Age of Reform* (1955) and in his essay on "Coin" Harvey in *The Paranoid Style of American Politics.* Victor Ferkiss, "Political and Intellectual Origins of American Radicalism, Right and Left," *The Annals of the American Academy of Political and Social Science,* 344 (1962) associates Populism with later fascist movements. Opposition to these views is found in Walter Nugent, *The Tolerant Populists: Kansas Politics and Nativism* (1963), and in three essays by Norman Pollack, "Hofstadter on Populism: A Critique of the *Age of Reform,*" *Journal of Southern History,* 26 (November 1960); "The Myth of Populist Anti-Semitism," *American Historical Review,* 63 (October 1963); and "Fear of Man: Populism, Authoritarianism and the Historian," *Agricultural History,* 39 (April 1965). C. Vann Woodward's article "The

Populist Heritage and the Intellectual," *The American Scholar,* 29 (Winter 1959–1960), is a fine account of Populism's meaning for modern historians.

The anti-Catholic movement represented by the American Protective Association has been analyzed in Humphrey Desmond, *The APA Movement* (1912), and Donald Kinzer, *An Episode in Anti-Catholicism: The American Protective Association* (1964). Studies of its local impact are John Higham, "The American Party, 1886–1891," *Pacific Historical Review* 19 (February 1950) and Donald Kinzer, "The Political Uses of Anti-Catholicism: Michigan and Wisconsin, 1890–1894," *Michigan History,* 39 (September 1955). John Higham has written an excellent study of the founder of the APA, "The Mind of a Nativist: Henry Bowers and the APA," *American Quarterly,* 4 (Spring 1952). A study of the impact of late nineteenth-century anti-Catholicism on national politics is David Farrelly, "Rum, Romanism and Rebellion Resurrected," *Western Political Quarterly,* 8 (June 1955).

A superb study of nativist fears is John Higham, *Strangers in the Land: Patterns of American Nativism* (1955). See also his "Origins of Immigration Restriction, 1882–1897: A Social Analysis," *Mississippi Valley Historical Review,* 39 (June 1952).

Fears of conspirators and traitors during World War I are detailed in Mark Sullivan, *Our Times,* V, chapters 8 and 23 (1933), and Frederic L. Paxson, *American Democracy and the World War* (3 vols., 1936–1948). Opposition to American participation and its brutal repression is described in Gilbert Fite and H. C. Peterson, *Opponents of War, 1917–1918* (1957). Also useful is John M. Blum, "Nativism, Anti-Radicalism and the Foreign Scare, 1917–1920," *Midwest Journal,* 3 (1950–1951).

Good accounts of the antiforeign movements of the early 1920s are Paul Murphy, "Sources on the Nature of Intolerance in the 1920s," *Journal of American History,* 51 (June 1964). Studies of the assault on radicals include the contemporary Louis F. Post, *The Deportations Delerium of Nineteen Twenty* (1923), and a fine scholarly work, Robert K. Murray, *Red Scare: A Study in National Hysteria* (1955). Stanley Coben, *A. Mitchell Palmer, Politician* (1963) is the standard biography of the attorney general who ordered the roundup of the Radicals.

Arnold Rice, *The Ku Klux Klan in American Politics* (1962) is a solid work. A number of regional studies of the Ku Klux Klan have appeared, but there is still need for a study that would analyze its ideology and role in shaping attitudes. Veterans and patriotic organizations, important in spreading fears of foreign conspiracies, are described in Wallace Davies, *Patriotism on Parade* (1955); Norman Hapgood, *Professional Patriots* (1927); and Rodney G. Minott, *Peerless Patriots: Organized Veterans and the Spirit of Americanism* (1962).

Eugene Lyons claims in *The Red Decade* (1941) that intellectuals sympathetic to the Communist Party exercised disproportionate influence in America in the 1930s. Granville Hicks, "How Red Was the Red Decade?" *Harper's Magazine,* 107 (July 1953) challenges this. However that may be, Congress saw dangers from foreign ideologies, and Walter Goodman, *The Committee: The Career of the House Committee on Un-American Activities* (1968) is a good account of official conspiracy fears.

The New Deal drew the ire of conservatives, who soon began to see it as a conspiracy to socialize America. George Wolfskill, *The Revolt of the Conservatives: A History of the American Liberty League, 1934–1940* (1962) describes the most important group. Among the most vociferous opponents of the New Deal was Father Coughlin, who turned to anti-Semitism in the late 1930s. Charles Tull, *Father Coughlin and the New Deal* (1961) joins Shenton in doubting both the power of the radio priest and his alleged fascist leanings. Wallace Stegner, "The Radio Priest and His Flock," in Isabel Leighton, ed., *The Aspirin Age* (1949) takes a less optimistic view.

The outbreak of World War II saw Americans terrified of subversion by Japanese Americans. Fear of the Japanese immigrants was of long standing, as is revealed by Roger Daniels, *The Politics of Prejudice: The Anti-Japanese Movement and the Struggle for Exclusion* (1966), and Carey McWilliams, *Prejudice: Japanese Americans, Symbol of Racial Intolerance* (1944). The response to the imagined threat is found in Allan R. Bosworth, *America's Concentration Camps* (1967), and Roger Daniels, *Concentration Camps, U.S.A.: Japanese Americans and World War II* (1971).

The most notorious outburst of conspiracy fear during the Cold War is associated with the late Senator Joseph McCarthy. Summaries of much of the voluminous literature seeking to explain the senator and his followers appear in Dennis H. Wrong, "Theories of McCarthyism," *Dissent* (Fall 1954), and a collection edited by Earl Latham, *The Meaning of McCarthyism* (1965). Richard Rovere, *Senator Joe McCarthy* (1959) argues that McCarthy was an opportunist, but William F. Buckley and L. Brent Bozell, *McCarthy and His Enemies* (1954) insist that he was a sincere foe of a genuine threat and that his enemies were themselves paranoid. Les K. Adler and Richard M. Fried,

"McCarthy: The Advent and the Decline," *Continuum,* 6 (Autumn 1968)—the whole issue is devoted to studies of McCarthyism—suggest that his anticommunist position emerged earlier than Rovere believes. See also Robert Griffith's *The Politics of Fear: Joseph R. McCarthy and the Senate* (1970).

Most studies have concentrated on the depth, origin, and influence of the senator's political support. Cameron Hall, "McCarthyism—An Analysis," *Social Action,* 21 (September 1954) finds McCarthyism the product of a "garrison state mentality." R. Sokol, "Power Orientation and McCarthyism," *American Journal of Sociology,* 73 (January 1968) advances a status thesis, seeing McCarthy's supporters as people frustrated by a loss of power and influence. Talcott Parsons, "McCarthyism and American Social Tensions: A Sociologist's View," *Yale Review,* 44 (December 1954) suggests that fears over changed values led people to attack the group believed to be responsible for the change —the eastern, liberal "establishment."

Three works have challenged the assumptions of most studies of McCarthyism. Samuel A. Stouffer, *Communism, Conformity and Civil Liberties: A Cross Section of the Nation Speaks* (1955), found that extreme fears of conspiracy were not widespread. Nelson Polsby, "Towards an Explanation of McCarthyism," *Political Studies,* 8, no. 3 (1960) finds little mass support for McCarthy and is not persuaded by the status thesis. Michael Rogin, *The Intellectuals and McCarthy* (1967), assails the idea that McCarthyism was a mass movement based on Populist centers of activity.

Opposition to Communist conspirators was not confined to Senator McCarthy; the Truman administration created a series of programs to enforce loyalty and security. Edward A. Shils, *The Torment of Secrecy: the Background and Consequences of American Security Policies* (1956), is a good overview. Alan Harper, *The Politics of Loyalty: The White House and the Communist Issue, 1946–1952* (1970), and Athan Theoharis, *Seeds of Repression: Harry S Truman and the Origins of McCarthyism* (1971), both show the prevalence of conspiracy fears in the highest reaches of government. An interesting discussion of this topic is Murray Kempton, "Truman and the Beast," *New York Review of Books* (February 1971).

Since loyalty is intimately connected with conspiratorial rhetoric, students of the subject will benefit from Merle Curti, *The Roots of American Loyalty* (1946), and Ralph S. Brown, *Loyalty and Security* (1958). John Lord O'Brien, *National Security and Individual Freedom* (1955) discusses some dangers of fear of conspiracy.

New organizations of the right, such as the John Birch Society, are the subject of numerous books and articles. An important collection of articles is Daniel Bell, ed., *The New American Right* (1955). Many books crying alarm over the doings of the right wing have appeared. A few of the best are: Donald Janson and Bernard Eismann, *The Far Right* (1963); Roger Burlingame, *The Sixth Column* (1962); Benjamin Epstein and Arnold Foster, *Danger on the Right* (1964) and *The Radical Right* (1967); Ralph Elsworth and Sarah Harris, *The American Right Wing* (1967); and Harry and Bonaro Overstreet, *The Strange Tactics of Extremism* (1964). Alan Westin, "The John Birch Society: Fundamentalism on the Right," *Commentary,* 32 (August 1961) emphasizes the anticonspiracy rhetoric of the society.

Most examinations view the right wing as a threat to democracy. Peter Viereck, "The New American Radicals," *Reporter,* 11 (December 30, 1954) finds middle-class egalitarian democracy to blame. But Joseph Gusfield, "Mass Society and Extremist Politics," *American Sociological Review,* 27 (February 1962) sees no necessary connection between mass politics and extremism. Richard Hofstadter's two essays, "The Pseudo-Conservative Revolt," *American Scholar,* 24 (Winter 1954–1955), and "The Pseudo-Conservative Revolt Revisited," in *The Paranoid Style in American Politics* (1965) argues that the right is not conservative in the classic sense of the term.

The connection between fundamentalist religion and the right is seen in a study of the Christian anti-Communist crusade by Raymond Wolfinger, "America's Radical Right: Politics and Ideology," in David Apter, ed., *Ideology and Discontent* (1964). A more general study is David Danzig, "The Radical Right and the Rise of the Fundamentalist Minority," *Commentary,* 33 (April 1962). Particularly valuable is Ralph L. Roy, *Apostles of Discord* (1953).

The ideology of the right wing is discussed in John Bunzel, *Anti-Politics in America* (1967), especially chapter II, "Politics and Conspiracy: the Moral Crusade of the Right Wing." Seymour Martin Lipset has written a number of essays seeking to place the right within the framework of a pluralist analysis, "The Right-Wing 'Revival' and the 'Backlash' in the United States," in his *Revolution and Counterrevolution* (1968), and "Fascism, Left, Right, and Center," in his *Political Man* (1960) are good examples of his approach.

Fear of conspiracy is not confined to the right wing. A number of essays point out the similarity in such fears of both the right and the left. Alan Westin, "Deadly Parallels: Radical Right and Radical Left," *Harper's Magazine,* 224 (April 1962) emphasizes the degree to which they both use conspiratorial rhetoric. Ralph Lord Roy sees a similar approach to attacks on religious liberalism, "Conflict from the Left and Right," in Robert Lee and Martin Marty, eds., *Religion and Social Conflict* (1964). On an international level Urie Bronfenbrenner, "The Mirror Image in Soviet-American Relations," *Journal of Social Issues,* 17, no. III (1961) shows the mutual conspiracy fears of Russia and the United States. In addition see the extremely perceptive article by Les K. Adler and Thomas G. Paterson, "Red Fascism: the Merger of Nazi Germany and Soviet Russia in the American Image of Totalitarianism, 1930s–1950s," *The American Historical Review,* 75 (April 1970).

Fear of conspiracy has greatly influenced postwar foreign policy. Athan Theoharis, "The Rhetoric of Politics: Foreign Policy, Internal Security and Domestic Politics in the Truman Era, 1945–1950," in Barton Bernstein, ed., *Politics and Policies of the Truman Administration* (1970) shows the connection between conspiracy fear and the policy of containment. An indictment of the anticommunist basis of foreign policy is Sidney Lens, *The Futile Crusade* (1964). Thomas A. Bailey, *The Man in the Street: The Impact of American Public Opinion on Foreign Policy* (1948), especially chapter XVIII, "Xenophobes and Xenophobia," shows the importance of public attitudes.

Prejudice is closely involved with fear of conspiracy, and there has been considerable work in this area by psychologists and sociologists. Earl Raab and Seymour M. Lipset, *Prejudice and Society* (1959) is a good introduction. A major figure in such studies is Gordon Allport. Allport and Bernard Kramer, "Some Roots of Prejudice," *Journal of Psychology,* 22 (July 1946), and Gordon Allport, "Prejudice: a Problem in Psychological and Social Causation," *Journal of Social Issues,* Supp. series 4 (November 1950), are interesting. Allport's book, *The Nature of Prejudice* (1954) is of great importance. Different in its emphasis is Bruno Bettelheim and Morris Janowitz, *Dynamics of Prejudice* (1950).

An important ingredient of fear of conspiracy is nationalism. Carleton J. H. Hayes, "Nationalism and Intolerance," in his *Essays on Nationalism* (1926); Irwin Child and Leonard Doob, "Factors Determining National Stereotypes," *Journal of Social Psychology,* 17 (May 1943); Lyman Bryson, ed., *Approaches to National Unity* (1945) are good introductions. Boyd C. Shafer, *Nationalism: Myth and Reality* (1955) is especially useful in showing the conspiracy-fear content of modern nationalism.

Fear of conspiracy has been associated by many commentators with authoritarian tendencies. T. W. Adorno *et al., The Authoritarian Personality* (1950) is a classic, but the comments and further contributions in Richard Christie and Marie Jahoda, eds., *Studies in the*

Scope and Method of the Authoritarian Personality (1954), should not be overlooked. An interesting use of the idea is Seymour M. Lipset, "Democracy and Working Class Authoritarianism," *American Sociological Review,* 24 (August 1959).

Demogogues have generally utilized fear of conspiracy. Richard Luthin, *American Demogogues: Twentieth Century* (1954) is a popular account. The first two chapters of Leo Lowenthal and Norbert Guterman, *Prophets of Deceit: A Study of the Techniques of the American Agitator* (1949) show the manipulative use of conspiracy fears by leaders. Eric Hofer's classic *The True Believer* (1951) contains shrewd insights.

Sigmund Freud, *Civilization and Its Discontents* (1939) sees hatred of the outsider as a means by which society insures unity. Erich Fromm, *May Man Prevail* (1961) regards this hostility, and the suspicion and fear of conspiracy that it engenders, as a problem of massive proportions. Hostility is analyzed in John Dollard, "Hostility and Fear in Social Life," *Social Forces,* 17 (October 1938) and his book *Frustration and Aggression* (1939).

A number of other studies by psychologists shed light on conspiracy fear. On the level of individual acceptance of anticonspiracy rhetoric two articles are useful: Robert Park, "Personality and Social Conflict," *Publication of the American Sociological Society,* 25 (May 1931), and Norman Cameron, "The Development of Paranoic Thinking," *Psychological Review,* 50 (March 1943). Also useful are David Shapiro, *Neurotic Styles* (1965), especially chapter III, "Paranoid Style," and Ernest M. Gruenberg, "Socially Shared Psychopathology," in John Clausen and Robert Wilson, eds., *Explorations in Social Psychiatry* (1957).

Index